SOLIDARITY

OTHER BOOKS BY
DAVID SPANER

Shoot It!: Hollywood Inc. and the
Rising of Independent Film
(Arsenal Pulp Press, 2012)

Dreaming in the Rain: How Vancouver
Became Hollywood North by Northwest
(Arsenal Pulp Press, 2003)

SOLIDARITY

Canada's Unknown Revolution of 1983

DAVID SPANER

RONSDALE PRESS

RONSDALE PRESS
3350 West 21st Avenue, Vancouver, B.C. Canada V6S 1G7
www.ronsdalepress.com

Typesetting: Julie Cochrane, in Caslon 11.5 pt on 15
Cover Photo: Solidarity protesters rally in Victoria on July 27, 1983. Courtesy of
    Pacific Tribune Photo Collection-SFU, Sean Griffin photograph
Cover Design: Julie Cochrane
Paper: Ancient Forest Friendly Enviro 100 edition, 60 lb. Husky (FSC),
    100% post-consumer waste, totally chlorine-free and acid-free.

Ronsdale Press wishes to thank the following for their support of its publishing program: the Canada Council for the Arts, the Government of Canada, the British Columbia Arts Council, and the Province of British Columbia through the British Columbia Book Publishing Tax Credit program.

Library and Archives Canada Cataloguing in Publication

Title: Solidarity: Canada's unknown revolution of 1983 / David Spaner.

Names: Spaner, David, author.

Description: Includes bibliographical references and index.

Identifiers: Canadiana (print) 20210301074 | Canadiana (ebook) 20210320710
    | ISBN 9781553806387 (softcover) | ISBN 9781553806394 (ebook)
    | ISBN 9781553806400 (PDF)

Subjects: LCSH: Working class—Political activity—British Columbia—History—
    20th century. | LCSH: Labor movement—British Columbia—History—20th
    century. | CSH: British Columbia—Politics and government—1975-1991.

Classification: LCC HD8109.B72 S63 2021 | DDC 322/.209711—dc23

At Ronsdale Press we are committed to protecting the environment. To this end we are working with Canopy and printers to phase out our use of paper produced from ancient forests. This book is one step towards that goal.

Printed in Canada by Island Blue, Victoria, B.C.

For Freda Gitten, Sam Kovnat,
Eleanor Roffman, Ben Spaner,
Murray Feldman and Al Kovnat.
They dared to fight the good fight.

"One thing I know, I know we're not alone
Was a million here before we came
Be a million when we're gone."

—PHIL OCHS

ACKNOWLEDGEMENTS

I thank the many people who helped out one way or another with this book. Much appreciation for the invaluable assistance provided by Vancouver's City Archives, the Vancouver Public Library, the University of British Columbia Archives and the Simon Fraser University Archives. Special thanks to SFU archivist Melanie Hardbattle.

The quotes in *Solidarity*, apart from those attributed to other sources, are from interviews I conducted for this book or, in some cases, publications I've written for. Among those I interviewed: Stuart Alcock, Saria Andrew, Joe Barrett, Aaron Barzman, Norma Barzman, Tzeporah Berman, Margaret Black, Jacquie Boyer, Raj Chouhan, Gwen Chute, Gary Cristall, Jack Darcus, Sara Diamond, Evelyn Farrelly, Patsy George, Ken Holmes, Beth Hutchinson, Ali Kazimi, Joe Keithley, Jef Keighley, Larry Kent, Art Kube, Larry Kuehn, Jean Pierre Lefebvre, David Lester, Ken Mather, Gail Meredith, Jack Munro, Len Norris, Scott Parker, Carol Pastinsky, Craig Patterson, Stan Persky, Marion Pollack, Nora Randall, Melanie Ray, Mary Robinson, Susan Safyan, Roisin Sheehy-Culhane, Muggs Sigurgeirson, Cliff Stainsby, Gary Steeves, Marjorie Stewart, Jess Succamore, Jean Swanson, Marcy Toms, Shari Ulrich, Fred Wah, Tom Wayman, Nettie Wild, Diane Wood, Kim Zander and Alan Zisman. I thank them all.

For providing photographs, particular gratitude to SFU Digitized Collections, B.C. Labour Heritage Centre, B.C. Teachers' Federation, Geoff Peters, Pacific Tribune Photograph Collection, Fisherman Publishing Society, and B.C. Government and Service Employees' Union. I'd also like to thank my colleagues at Ronsdale Press—Ronald Hatch, Hélène Leboucher, Megan Warren, Julie Cochrane and Kevin Welsh.

CONTENTS

GLOSSARY OF
ACRONYMS AND EPITHETS

AUCE	Association of University and College Employees
BCFED	B.C. Federation of Labour
BCGEU	B.C. Government and Service Employees' Union
BCOFR	B.C. Organization to Fight Racism
BCTF	B.C. Teachers' Federation
CAIMAW	Canadian Association of Industrial, Mechanical and Allied Workers
CASAW	Canadian Association of Smelter and Allied Workers
CCF	Co-operative Commonwealth Federation
CCU	Confederation of Canadian Unions
CFU	Canadian Farmworkers Union
CIEA	College Institute Educators' Association
CIO	Congress of Industrial Organization
CLC	Canadian Labour Congress
CP	Communist Party
CUPE	Canadian Union of Public Employees
CUPW	Canadian Union of Postal Workers
CUSO	Canadian University Service Overseas
DERA	Downtown Eastside Residents' Association
FLQ	Front de Liberation du Quebec
Fish	United Fishermen and Allied Workers' Union
HEU	Hospital Employees' Union
HUAC	House Un-American Activities Committee
IBEW	International Brotherhood of Electrical Workers
IWA	International Woodworkers of America
IWW	Industrial Workers of the World
LMBC	Lower Mainland Budget Coalition

LRB	Labour Relations Board
MacBlo	MacMillan Bloedel
NDP	New Democratic Party
PPWC	Pulp, Paper and Woodworkers of Canada
PSA	Political Science, Sociology and Anthropology
RWL	Revolutionary Workers League
SDS	Students for a Democratic Society
SDU	Students for a Democratic University
SFU	Simon Fraser University
Socreds	Social Credit Party
SORWUC	Service, Office, and Retail Workers Union of Canada
SPEC	Society Promoting Environmental Conservation
TSSU	Teaching Support Staff Union
UBC	University of British Columbia
UFAWU	United Fishermen and Allied Workers' Union
UFW	United Farm Workers
VCC	Vancouver City College
VDLC	Vancouver and District Labour Council
VISTA	Volunteers in Service to America
VMREU	Vancouver Municipal and Regional Employees' Union
WAB	Women Against the Budget
Wobblies	Industrial Workers of the World
YCL	Young Communist League
YIP	Youth International Party
Yippies	Youth International Party

Just a Step Beyond
the Rain

IT WAS LIKE 1984 had come a year early.

The year 1983 began conventionally enough in British Columbia—with the New Democratic Party (NDP) losing a provincial election to the Social Credit Party (Socreds)—but that all changed on July 7 when the province's premier, Bill Bennett, and his cohorts unleashed a far-right legislative avalanche that tossed asunder virtually every advance achieved by B.C.'s social activists and trade unionists. In an instant, and from every corner of the province, there was a rising of resistance.

It was one of the great social uprisings in North American history. The scale of this Solidarity revolt of 1983 was unexpected, but Social Credit's anti-social behaviour and the fervent opposition to it wasn't a surprise to anyone who came of age in B.C.'s postwar decades. From the 1950s to the 1990s, B.C. was divided between descendants of the

far-right movements of the 1930s (the Socreds) and the left popu-
list movements of the 1930s (the NDP), and generations of British
Columbians grew up on dinner-table debates about their seemingly
endless electoral combat. The conflict in B.C., however, didn't begin
or end with social democrats and Social Credit.

This book is a story of B.C.'s Solidarity uprising told through the
lives of people who lived it. There are the little indignities in everyday life that people endure, silently, on their own. There are also
moments, however, when solitude suddenly gives way to solidarity. In
1968, student protests in France led to repression and riots and more
protests, with unions joining in, until for two months the country
was in the throes of a general strike—occupied factories under workers' self-management, universities run by "occupation committees"
and the National Theatre transformed into a decision-making assembly. Even the seemingly least political joined in the strikes and
occupations. France's national football league hung a banner from its
headquarters proclaiming *Football belongs to the people.*

"It was mind-boggling, actually," Aaron Barzman, a veteran of the
uprising, told me. "Time had stopped. The whole country was on
strike."

The heady events in France were part of an international rising that
occurred during the late 1960s and early '70s. Similar exhilaration
ensued at Tiananmen Square (1989), Spain (1936–38), all of Europe
(1848), Occupy Wall Street, Cairo and Hong Kong (2011) and the
anti-racism protests of 2020. These euphoric moments arrive suddenly, but they're expressions of long-simmering, widely held feelings.
They express the repressed potential for an entirely different set of
social relations than we're accustomed to. B.C. is not on the world's
radar like Paris or New York but, still, Solidarity was our moment.

"So many people coming together from all different stripes, for all
the different reasons that they had, all coming together and working
together with one objective," says Solidarity activist Diane Wood.
"You don't get that opportunity very often in your life so for me, you
used the word euphoric, it was."

A school teacher can change everything. All of British Columbia witnessed this in the fall of 1983. For Fred Wah, this realization happened much earlier, when he played horn in a Nelson high school band and a music teacher opened his ears and his heart to contemporary sounds he never knew existed.

That teacher, Ed Baravalle, had a history in Hollywood before arriving in Nelson, B.C. "Our high school music teacher," says Fred, "was a major M-G-M composer. We had this American music teacher who had to leave the States." He worked for a decade in Metro-Goldwyn-Mayer's storied music department before being driven out of town by the anti-Communist blacklist that tore through Hollywood in the late 1940s and '50s. Deprived of their livelihoods at the studios, many of Hollywood's most creative artists took whatever work they could get wherever they could find it. Ed Baravalle found his way to Nelson, Fred's hometown in the picturesque Kootenay region of B.C.

Nelson had a history of progressive politics as well as a proclivity for the arts, so Ed's past didn't seem to be a problem there. "I don't think anyone was bothered by it," Fred says. "Nelson's always been pretty open to political refugees." Yes, Fred Wah's hometown was special. And most who lived there didn't give a hoot about the Hollywood blacklist. In some ways, though, Nelson was also the same as other towns. In Nelson, Fred had known anti-Chinese racism, and just across town a local version of the Hollywood blacklist had erupted at Kootenay Forest Products. While the McCarthy era was never so systematic in Canada as it was in the U.S., it did exist, and in 1950s Nelson the "establishment" White Bloc wing of the International Woodworkers of America (IWA) warred against the left-wingers who had built the union.

Just after Fred left Nelson to study music at the University of British Columbia (UBC), Jack Munro showed up in town. In 1958 he was a strapping young Albertan who looked like he might have been on the wrong end of a Rocky Marciano punch or two. Hired as a welder at Kootenay Forest Products, he fell in with the remnants of the White Bloc and became a shop steward. In 1968 Munro ran for third vice-president of the International Woodworkers of America. Munro moved on to the IWA presidency in 1973 and became a force in the B.C. Federation of Labour (BCFED). Munro's rough-hewn manner camouflaged his "establishment" views until 1983.

Meanwhile, Ed teamed up with artist Zeljko Kujundzic, who also taught at the high school, to co-found the Nelson School of Fine Arts. It would later be renamed the Kootenay School of Art and become a renowned incubator of generations of young artists. When Fred Wah told me about his music teacher at Nelson High, I searched Edward Baravalle's IMDb. "Born: October 8, 1912 in New York, New York, USA."[1] He was a mainstay of M-G-M's music department with twenty-eight credits, including such notables as *The Clock* and *Son of Lassie*. What really caught my attention, though, was his first Hollywood shoot: *The Wizard of Oz*, 1939.

Well before *The Wizard of Oz* songs were standards, Ed Baravalle was among the first to hear "Follow the Yellow Brick Road," "Over the Rainbow" and the rest of its great soundtrack while working at M-G-M with composers Yip Harburg and Harold Arlen. Like Fred Wah's music teacher, Harburg would be blacklisted in Hollywood.

To Harburg, art is on the side of the rebels and idealists. "We worked for, in our songs, a sort of better world, a rainbow world."[2] To this socialist songwriter, "Over the Rainbow," along with being a magical wish for personal happiness, was an anthem for a just new world where dreams come true.

1983: Nelson's Fred Wah is a celebrated poet and author, back in his hometown teaching at David Thompson University after studying and working abroad. Like much of B.C., Fred is shaken when the provincial Socred government unveils a legislative package like nothing seen before in the province. Nelson's Jack Munro plays a decisive role in the Solidarity uprising's anticlimactic finale.

Everyone in this book, and in the streets with Solidarity, shared one thing—they were twentieth-century people. The twentieth century was more technological (screens were everywhere: movie screens, TV screens, computer screens), less theological (secularism was commonplace) and more ideological ("isms" abounded) than earlier centuries. The climactic moment of the century's warring ideas came during the Spanish Civil War, when the armies of every lefty *ism* faced off against fascism in a preamble to the Second World War. Those ideas shaped this province, too, thriving in twentieth-century B.C. as much as any place in North America. The words "Wobblies" and "Greenpeace" were coined in Vancouver. (Later, "Occupy Wall Street" would be, too.) Feminism also came early and fiercely to the city, which hosted one of the first international women's liberation conferences. B.C.'s subculture scenes—from UBC's *TISH* magazine to Burnaby punk rock—were widely known throughout the international underground. No surprise, then, that more volunteers for Spain left from Vancouver than any other North American city apart from New York.

Few know the diversity of B.C.'s rebel politics as intimately as venerable Nanaimo activist Marjorie Stewart—a Communist Party (CP) supporter, then a member of the local NDP executive, then an anarchist. Marjorie expressed the sentiments of much of progressive B.C. the day she gave her young daughters a memorable, albeit tongue-in-cheek, talking-to about what was unacceptable in the family home.

"They were told when they were little, 'If you turn Socred or if you get into a fundamental religion, don't bother coming home because I won't want to know you'—to which one of them immediately replied, 'I'll become a Socred if I want to.' She would decide she didn't want to." (Marjorie's spirited, independent-minded daughters grew up to be as decidedly progressive as their mother.)

During the Solidarity months of 1983, the fragments of B.C.'s left would, for once, be focused on the same issues and attend the same protests. What made the Solidarity movement so powerful, though, was that thousands upon thousands of people who had never before been inclined to act were also at those protests. The Solidarity uprising of 1983 was the culmination of the ongoing political clashes, revolutionary ideas and cultural insurgencies that shaped B.C.'s twentieth century. How did we come to that in 1983?

The answer is in the lives of those touched by Solidarity. In the telling of their diverse political and cultural journeys to 1983, this book becomes a history of twentieth-century B.C.—exploring its great divides and unions, cultures and subcultures, conflicts that continue into the twenty-first century.

———

In a cozy Kitsilano living room on a grey fall day more than a decade before the Solidarity uprising, a young lefty prof and three student radicals began a conversation that lasted into the morning. Vancouver City College instructor Jim Green (of Alabama) invited the three— Clyde Hertzman (of Vancouver), Rick Fantasia (of New York) and myself (of Vancouver)—to talk with him at the beautiful old clapboard house he rented in countercultural Kitsilano. This was before Jim became Eastside Jim Green, a renowned activist/politician on the city's Downtown Eastside—before Clyde became one of the world's essential experts on childhood development—before Rick became an eminent academic/activist, authoring books on culture and labour and chairing activities of the American Sociological Association.

At the time, revolution was in the air. So, as we talked and talked, the night turned to morning and the conversation turned from Black Panthers and France '68 (Rick was studying in France when the uprising began), to New Hollywood movies and beat literature, to music. There was simpatico between this radical professor and these activist students, and Jim suggested we should all listen closely to the Bob Dylan song "When the Ship Comes In." He put it on the turntable. *The ship*, he explained, was *the revolution*. Jim particularly liked the verse about facing down, without compromise, the Socreds of the world, and after the song played he repeated aloud to us its unyielding lyrics: "They'll raise their hands/Saying we'll meet all your demands/But we'll shout from the bow your days are numbered."

We all smiled. Jim laughed and he played the song again, and again.

CHAPTER 1

Bill's Bills: The Decline of West Coast Civilization

ON JULY 7, 1983, Jacquie Boyer was in the Legislature's gallery. A resident of Coquitlam, she was on vacation in Victoria and dropped by the Legislature just to watch. She usually found these sessions entertaining. This day, though, she left the building shaken. When Jacquie met up with a friend who had spent the day negotiating a Canadian Union of Public Employees (CUPE) contract, she told him that whatever he'd achieved today would be useless. "He said, 'What the hell are you talking about?' I said, 'You'll find out.'"

Jacquie had just witnessed an assault by legislation. It began with Bill Bennett and his Social Credit government calling an adjournment, "which was almost unheard of, and people were sort of curious about what was going on. Then they came back in and literally dropped the bills, one through twenty-six, just like that. And they kept getting worse and worse and worse. And I must have been sitting there with my mouth hanging open."

Through Jacquie's work as a B.C. Teachers' Federation (BCTF) administrative assistant, she knew broadcasters and newspaper reporters. As those bills dropped, she was besieged. "They're pulling me out of the gallery asking if I know where so-and-so is, because nobody expected this," she says. "I knew full well what the implications would be. I was thinking, 'This is really big and my life at work is going to be even busier.'"

The twenty-six-bill budget tabled that day was a legislative potpourri of the worst of Ronald Reagan and Margaret Thatcher's austerity theology. It was viciously anti-labour, allowing for workers to be fired without cause even if they were in a union. As an opening salvo, 1,400 members of the B.C. Government and Service Employees' Union (BCGEU) were fired July 8. The budget was also an attack on Canada's Medicare system. For education, it meant fewer teachers and larger classes, the elimination of special education, reduced student loans and less autonomy for local school boards. It centralized into Socred hands much of the decision-making that had been local or regional. The budget also meant legal aid would be cut, environmental protections removed, welfare rates frozen, health care facilities closed, and the Human Rights Commission, rent controls and other vital programs cut. The Vancouver Women's Health Collective, for instance, received sudden notice that its long-time funding was eliminated.

"It was a barrage," says Diane Wood, a BCGEU vice-president in 1983. "My feeling was that we have to fight. We can't allow this. It affects everybody. Not just our members." What surprised Bennett and his Socreds was that those feelings weren't restricted to the union movement or the left. A resistance rose in every corner of the province. Soon, Operation Solidarity, a united union front, was launched, followed shortly by the Solidarity Coalition, a combine of social justice community organizations.

In 1953, Diane Wood was in elementary school in Victoria when her parents brought home the first television set on their block. "So the whole neighbourhood used to come and watch TV at our house. And often I remember my mother making sandwiches and serving coffee and stuff until one or two in the morning." In her teens, Diane loved rock 'n' roll ("saw the Beatles on *Ed Sullivan*") and the U.S. TV dance show *American Bandstand*, so she took to dancing on a local version called *Club 6*. When Victoria's CHEK TV began broadcasting *Club 6*, Diane and her high school friends became minor celebrities about town. "Everybody went and danced there."

Just as Diane's teen years were starting to sound like something out of *Bye Bye Birdie*, she told me that the blocks surrounding her parents' rooming house near Victoria High School were the closest thing to a multicultural neighbourhood in Victoria, with numerous post-Second World War European immigrants arriving. "Called DPs," says Diane, referring to "displaced persons," a postwar government term for refugees that became a schoolyard slur. "We had this whole crowd of kids that just hung out together and we didn't care. We all played together in the park." Also, Diane's mother's father ran alcohol from Canada into Illinois during prohibition. "He kind of worked on the dark side, my grandfather. He was a gambler and he ran illegal liquor."

After high school, Diane was hired on as a secretary for Victoria's school board. Upon marrying at twenty, she moved slightly up-island to Duncan and got a job with its school district. It was Diane's first glimpse of a non-union workplace. So she organized a union.

"I saw the differences from when I worked in Victoria, the rights and benefits that the workers had. I said, 'Oh, this isn't right.' And they were all women working in the areas that I was working in. So I had them to my house and the business agent came up, we signed them up, and we had a three-week strike—thirteen women."

A decade later, Diane was a court services worker living in the B.C. Interior town of Prince George. By now, she was a feminist as well as a socialist and trade unionist. "I read *The Feminine Mystique*. For me, it was connecting the dots, basically. There was a real active feminist movement in Prince George. I remember [NDP MLA] Rosemary Brown coming up and all of us riding a bus to Terrace and staying in a big park area and just talking with Rosemary about, 'things need to change for women.'" Diane became president of her local of the BCGEU and, in 1977, a vice-president of the provincial union.

1983: Diane is living in Prince George, working in the human resources ministry, when the Socred government begins firing her union's members. "They were just firing people right, left and centre. And the first group they attacked was the family support workers, which was where I worked. Those are the folks that went in to work with families that needed the services. Such a vital service." Many of those fired were BCGEU activists like Diane and the union's other vice-president, John Shields. "It was clear to my members—if they could fire the first and second vice-presidents of the union, how safe are we?" Her firing came as no big surprise. "I was ready for it. I said, 'They're going to come after us. There's no question.'" She returned to her hometown on July 19 to address the province's first big Solidarity rally—6,000 protesters at Victoria's Memorial Arena. Some at the rally were already broaching the idea of an all-out strike. "I want a general strike. I think the only thing that will wake them up is a general strike," a government worker told a reporter. "I personally feel very threatened by the legislation. I'm a civil servant. I'm also a renter. To ask them nicely to withdraw the legislation is just not going to work."[1]

During Solidarity's halcyon months—July to November—Diane was a popular speaker at Solidarity events across B.C. "This is a fundamental democratic issue," she would tell the crowds. "They're using their power to take away our rights. This is wrong. This is just simply wrong. And if you allow it, it's a slippery slope." The articulate trade unionist made an easy transition from teen dance TV to national broadcast news. "I remember being interviewed on [CTV's] *Canada AM* and I said, 'I may have lost my job but I haven't lost my voice.'"

Diane says many B.C. unionists were aware of the goings-on in

Thatcher's England, where her government was privatizing everything from British Airways to British Gas while waging war on union workers. "All of the shit that was going on there. I mean, the attack on the mine workers. We knew. Why did they pick British Columbia for this? Why, in all of Canada, did they pick what I feel was probably the strongest labour movement in Canada?" Diane's answer: the Socreds, buttressed by right-wing politicians and think tanks, were using B.C. "as their little laboratory. If they could win in British Columbia, then they just move it [everywhere]. There was no question that there was a concerted effort among other right-wing leaders of provinces in this country. And don't forget we had the Fraser Institute."

———

On July 19, BCGEU negotiator Gary Steeves received a phone call asking him to meet with the Bennett government's Ministry of Human Resources. Gary's parents were members of the Co-operative Commonwealth Federation (CCF) who co-founded the New Brunswick NDP and he was a distant relative of the Steves family of Steveston. He had come out to the West Coast to be the BCGEU's assistant director of collective bargaining. At the July 19 meeting, he was told that the government would use its new legislation to close Tranquille, a mental health facility in Kamloops, and fire its 600 employees.

"Well, hold on," Gary responded. "There's a collective agreement in place and there's a no-layoff clause for any regular employee who has over three years seniority. You can't fire them." The government could and would, he was told, under brand-new Bill 3, the Public Sector Restraint Act. Gary left for Kamloops. "That night, we had a general membership meeting of everyone at Tranquille. We decided we were going to occupy the facility. The occupation started that night."

The union, as part of Solidarity, occupied and self-managed Tranquille. "We set up a council with representatives from each department," Steeves says. "We met daily and we would make decisions of

what we were going to do and how we were going to do it. I took
over the paperwork of the facility. And we'd just carry on and run the
facility." When an expensive air conditioning unit failed one steamy
night in a building that housed people with cerebral palsy, the occupiers installed a new unit and gave the bill to government officials.
"They said, 'We're not signing.' I said, 'If you don't sign, we're going
to go to the national media and have a discussion in front of the
cameras, you and me, about why you want [people with] cerebral
palsy to die in their beds from heat exhaustion because you guys are
too cheap to put in the new air conditioner.' So they reluctantly
signed. We operated as if we lived there. When something was
broken we fixed it, and if someone needed something we addressed
the need. And that's how we operated the whole place, whether it
was the nursing department, the maintenance department, dietary, or
whatever."

Kamloops's Socred MLA threatened to send police into Tranquille
to crush the Solidarity occupation. "We said, 'If you did that, something bad could happen and then that's all on you because right now
it's all running smooth, like clockwork.'" So, the resistance continued.
The occupation was on the news every evening and supporters rallied
across the province. "We put up signs in all the windows—*Under
New Management*. We had fun."

———

The Vancouver of 1983 had different memories than it does today.
Many who were middle-aged or older had sharp recollection of the
1930s and '40s—the relief workers' strikes and occupations, Saturday
matinees with Fred & Ginger, baseball at Oppenheimer Park, Sina-
tra at the Commodore, wars against fascism.

Baby boomers in 1983 had fresh memories of the 1960s and '70s—
the student radicals' strikes and occupations, *Easy Rider*, baseball at
Capilano Stadium, the Clash at the Commodore, protests against
the Vietnam War.

Along with different memories, the Vancouver of 1983 had more affordable price tags. In neighbourhoods like Kitsilano and Dunbar, homes were owned by teachers, firefighters, reporters. "I grew up in downtown Vancouver [in the 1950s and '60s] and it was a city of loggers, a city of miners, a city of fishermen," says teacher Scott Parker. "It was far more working class here. And of course it had a very strong militant history with the Industrial Workers of the World, the Communist Party, even the Co-operative Commonwealth Federation, which was powerful here." Besides these older organizations, the West Coast had a large New Left which, peaking between 1968 and 1972, was a combustible mix of campus protest, anti-war activism, feminism and counterculture. Scott's parents were lefty sympathizers and he easily transitioned from star quarterback at King George high school to New Left activist at Vancouver City College.

1983: Scott Parker is on summer holiday in Europe when revolt erupts back home. "I was in Greece and someone said there were large demonstrations in the streets in Vancouver—thirty, forty thousand people. I couldn't believe it. It must be another place in the world or he's making it up. But sure enough, he was right." Scott is a B.C. Teachers' Federation activist. Back at school after the holidays, there are meetings and "immediately the teachers voted to join the Solidarity movement." Like Diane Wood, Scott sees right-wing ideology written all over Bill Bennett's legislative avalanche. "Part and parcel of a movement led by Thatcher and Reagan to dismantle the social safety net the New Dealers had built in Europe and North America," he says.

—◦◦◦—

What surprised Bennett and his Socreds was the ferocity of the resistance in every corner of B.C., with many asking: "Can they do it here, or can we stop it here?" Over the next several months the government rammed the bills through the Legislature, holding a series of all-night legislative sessions and invoking closure twenty times to end debate. A sampling of the worst of Bill's bills:

Bill 2. The Public Service Labour Relations Amendment Act. Forbade government workers from bargaining specific matters, including seniority rights. Mention of seniority, hours of work or overtime in existing collective agreements was declared null and void. (Bill 1 was routine legislation used to open sessions in Victoria, so the woeful twenty-six began with Bill 2.)

Bill 3. The Public Sector Restraint Act. Encouraged firing without cause. "Notwithstanding the Labour Code and the Public Service Labour Relations Act, a public sector employer may terminate the employment of an employee without cause."

Bill 5. The Residential Tenancy Act. Abolished rent controls and renters' tax credits. Tenants could be evicted without cause. Eliminated the Rentalsman's office, meaning disputes would have to be settled in expensive court proceedings.

Bill 6. The Education Finance Act. Gave the Socred government power over education budgets previously determined by local school boards.

Bill 9. The Municipal Amendment Act. Decimated the farmland-protecting Agricultural Land Act brought in by Dave Barrett's NDP government of the early 1970s. Severely reduced regional-district planning powers.

Bill 24. The Medical Services Act. Socreds never much liked the Canadian Medicare system, and this limited the number of doctors in the program. Also increased user fees for hospital care.

Bill 27. The Human Rights Act. An ironically titled piece of legislation that abolished the Human Rights Commission and the Human Rights Branch. They monitored prejudice in the province and investigated and arbitrated human rights complaints. Their employees were among the first fired.

Shortly after I was hired at New Westminster's *The Columbian* daily newspaper in the summer of 1983, its labour reporter, Terry Glavin, left and I was asked to take over the labour beat as the Solidarity movement was heating up. Years later, *The Columbian*'s legendary old photographer Basil King told me: "In all my years in newspapers, you're the second-most biased reporter I ever met. The first was Terry Glavin." At the time, Glavin was a staunchly pro-union journalist, so I took Basil's jibe as a left-handed compliment. Having come through the underground press and the New Left, I never did buy into notions of "objective" journalism (unless the objective was to help "prepare the general strike") and I happily covered Solidarity—its meetings and actions and personal stories—until the November day when Solidarity and *The Columbian* evaporated.

—⁓—

BCTF president Larry Kuehn was in Victoria for a meeting with the education minister when the bills were tabled. "I was in the Legislature. I was totally, totally knocked over by the extent of what they were doing. [NDP Education Critic] Eileen Daily came out just looking totally devastated and said, 'This is just so terrible.' I got a headache it was so intense. And I never get headaches." Larry had planned to leave that day for a meeting of the Canadian Teachers' Federation in Saskatoon. "While we were in Saskatoon, the first of the meetings was called here. It was the Lower Mainland Budget Coalition. [B.C. Federation of Labour president Art] Kube called the first of the Operation Solidarity meetings at that stage as well."

The day the bills came down, George Hewison, vice-president of the Vancouver and District Labour Council (VDLC), got hold of a copy of the legislation. "Now, remember George was the financial secretary of the fishermen's union so he had an eye for numbers already," says Kim Zander, coordinator of the VDLC's Unemployed Action Centre. "When he had a look at it and he went through it in detail, he went, 'Oh, my God.' We immediately called a meeting of the Unemployment Committee of the Vancouver Labour Council and George said, 'Here's what's on the agenda—this budget is absolutely hell on wheels. We've got to start doing something.' So the unions that were involved in the Unemployment Committee of the VDLC said, 'Okay, well that's it, we've got to sound the alarm.'" The VDLC called unions and community organizations to a July 11 meeting where the Lower Mainland Budget Coalition (LMBC) was formed.

Jef Keighley, an organizer for the Canadian Association of Industrial, Mechanical and Allied Workers (CAIMAW), was at that first public meeting of the Lower Mainland Budget Coalition. Like George Hewison, Jef had read the bills as soon as he could get his hands on them. "We sat down in the CAIMAW office and—there's four or five of us—we read it back to front, front to back, discussed it, and we said, 'Look, this is absolutely fucking outrageous. We got to shut down the province.'" CAIMAW was a member of the Confederation of Canadian Unions (CCU), which by happenstance was having a meeting of its B.C. council in five days, including delegates from CAIMAW, Pulp, Paper and Woodworkers of Canada (PPWC) and Canadian Association of Smelter and Allied Workers (CASAW). There were about 20,000 CCU members in the province and its council met at the CAIMAW hall in New Westminster. "So we said, 'We need to set aside a lot of the regular business, we need to focus on this because this is an attack on the people of B.C.' . . . By the end of the first day [of council meetings], it was pretty obvious that there was only one logical response and that was a general strike. By this time, the fishermen's union, CUPW [Canadian Union of Postal Workers], some of the better CUPE [Canadian Union of Public Employees] locals, the carpenters and some of the good people in the plumbers' union were beginning to get together."

The mood was electric at the Fisherman's Hall on Cordova Street the night the LMBC was launched. "Basically, the left gathered," Jef says. "The outrage was palpable. This is before the Internet, before you could do all the rest of that stuff. We couldn't get everybody in the door. There were all these people out on Cordova Street getting the messages relayed. I mean, we were well over legal capacity inside the Fisherman's Hall." LMBC membership was open to any organization "committed to the goals of defeating the B.C. government's budget and legislative program and to the development of a more equitable society." A Steering Committee was named with George Hewison elected chair and Jef Keighley secretary. The meeting decided on its first action: a rally on Saturday, July 23, 1983, that would start at Thornton Park in front of the old CN Station and march on the new B.C. Place. A report on the LMBC at the July 20 meeting of Women Against the Budget (WAB) says that "400 people attended the meeting at the Fisherfolk Hall."[2] Minutes from the WAB meeting note that the LMBC discussed which speakers to invite to its rally: "NDP and Socred speaker defeated, Women's speaker and minority groups accepted."[3]

The day of the LMBC's Fisherman's Hall meeting, the B.C. Federation of Labour called for an all-union conference to create a coordinated response to the budget. So, with LMBC plans for the July 23 rally under way, the BCFED was about to launch Operation Solidarity, an alliance of 400,000 union members. The Fed unveiled its "Program of Action" on July 15. The plan included the establishment of a Trade Union Solidarity Committee—comprised of the Fed's executive council and non-affiliated unions—"for the purpose of mounting an effective fight-back campaign against the vicious attack of government on social, economic, human and trade union rights."[4] It was agreed that the B.C. union movement, under the leadership of the Fed, enter into a "broad-based coalition" with groups representing churches, the unemployed, peace, tenants, minorities, small business, women "and any other groups who have a sense of moral and social responsibility to the overall community, for the purpose of opposing the brutal attack of government against the social, economic and democratic fibre of this province."[5] Operation Solidarity, it was announced, would hold its first of a series of mass rallies on July 27 in Victoria. Art Kube was named Operation Solidarity chair.

The BCTF was among the unions unaffiliated with the B.C.

Federation of Labour that quickly signed on to Operation Solidarity. Art Kube also invited the CCU, which operated independently of the BCFED, to join Solidarity, although it was never actually invited into its Fed-controlled inner sanctum. CCU president Jess Succamore's notes record that Kube phoned him on July 11 and 12 and the two met at 6:30 p.m. on July 25, an hour before the Solidarity Coalition meeting at the Fisherman's Hall. "We had a really good working relationship [with Art Kube] on this thing," Jess says. "He just phoned up to find out where we were at because he didn't want to start organizing something and us be out there throwing bricks at it. I told him basically, 'Look, you do what you got to do there. Don't worry about us. We'll be on side.'"

Besides the CCU and BCTF, the BCFED's B.C. Trade Union Solidarity Committee's first meeting July 28 at the BCGEU Auditorium in Burnaby was attended by BCFED officers and executive council members, plus representatives of the B.C. Nurses' Union, Hospital Employees' Union, Health Sciences Association, police, College Institute Educators' Association, Canadian Association of University Teachers, Building Trades Council, International Brotherhood of Electrical Workers Local 258, Retail Wholesale Department Store Union, Vancouver Municipal and Regional Employees Union, Workers' Compensation Board, Canadian Labour Congress, Teamsters and the Association of University and College Employees. This early version of Solidarity agreed to a series of objectives, including a broad-based plan of action to involve coalition partners. To "increase the moral authority of the Operation Solidarity Coalition," they also agreed on a province-wide petition drive calling for withdrawal of the legislation or a new provincial election.[6] The goal of the petition was to get more signatures than the Socreds got votes in May.

The Lower Mainland Budget Coalition endorsed the BCFED's Solidarity program, but inside the LMBC there was some cynicism about the new organization. Kim Zander saw the formation of Operation Solidarity as the BCFED's worried reaction to the LMBC. "As soon as they saw the Lower Mainland Budget Coalition pull together, and the way that it had formed through the Vancouver Labour Council's Unemployment Committee, they went, 'Oh fuck, we're in trouble,' because they couldn't control it. It was that simple. The Vancouver Labour Council was always seen as the lefty and, you know, the unruly child in the labour movement."

Meanwhile, the LMBC was steaming ahead with its July 23 rally—the first mass protest against the budget. The BCFED signed on as a co-sponsor but was more enthused about a protest it had come up with on its own. "The plan that the BCFED had actually come up with was that they would hold a symbolic protest march," Jef Keighley says. "They would have two members of every union affiliated to the BCFED march down the Theatre Row on Granville Street in protest against the legislation. It would be limited to two so that you could count them and see that every union was represented. And people heard that and said, 'You must be fucking kidding.' 'No, this is a good plan.' 'Fuck you, it's a good plan. That's not going to happen.'"

Jef was at an LMBC Steering Committee meeting when its chair, George Hewison, received a phone call from Art Kube. "We're in a meeting in the board room of the Fisherman's Hall and George's support worker comes and says, 'George, Kube's on the phone.' So George goes out, comes back in about five minutes. And he's livid. He says, 'Kube says the Fed's pulling out. They're not going to co-sponsor it.' . . . I said, 'George, you get him back on the phone and you tell him that based on the earlier commitment that the Fed was going to co-sponsor we have printed 20,000 copies of this notice.'" Jef suggested Kube be told that the LMBC had exhausted its funds, couldn't afford to print another 20,000, and wasn't about to cross a pencil through the BCFED's name on the leaflet. "'So we're going to use those 20,000. We're going to distribute them and it'll be up to the BCFED to explain why they're no longer co-sponsoring this march.' And people looked around, and said, 'That's not true.' And I said, 'They don't know that.'

"George [had a] twinkle in the eye because he was always the leprechaun and he liked that kind of stuff. So he phoned him [Kube] up and said, 'We printed 20,000 and it's gonna be up to you to explain why you reneged on a previous agreement.' And Kube said, 'Oh God, oh God, oh God.'" Jef says Kube phoned back twenty minutes later. "He says, 'Okay, okay, we're still on, but we want to have some say over the speakers there.' And we all said, 'Of course you would. You co-sponsored.' So we went forward with that. We were hopeful we'd have 2,000 people show up at Thornton Park. Instead, we had 25,000 people show up."

On a sunny July 23, the spirited marchers chanted and waved placards ("Nuke the Socreds," said one) as they poured through city streets, across the Georgia Viaduct and on to B.C. Place. The rally featured speakers Hanne Jensen (ex-Human Rights Branch), Charan Gill (B.C. Organization to Fight Racism), George Hewison (Lower Mainland Budget Coalition), Mike Harcourt (Vancouver mayor), Jack Munro (International Woodworkers of America), Jim Roberts (soon to co-chair the Solidarity Coalition) and Kim Zander (Unemployed Action Centre). Kim Zander's Action Centre drew on its community connections to provide a volunteer army for the rally. Kim recalls telling the protesters: "We have to resist the budget that Bennett is putting forward. We don't have any choice." Fired Human Rights commissioner Hanne Jensen said: "British Columbians are not going to accept less just because somebody decides that allowing discrimination to go unchecked is necessary for economic recovery."[7] Four days after the big Vancouver rally, morning passengers on B.C. Ferries en route to Vancouver Island received a leaflet. "Enjoy Your Trip," it said. "The people who operate the ferry which you will be traveling on today are public sector workers. Recently the government of British Columbia introduced legislation which will remove many of the fundamental rights of public sector workers. . . . Today in Victoria, thousands of public and private sector workers, representatives of community groups and churches will be demonstrating against the government. . . . We ask that all B.C. residents traveling on the ferries today take time to write to the premier and the MLA denouncing the removal of the fundamental rights of public sector workers. IF YOU DON'T SPEAK OUT, WHO WILL?—Operation Solidarity."[8]

That day's Operation Solidarity protest drew 30,000 protesters to the Legislature's lawn. This was the rally where a young Victoria resident, John Horgan, was so inspired by ex-NDP premier Dave Barrett's impassioned speech-making that he dropped by an NDP office and joined the party that day. ("Dave had an ability to capture your heart, mind and soul," said Horgan, who would much later become the B.C. premier.[9]) The Vancouver and Victoria rallies were in the national news, but there were less-publicized Solidarity protests of every shape and size across B.C. as July wore on into August.

Although teachers were on summer holiday when the legislation landed, many turned out for the first big rallies in Vancouver and Victoria. "It didn't take very long at all for people to respond to it," says the BCTF's Larry Kuehn. "We have a summer training conference every year in August at UBC—about 600 people from across the province." That year, the three-day training session focused on developing strategies for the fall and the immediate task of mobilizing teachers to attend the Empire Stadium rally. "That conference, in many ways, was a key to organizing," Larry says. "Started talking about the possibilities of a strike. We had the president of the Canadian Teachers' Federation and several presidents of other provincial unions speak. We went downtown and stood on streets to talk to people about what's happening and basically built the basis for the local activity that would take place around the province—through the workshops that we had and planning sessions and et cetera, et cetera." The BCTF's local officers returned to their school districts well-informed of the issues and with action plans in place.

—◈—

The bills were so repugnant to so many that they mobilized the public in ways veteran activists couldn't have imagined. Stan Persky, editor of the *Solidarity Times* newspaper during the uprising, says: "It is so difficult to create the preconditions for a political upheaval of any kind, whether it's a real-live revolution or it's merely some sort of effort to change conditions on the ground. The ability to pull that together requires so many elements that nobody has control of, especially the political organizers involved." This time, though, the pieces seemed to have fallen into place: a Reagan-Thatcher-Bennett set of policies being implemented, a community-labour alliance resisting these policies and a tremendous welling of public support for the resistance. "It looked to a lot of us like there really were conditions for a general strike. You can't just announce, 'Gee, we're going to have a general strike,' and then everybody waves the flag. It requires enormous amounts of building and putting conditions together that would make a general strike possible. . . . It looked like that had happened. Those conditions—that so-called perfect storm of circumstance—had happened in 1983. It's the sort of thing that can happen once a generation."

CHAPTER 2

In Solidarity:
The Empire Strikes Back

MUGGS SIGURGEIRSON KNEW she'd be at Empire Stadium. Muggs already had one particularly vivid memory of the stadium out by the Pacific National Exhibition in East Vancouver. She was living in North Vancouver and thirteen years old on August 31, 1957, the day Elvis Presley played Empire Stadium. Like so many 1950s teenagers, she had watched Elvis on *Ed Sullivan* and was enthralled by the new rock 'n' roll. "We all thought he was really cool. Everybody was moved by the music. When I was in junior high, we had sock hops twice a week on our lunch hour and they played rock 'n' roll in the lunchroom all the time to keep the kids from going out in the bush and smoking." When Muggs and her friends heard Elvis was coming to town, they quickly purchased the $1.50 tickets.

Marcy Toms was living on the West Side of Vancouver and fourteen years old on August 22, 1964, the day the Beatles played Empire

Stadium. Like so many 1960s teenagers, she had seen the Beatles on *Ed Sullivan* and was captivated by this British Invasion. This time, tickets started at $3.25. "In order to get tickets, my parents allowed me to accompany three friends and sleep overnight in front of the stadium." Chaperoned by a parent, they stayed up all night.

Besides rock concerts, the Empire Stadium of the 1950s and '60s was home to football's B.C. Lions and the annual Vancouver and District Inter-High School track meet. Cliff Stainsby, of Burnaby South high school, ran the mile and two-mile races in the stadium's 1966 meet. "It was just tremendously exciting. Track was big in high school and it was big at Burnaby South. But I was never a star."

After high school, Cliff enrolled at Simon Fraser University (SFU). "I came from a fairly conservative background. After the first year I became a hippie, smoked pot, did LSD, all that stuff, and according to my parents became quite radical." By 1983, Cliff was a long-time environmental activist who made phone calls to help get people out to Solidarity's Empire Stadium rally. "As far as I can recollect we filled Empire Stadium more than we did at the high school track meet. That was just heady stuff."

This high school track meet received extensive local media coverage and was the one place—excluding Beatles and Elvis concerts— where teenagers from every corner of the Greater Vancouver area would cross paths. "I was there," says Nettie Wild, a student at West Vancouver high in the late 1960s. "And that's what was so interesting about the protest. When you go in a building that's been defined in a completely different way before, and then you walk in and it's taken over by a different voice like that—it was stunning for me. I couldn't believe it. Really moving."

On August 10, 1983, Nettie and some 40,000 fellow Solidarity protesters crowded into Empire Stadium. With its massive turnout and electric energy, it was for many the event that established Solidarity. After August 10, they knew they were part of a historic moment when anything—even the impossible—seemed possible. The Empire Stadium rally helped to rouse protests across the province. The next day, 1,500 protesters attended a Solidarity rally in Williams Lake (almost 20 per cent of the B.C. Interior town's population). The following week, 4,000 showed up at Kelowna's City Park. And there were rallies in Cranbrook (Aug. 12), Salmon Arm (Aug. 13), Fort St. John (Aug. 13), Nanaimo (Aug. 17), Fort Nelson (Aug. 20) and Courtenay (Aug. 31).

—◦◦◦—

Empire Stadium was practically brand new the day Elvis played there. The stadium had been completed in time to host the 1954 British Empire and Commonwealth Games, a considerable sporting event back when there was a British Empire. At the 1954 Vancouver Games, Roger Bannister and John Landy broke the four-minute mile, bringing for the first time international headlines to a Vancouver dateline. After the Games, this utilitarian stadium would be home to other sporting events. But for Elvis's army of teenage fans, the stadium existed in August 1957 for a single purpose—to host the most anticipated concert in Vancouver memory.

"One of the kids that I used to hang around with had an older brother who worked around the stadium. He knew when Elvis was coming," Muggs Sigurgeirson says. He knew which parking lot entrance Elvis was coming through, too, so Muggs and friends were waiting there when he arrived. "And he drove right by us. We were actually like touching his car, and he was turning around into the back window and waving and being super friendly so we were really juiced. Even at the time I was thinking, 'Millions of people do this to him all the time—*don't you get tired of doing this?*'" When Elvis walked on stage, the audience surged toward him. "We ran down," Muggs says. "Nobody stayed in their seat. Everybody poured down. We were right up at the front of that. He was just on a wood platform in the middle of that stadium, like no protection. Within minutes he was completely surrounded."

The concert's small security force was overwhelmed. Marion Guild, a young Elvis fan at the time, told me: "It was pandemonium. All around me were other kids and cops. Suddenly, I saw my shoe underneath the foot of a cop. I tried to get his attention, to no avail. The next thing I knew, I was biting the cop's arm. He moved, I got my shoe and ended up right in front of the stage, where I was mesmerized by the beautiful sight of Elvis."[1] After twenty-two minutes of concert, Elvis's manager Colonel Parker had seen enough. The last concert Elvis would play outside the U.S. was over. "They got him out of there," Muggs says. "We tried to follow him out to the car but of course we lost him in the mob."

Seven years later, the Beatles concert at Empire Stadium lasted twenty-seven minutes. Like Marcy Toms, I was at this Beatles concert. As the band walked on stage my cousin Maureen, seated beside me, let out a shriek. Several thousand others were letting out the same shriek. "Could not hear anything," says Marcy. The Beatles' Vancouver concert quickly turned as rambunctious as Elvis's had been. Thousands rushed the stage with some pressed hard against a makeshift fence. Local celebrity DJ Red Robinson stepped to the microphone between songs to urge calm, prompting John Lennon to snap: "Get the fuck off our stage."[2] Seeing that the show she had so anticipated was coming to an early end, Marcy had a notion. "I thought, I must check to see if they're wearing Beatle boots. They were." And the most memorable evening of Marcy's young life was suddenly over.

The Beatles were taken from the concert to the airport, stopping for burgers at Wally's Drive-In on Kingsway. A year later, the Beatles visited Elvis at his L.A. home and they got to talking about Vancouver and Empire Stadium. "Some funny things happen to you on the road, don't they?" Elvis told the Beatles. "I remember once in Vancouver we'd only done a number or two when some of the fans rushed the stage. It was lucky the guys and I got off in time. They tipped the whole damn rostrum over."[3]

—⁓—

In Solidarity: The Empire Strikes Back / 29

Nettie Wild's mom grew up next door to Hugh Pickett, the impresario who staged the Elvis and Beatles shows at Empire Stadium. Nettie's aunt would later work at Pickett's Famous Artists Productions and regularly provide her with concert tickets. By 1983, people were buying tickets to see Nettie perform with the popular Vancouver agitprop troupe Headlines Theatre. Many in Nettie's circle of friends were actively opposing the Socred bills. "When I heard that there was going to be a rally at Empire Stadium I remember at the time thinking, 'Ah, I better go to support my pals who had been working so hard around all this crazy stuff that was going down,' and thinking that not very many people would be there, that I would just go to lend my feet."

As Nettie walked toward the stadium that August day, her expectations as to what she'd find inside were rapidly changing. "It was like a magnet. It was like the entire city was coming from all different directions toward Empire Stadium. And then when we walked into the stadium I was just overwhelmed. I remember walking and thinking it didn't feel like Canada. It didn't feel like anything culturally that I had experienced before. It felt like a newsreel from somewhere else. A hell of a lot more people there than I expected." A roll of sound filled the stadium as Nettie made her way into the stands. "Sound that doesn't come from some little knot of people. It comes from a whole lot of people. And it was very, very exciting." As one by one the union contingents came into the stadium to parade in front of their fellow protesters, the stands erupted in a voluminous sound the place hadn't heard since the Beatles and Elvis. "I'm finding myself bursting in tears as the postal workers are walking in," says Nettie. "There was the firefighters and all these various different unions—police coming in. It still gives me goosebumps. It was just phenomenal."

—*∿∿*—

August 10 at Empire Stadium was organized by Operation Solidarity. The leaflet for the Empire Stadium rally called on British Columbians to "JOIN US AND SPEAK OUT Against Discriminatory and Repressive Legislation. . . . 10:00 a.m. to 1:00 p.m.—BRING THE FAMILY."[4] It listed thirteen locations where people could catch free bus transportation to and from the rally, including Burnaby's Brentwood Mall and Vancouver's Oakridge Shopping Centre, Hope's Legion and Surrey's Guildford Town Centre. Unions across the Lower Mainland called on their members to attend. The Hospital Employees' Union (HEU) said: "All HEU members who are not designated as 'essential' must be there!"[5] Operation Solidarity minutes noted a rumour that the "Fireman's Band with Mayor's [Mike Harcourt] blessing will be going."[6] A memo from Vancouver's city manager, Fritz Bowers, said "nearly all" city workers who were members of the Canadian Union of Public Employees or the Vancouver Municipal and Regional Employees' Union (VMREU) were expected to attend the rally.[7] The VMREU produced a leaflet urging its members to:

> come to work on August 10. Leave for the Rally at 10:30 a.m. Tell your supervisor that you are going to the Rally, and encourage ALL your co-workers (including your boss) to come. . . . THE VMREU BANNER WILL BE MARCHED IN FROM THE NORTH END OF THE STADIUM AT 11:00 A.M. TRY TO BE THERE.[8]

The plan was to have each union's contingent make a grand entrance—some, like firefighters, in full uniform—then join the parade around the stadium. There was a compelling pageantry to this, like an Olympic Games opening ceremony, or even more like the rousing finale in a Clifford Odets Group Theatre production in 1935 New York. As the riveting union production played out on the stadium AstroTurf, it called together some unaccustomed bedfellows. Before becoming active in the Solidarity Coalition, Jean Swanson was an anti-poverty activist with the Downtown Eastside Residents' Association (DERA). The diversity of protesters at Empire Stadium was a bit disconcerting for her. "I remember marching around the stadium out at the PNE and there was all the people who had been fired from the Rentalsman office that had been abolished. And I remember thinking how weird it was to be in Solidarity with them when I had been fighting them for so long at DERA—trying to get them to say that we needed landlord-tenant protection."

Melanie Ray knew she had to be at Empire Stadium. She had been shaken by the Socred legislation on July 7 and felt, from afar, an intense solidarity with the first anti-budget protests. "I was staying current on what was going on." So, when she heard about the big rally planned for Empire Stadium on August 10, she immediately decided it was her time to activate. "I don't think I was exactly an activist," she says, "but when do you get off your tush?"

When Melanie made her snap decision to attend the rally, she was working at the downtown offices of the Teck mining company. Melanie was an aspiring actor who, a few months earlier, answered an ad for the Teck job. "They were looking for a mail clerk. I did an interview and compared to an audition a job interview is nothing." Thus, Melanie added to her daily juggling act sorting mail for eight floors. "I was trying to keep a home and a job and a child and a small women's theatre company together."

When she decided to go to Empire Stadium, Melanie knew she had banked enough time to take the day off. "I went to my boss, who I was friends with, and said, I'd like to have such-and-such a day off. And I happened to say, 'I want to go to the Solidarity rally.'"

Boss: "What?"

Melanie: "Yeah."

Boss: "You can't do that."

Melanie: "It's my day off. I can do what I like."

Boss: "No, no, you can't do that."

Melanie: "It's none of your business what I do on my days off."

Boss: "If you go you will be fired."

Melanie: "Well, I'm going."

On August 9, Melanie's boss said, "Are you going tomorrow?"

Melanie said yes. "She said, 'Then pick up your things and go now. You're fired.' So I took my stuff and I left. My first thought was *hooray* because I hated being trapped in a building without open windows from 8 a.m. to 4 p.m. every day. So, I was just essentially really happy, and then I had a talk with a friend who said, 'You know, that was pretty bad what they did. No notice. You're out because of something you're doing on your time off.'" Melanie decided to fight the firing. "I wasn't real keen, but I thought that it would be a good thing for Solidarity. I was trying to help where I could. So I did that."

Although Melanie didn't consider herself an activist, she knew where she stood ("I felt things and thought things") and had politically active friends. "Frances Wasserlein was a friend. A few other people. Through [volunteering at] the folk music festival, I knew people." Women Against the Budget held a rally in front of the Teck building in support of Melanie and Dave Barrett visited Teck's office to ask that she be rehired. There were newspaper articles about her. With negative publicity spreading, the company buckled. So Melanie went to Empire Stadium and kept her job. "Once I came back I got quite a lot of nastiness coming from people who worked at Teck. I just remember feeling I was in this nest of right-wing people and my heart was breaking." Besides, the office still had no windows or sunshine. Melanie's stay at Teck was over before 1983 ended.

———

To understand the politics of B.C. during the Depression, you should know the Communist Party, which young Russian-Jewish immigrant Rose Barrett, like so many of the era, joined. As in the rest of the world, B.C. was in upheaval in the 1930s and many of its benchmark protests were organized by the party. B.C.'s unemployed were housed in relief camps where they were paid twenty cents a day to plant trees and construct buildings and roads. The CP-organized Relief Camp Workers' Union went on strike and hundreds of its members, demanding improved relief camp conditions and pay, descended on

Vancouver to stage protests—including the On-to-Ottawa Trek of 1935. An "On to Ottawa!" notice called on locals to meet at the Canadian Pacific Railway station "to give OUR BOYS a farewell send-off in their determined fight for the right to live as human beings."[9] Riding freight trains, the goal had been to pick up thousands of additional protesters along the way to Ottawa. The plan was working so well that the government stopped freights going east from Regina. In Regina, the Trekkers and their supporters were attacked by police, leaving one dead, hundreds injured and 120 arrested. In Vancouver, the CP also organized occupations of the post office, art gallery and Hotel Georgia, which resulted in the "Bloody Sunday" riot of 1938.

At a Vancouver May Day parade in 1938, Rose Barrett wrapped her son David in bandages so he could portray a wounded child on a Spanish Civil War float, which made its way through downtown to Stanley Park. The *Vancouver Sun* reported:

> Conservative estimates place the number who heard May Day speeches at [Lumbermen's Arch] at around 20,000. From Mission and Surrey and from up the coast, people came to take part. . . . Although "O Canada" was sung at the commencement, "The Internationale," rather than "God Save the King," featured the close of the Lumberman's Arch demonstration.[10]

Vancouver's Len Norris would have been at Stanley Park, but he was away in Spain with the CP-organized Mackenzie–Papineau Battalion, some 1,500 Canadian volunteers who fought fascism in the civil war. Spanish writer Ogier Preteceille brought greetings from Loyalist Spain to Stanley Park. "They are fighting your fight, as well as their own," he told the cheering Vancouver crowd.[11]

To understand the politics of B.C. during the Depression, it also helps to know the Co-operative Commonwealth Federation (CCF). If the CP was associated with the union and street battles of the 1930s, the CCF was the era's ballot-box left. Left-wing democratic socialists—more Tommy Douglas and less Thomas Mulcair than the

NDP of the twenty-first century. The CCF quickly established itself electorally, winning seven seats in 1933 to become the official opposition in Victoria. Rose Barrett was still in the Communist Party when her son David was first elected to the B.C. Legislature in 1960 as a member of the CCF. (Rose wouldn't quit the CP until 1968, when she left in protest of the Soviet invasion of Czechoslovakia.) David's politics would be closer to his Winnipeg-born, democratic-socialist father, Sam. After serving in the Canadian Forces during the First World War, Sam was a member of the Industrial Workers of the World (IWW/the Wobblies) in California and, following his return to Canada, became a CCF supporter and operated a grocery store across from Oppenheimer Park. (My father's uncle, Louis Spaner, was among Sam's best friends in the old Strathcona neighbourhood.) So, the Barretts of East Van's McSpadden street were an outspoken mix of the energetic democratic-socialist and Communist movements of the era. While the CCF was plenty popular at the B.C. ballot box, it was red-baited almost as venomously as the CP, particularly by Bill Bennett's father, long-time Socred premier W.A.C. Bennett.

Dave Barrett's NDP formed the provincial government in 1972 and, in short order, passed a guaranteed income supplement for seniors and the disabled, raised the minimum wage, ended the incarceration of young children, provided autonomy to school boards and protected rural areas with the Agricultural Land Reserve. The Barrett government lost its re-election bid in 1975. It was expected to return to power in the May 1983 election but lost, resulting in Bill Bennett's twenty-six bills. The NDP opposed these bills in Victoria, but the burgeoning Solidarity resistance was well beyond the confines of the Legislature. As Art Kube noted: "I presume the NDP caucus feels lonely in the Legislature because the action is not in the Legislature. It's out in the community."[12] On August 10, Rose Barrett and her kindred spirits across the province would find solace in the events at Empire Stadium. "She was there with her old fellow traveller buddy Mina," recalls her grandson Joe Barrett. "I remember the two of them did chum around. They were two old commies. And when the police marched in, they were convinced this was the moment. The general strike would take place and it would be the downfall of capitalism. As you could imagine, the two of them, who at that point in time would have been close to their eighties, really thought this was a pivotal moment."

———✧———

To understand the politics of Vancouver during the New Left 1960s and '70s, it helps to know Saria Andrew. She was the Youth International Party (YIP/the Yippies) mayoralty candidate in 1970, calling for the repeal of all laws including the law of gravity, "so everyone can get high."[13] The Yippies combined the era's counterculture with its counter-politics while creating some of the more memorable events in Vancouver left history, including the Blaine Invasion (an actual invasion of the border town in response to Nixon's invasion of Cambodia), All Season's Park (a "people's park" that stopped a development at the entrance to Stanley Park) and the Gastown Smoke-In (a riotous protest against the police's brutal enforcement of marijuana laws). Some Vancouver Yippies would later be heavily involved in the politics of punk, including Rock Against Radiation and Rock Against Racism concerts.

Coming of age in Nova Scotia, Saria was involved in legendary anti-racist activist Rocky Jones's Kwacha House, a trail-blazing multiracial youth centre in Halifax. Moving on to Vancouver, Saria protested the Vietnam War and nuclear warships but found much of the left "very stiff and very closed and not much fun." So she joined YIP, with its emphasis on guerrilla theatrics and an anarchic politics of joy. "It wasn't that we weren't serious but that we wanted things to be more inclusive," Saria says. The Yippie aim was to organize the burgeoning counterculture, with its communal anti-authoritarian ethos, into a radical social movement. At an all-candidates meeting in 1970, notorious anti-hippie mayor Tom Campbell didn't show up on time, so YIP mayoralty candidate Saria sat in his empty chair and proceeded to deliver his talking points. "He always gave the same speech when he did show up and so I had it pretty well memorized. Just after I gave his speech, he came in. His handlers should have told him that I had already given the speech because he gave the same speech."

1983: In the 1970s, the post office was one of the few places a counterculture lefty could find work. Saria was a mail sorter, then forklift driver and a Canadian Union of Postal Workers (CUPW) shop steward. She applied for time off to attend the Empire Stadium rally. "Of course they didn't grant it, but I took the time off anyway. I just remember thinking that it was quite wonderful because there were so many people and so many kinds of people." An overwhelming show of force by B.C.'s unions. "We all came. And the national postal workers came from Ottawa. I had my kids. I had fun. And we were so solid. . . . It was so supportive, inspiring and energizing."

———

Between the tabling of the bills on July 7 and Empire Stadium on August 10, Raj Chouhan became active in Solidarity. Still, Raj had little sense of how big this movement might be until he marched into the stadium with a hundred members of the Canadian Farmworkers Union (CFU)—the union he had co-founded. This contingent was greeted that day by waves of thunderous cheering. "Like you had just won the Oscar," Raj says. There had been all manner of social movements across B.C. history, but now, in August of 1983, it seemed they could coalesce into one unstoppable force. "That's what I'm trying to find words to describe," Raj continues. "People were engaged in their small little groups, small little union, here and there and all that. Scattered, splintered, whatever. And suddenly this happened. Everybody together into the same central focus. We were together. Thinking the same way. Towards the same goal. Not one group was trying to dominate that. No one group tried to say that 'I should be in the forefront. We should be leading it.' That kind of ego. I didn't see that.

Until Kelowna, but we'll get to that." This day in August, Raj and friends left the stadium overcome with elation and solidarity. "That was the feeling everybody had, actually, when we left that rally. We achieved something. We're nowhere near achieving the final goal but, you know, we felt that's really good. People are waking up. People will stand up."

—◁∿∿—

It was at the Empire Stadium rally that long-time activist-writer Stan Persky first pitched his idea for a Solidarity newspaper. "I ran into a guy that I knew named David Cadman, who was then the president of the Municipal Government and Service Employees' Union in Vancouver." He was also a member of Operation Solidarity's thirteen-member executive. "And David Cadman and I were standing next to each other at the rally. I also was aware that the BCFED used to run a real newspaper at one point in B.C. history. So I said to David Cadman, 'You know, what this Solidarity thing needs is a newspaper.' And he said, 'Well, that's a good idea. Why don't you come to the Solidarity Coalition meeting and you can present it as a proposal.'"

—◁∿∿—

A week following the Empire Stadium rally, Operation Solidarity's Steering Committee resolved that:

> Operation Solidarity adopt and endorse the principle than an injury to one partner of the Coalition is an injury to all partners of the Coalition; and be it further resolved that Operation Solidarity commit itself to the principle that all legislation affecting the Coalition partners must be withdrawn; and be it finally resolved that Solidarity communicate our resolve to all partners of the Solidarity Coalition.[14]

Empire Stadium would remain the most enduring memory of 1983 for Beth Hutchinson of the Women's Health Collective. "It was just such an amazing and fabulous event. And it just stood out in so many ways. I mean, the bus drivers weren't driving anybody unless they were going to the event is my recollection. The organizers of that event—I just thought they were entirely brilliant in the way they set it up. It really was an event to show solidarity. I mean, it didn't have to chout how appalling these moves of the Socred government were. That thrill of the different groups walking around

"And here come the bus drivers—*hooray*! Cheer for them! Clap for them! Here comes postpartum counselling. Cheer for them! Here come the letter carriers. Cheer for them! Here comes group after group after group. And such a mixture of labour and political and women's and community and church groups who had come together. I remember just that heady feeling of ... *this is building. This is very big. There could be a general strike.*"

CHAPTER 3

The Solidarity Coalition:
Something Big

DURING THE SOLIDARITY months of 1983, there were weekly meetings at an office at 686 West Broadway in Vancouver. Those who met around long tables at the Solidarity Coalition office had been crack organizers in their own political silos and now, together at these Steering Committee meetings, they represented everyone damaged by the Socred legislation. With so many of the best kind of organizers—tireless and highly motivated—at the same table and, for the most part, wanting nothing less than to bring down the government, the adrenaline in the room was contagious.

Art Kube lifted the new movement's name from the Polish Solidarity trade union that was all over the nightly news in the slightly earlier 1980s. Having launched the union-based Operation Solidarity on July 15, Kube wanted a coalition of social movements to operate alongside it. Operation Solidarity provided funding for the Solidarity

Coalition, which formed August 3 and soon had a staff and this Broadway office. "The unions created the Solidarity Coalition," says coalition organizer Jean Swanson. "Art Kube created it. He had this idea that you could get community groups together and they could work together and come up with something big." An Operation Solidarity interim operating statement recommended that the coalition be driven by a Steering Committee "representing, as much as possible, the following areas of interest": women, ethnic minorities, students, youth, seniors, professionals, environmentalists, the peace movement, gays, lesbians, the co-operative sector, injured workers, tenants, public education, health, universities/colleges, the unemployed, anti-poverty, human rights, Indigenous groups, unions, disabled people, social services, religious groups, consumers, civil liberties, and small businesses.[1]

Kube recruited a BCGEU vice-president, John Shields, to pull together the Solidarity Coalition. He knew Shields was one union organizer who could connect with activists outside the labour movement. Born in New York City, Shields had been an activist Catholic priest protesting alongside Martin Luther King. He left the church disillusioned and moved to Victoria, where he became a social worker. "For social activism, human rights and justice. It was his very fabric," says Solidarity organizer Diane Wood. The organizers Shields called on to help coordinate the coalition shared his passion for social justice—Jim Roberts, another "social gospel" priest, and Renate Shearer, a Jewish refugee from Nazi Germany who spent a lifetime fighting for human rights. The Solidarity Coalition's Patsy George says Jim Roberts was a pleasure to work with. "He really believed in human rights. He was instrumental in bringing some of the church communities into the Solidarity movement because they felt, oh, Father Roberts is there, it must be okay." Renate Shearer, Patsy says, "was a friend. She was a human rights commissioner and she was fired from that job. Renate worked very closely with the First Nations people, she worked very closely with the farm workers, so she had a larger view of the various struggles that people were going through."

—〰—

Patsy George was at the table at 686 West Broadway. She grew up in the Kerala province on the southern tip of India. Like Dave Barrett, one parent was a democratic socialist and the other a communist. "My mom worked for one candidate. My father would support another candidate. It never created a problem for the two of them. We thought it was funny. We children did. And the discussions, you can imagine at our dining table, so it made us all very, very aware." Both of her parents were active in India's independence movement. So, long before Patsy was asked to partake in the Solidarity Coalition, she was acutely aware that a political/personal coalition can work.

In 1959, Patsy left India for Mount St. Scholastica College in Atchison, Kansas. "It was a completely white college, okay, and there were two of us, people of color. Me and another woman, Wangari Maathai, from Kenya." Wangari would, decades later, start the Green Belt ecological movement and be the first African woman to win the Nobel Peace Prize.

Patsy and Wangari became close friends and co-troublemakers. "We got in trouble with our professor whenever we would have any discussions and whatnot, so I decided that's not a place for me," says Patsy. She moved on to Our Lady of the Lake College in San Antonio, Texas. "The first week or so that I was there, three kids took me to a movie theatre and I had to sit somewhere separate from them because they were all white and I was brown. That did it to me."

Patsy was packing to return to India, crying, when a professor she had befriended stopped by to suggest she give Canada a try. She transferred to the University of Windsor. Patsy saw injustice in Canada, too, but was inspired by social movements emerging in the 1960s. Living in Nova Scotia, she founded a Planned Parenthood branch and assisted U.S. draft dodgers. Patsy moved on to B.C. in 1974 "because of Dave Barrett," but his government fell before she had a chance to join it. Instead, she wound up coordinating welfare services in the Downtown Eastside's Strathcona neighbourhood. She quickly gained a reputation as a staunch defender of the dispossessed, working tirelessly to create lunch and literacy programs alongside organizers such as Bruce Eriksen, Libby Davies and Jean Swanson. "Outside work hours, I was active as a community person. It was not easy—working outside and from within as a public servant working at making changes. Many times, I got very close to getting fired."

1983: Patsy has just stepped down as president of the B.C. Association of Social Workers and is a member of the NDP. ("I was always more left of the New Democrats in my own head, you know.") When the Socred legislative avalanche comes down, Patsy is among the 1,400 B.C. Government and Service Employees' Union members immediately fired and she is asked to join the Solidarity Coalition staff. "John Shields, a fellow social worker, was getting active with Solidarity and decided that I would be a good person because I knew a whole bunch of people all around the province as well as I had this organizing kind of a mind." There is a handful of Solidarity Coalition paid staff who work closely with the coalition's original coordinators—Shields, Renate Shearer and Jim Roberts. "[The coalition] would meet once a week, sometimes even more. I took the minutes some days. Renate would chair those meetings. It would be mostly to talk about strategies. Not only working with the unions but also expanding to various parts of the province."

Patsy throws herself into the coalition the way she'd defended her Strathcona clients—unconditionally. "Started at six in the morning and went on until eleven, eleven thirty at night, because we start again at six in the morning. Those were the days we didn't have computers, so we used telephones and we used going out and talking to people. So there was so much more work. I mean, to organize a rally, it took so much work and telephone trees and all of those sort of stuff. So we needed volunteers. And also part of our job—there were three of us [staffers]—was to bring various groups into the Solidarity Coalition, whether it is the professional groups, whether it is the women's groups, whether it is church community, or even small business people. . . . So most of our work was really to go out into the community, various parts of the province."

———

Visiting communities across B.C., Patsy would do radio and TV interviews, disseminate anti-Socred information, encourage Solidarity protests. "I was sent to Prince George. I knew the social worker community in Prince George but I didn't know the union people other than the BCTF. The rest of them, particularly all those people who work in the forest, were all new to me. I had no contact whatsoever. So I asked a local person, 'Where do I find these people?'" Patsy was told she'd have to go into the pubs where the workers relax in the evenings after their shifts. "So can you imagine me—thirty-eight years old at the time, an Indian woman—walking in a pub all by myself and trying to say hello to all these men sitting around having their beer and whatnot. I go in and say, 'Have you heard of the Solidarity Coalition? I'm here because I would like to meet with local unions.'" She struck up conversations about what the bills would mean to these workers and their families and neighbours. Before she left the barroom, Patsy had explained how to get involved in the Solidarity organizing under way in Prince George. "Connecting people and trying to get them excited about protesting and all of that kind of stuff. That's what I did for those months."

Five thousand people would come out for Prince George Solidarity Day on September 21. It saw numerous unions leave work for rallies and study sessions. In the nearby, smaller communities of Mackenzie and McBride, teachers set up an information booth, went door-to-door with a Solidarity petition and held a planning session.

———

With so many strong personalities at the table, it's no surprise that coalition meetings were passionate affairs. A sampling of players in this weekly drama: ecologist Cliff Stainsby, gay activist Stuart Alcock, feminists Marion Pollack and Lorri Rudland, Downtown Eastside organizer Jim Green, social worker Patsy George, anti-racism activists Raj Chouhan and David Chiu, union organizers Jef Keighley and Larry Kuehn, college rep Ed Lavalle, prisoner rights advocate Claire Culhane and national liberation movement advocate Roisin Sheehy-Culhane. The names would change somewhat from week to week, reflecting who showed up at the meeting to represent member groups. The politics of the coalition ranged from moderate church and small business groups to revolutionary socialists. (A Solidarity Coalition contact list includes such decidedly left-wing organizations as Socialist Challenge, Communist Party, Socialist Youth, and the Industrial Workers of the World.) The earlier VDLC-organized Lower Mainland Budget Coalition—including everyone from the Green Party to the Unitarian Church—was absorbed into Solidarity. Within the Solidarity Coalition there were also new groups formed to fight the Socred bills, such as Women Against the Budget and the Defend Educational Services Coalition. Many of the sixty-five branches of the Solidarity Coalition that formed across the province were closely tied to the BCFED—utilizing its affiliated labour councils' resources —and a few trade unionists participated in the Solidarity Coalition as well as Operation Solidarity.

—*∿*—

Burnaby might have become a Vancouver neighbourhood in the 1960s. There was a concerted push by its mayor of the day to amalgamate with the bigger city, but Burnaby's inhabitants do have pride in the place and they said no. So, it remained the kind of sprawling suburbia anonymous enough for its residents to say they're from Vancouver when travelling outside the province. One local hero is nick-named "Burnaby Joe" (hockey's Joe Sakic) and a community theatre is named after another (the Michael J. Fox Theatre). In subcultural circles, Burnaby is best known for helping to launch the international "hardcore punk" movement, its litany of formidable bands including D.O.A., the Rabid and, my favourite, the Subhumans. (I managed this band.) Burnaby is also notable for having been represented by socialist politicians, including Tommy Douglas, Svend Robinson, Raj Chouhan and Doug Drummond.

Doug may not be as well-known as the other three but he was a dogged lefty alderman admired by many for his integrity when I covered Burnaby council for a suburban newspaper. Every once in a while, after a council meeting, I'd join progressive councillors at a nearby hotel bar. Doug had been bat boy for the 1959 Triple A Vancouver Mounties baseball team, of Brooks Robinson and Jim Pagliaroni, and he had stories to tell. He would talk politics, too, and one evening he described a battle I was unfamiliar with—one that took place in the early 1960s over the future of Burnaby Mountain. This debate was about whether to construct Simon Fraser University on Burnaby Mountain or at what would become the Kingsway location of Burnaby's Metrotown super-mall "town centre." Had SFU been built at that Metrotown location instead, it would have been an urban university surrounded by beautiful old houses and a Central Park (yes, named after the New York one). So the decision to build on the mountain likely cost B.C. the kind of vibrant university district it has never known, especially considering that when the campus opened in 1965 the student movement and counterculture were making their debuts, too, and would have changed the face of that Burnaby neighbourhood. "Yeah, it would have been a far better choice," says Jef Keighley, "because you go up to Simon Fraser in the winter, it is just dull and drab. The cloud level is below the base of the university. You're in the clouds."

Jef Keighley grew up on Burnaby Mountain. His father had received a Veterans' Land Act two-acre plot because he was in the army during the Second World War. "We had forty fruit trees and a huge garden." Jef and his friends got to know this mountain. "We chopped down trees and built forts and wandered Burnaby Mountain at will." That began to change, though, when construction crews arrived to build SFU. "We helped ourselves to some of their tools and so we got ourselves in trouble that way. We were pissed off as hell that they were fucking up our mountain—they were going to cut down all these trees, put in roads and put in buildings on our mountain. What the hell did they think they were doing? I mean, where were the bear and the deers and the cougars all going to go?"

In the early 1960s, when everything for so many seemed personal and not yet political, Jef raged against the machines climbing their mountain. Meanwhile, just down the coast in Berkeley, California, a campus Free Speech Movement was taking hold and a young student activist named Mario Savio raged against another machine: "There's a time when the operation of the machine becomes so odious, makes you so sick at heart, that you can't take part! You can't even passively take part! And you've got to put your bodies upon the gears and upon the wheels."[2] Soon after SFU opened, it would become known as the Berkeley of Canada. On land where Jef and friends had explored, there were now concourse rallies and the administration building occupation, and when the new feminism arrived on the mountaintop, things suddenly seemed political *and* personal. They had, we soon learned, been that way all along.

So the mountain university that Jef had so disdained would wind up incubating an entire generation of B.C. activists, many of whom would be involved in Solidarity. Jef took a different route to activism. After Burnaby North high school, he took engineering courses at Burnaby's B.C. Institute of Technology, then joined Canadian University Service Overseas (CUSO), which dispatched young Canadians overseas to combat poverty. Jef was twenty-two years old when he went to Jamaica to teach land surveying and construction in the hills, arriving in a time of intense social conflict, much of it targeting newly elected progressive prime minister Michael Manley. Jef learned from the experience of living in Jamaica, and the books and magazines and reggae music he devoured there, and he returned to Canada looking for a vehicle for his new politics.

"By this time I had made a mental commitment to the fact that I'm a socialist. I came to the conclusion that if I'm going to be socially active for my lifetime then you need to attach yourself to an organization." He found work at the CAIMAW-organized Kenworth truck-assembly plant in Burnaby. "I started on a Monday, the shift was over at three thirty and by four o'clock I was at the CAIMAW office up on Imperial. I said, 'Well, I've just got hired on at the plant and I think I need to learn about the union.' So Jess Succamore and John Bowman sat me down and give me a stack of every issue of the *CAIMAW Review*." Jef returned to that office every day after his shift until he had read all of them. "I thought if I'm going to get involved in this union I better know the history." He soon learned that a strike at the nearby Lenkurt Electric Plant and lack of support from the American-based union's leadership spurred the Canadian union movement CAIMAW was so much a part of. "The international union didn't give us any support when we were on strike for six months, never got a penny from it. So I was not impressed." Not long after that strike, the Lenkurt workers joined CAIMAW.

1983: Jef is a rank-and-file organizer for CAIMAW, pressing for democratic Canadian trade unionism. "The provincial government wanted to kill us. The federal government wanted to kill us. The American unions wanted to kill us. The Canadian Labour Congress (CLC) and the BCFED wanted to kill us. But we always had really good working relationships with all the progressive unions." Although much smaller than the BCFED, CAIMAW had become a force by 1983, organizing steelworkers, pulp workers, railway workers, mine workers and White Spot workers. "Our group was far more, you might say, ready to fight than most were. They understood their interests more." When the Bennett budget comes down in July, CAIMAW moves into action and Jess Succamore is its rep in Operation Solidarity. Jef becomes its representative on the Solidarity Coalition Steering Committee. CAIMAW is affiliated with the Confederation of Canadian Unions, which passes a resolution regarding the B.C. uprising: "The CCU will support bona fide actions inclusive of a general strike if launched to secure the objectives of Operation Solidarity and the Solidarity Coalition."[3]

Jean Swanson's father was a prospector in search of his mother lode, so their family didn't stay put for long. Born in New York, she was a teenager when the Swansons finally settled in Forest Grove, Oregon. While attending Portland State University, Jean went to her first demonstration. It was against a hearing being conducted in Portland by a red-baiting government committee. "I saw a poster and I went. I was all by myself and I was curious. I didn't think the committee was right. I also took Russian when I was in the university because you had to take a language and I was perverse. It was during the Cold War. I took Russian for the sole reason that it was perverse."

In 1967, Jean and her young husband were part of a parade of anti-war, anti-draft Americans crossing into B.C. A few years passed and Jean was a single mom slinging beer at the Downtown Eastside's Patricia Hotel. The boss repeatedly pressed her to place more than one beer in front of each customer. "He took me into the back room one time and showed me a picture of Bruce Eriksen and said, 'This guy will turn you in if you over-serve or do anything that's illegal.' And I was thinking, oh, he probably should." Through her job, Jean became friendly with Eriksen and Libby Davies, activists with the Downtown Eastside Residents' Association. "I would talk to them and they would give me their newsletter, which I would take home and read. On my lunch hour one day I saw Bruce at the Ovaltine [diner] and I went in and asked him for a job. He gave me one about six weeks later. . . . So I got a job doing something that seemed like it was doing good rather than something that was making people into alcoholics." Jean became a resolute DERA activist, speaking up for low-income housing and other anti-poverty issues, editing its newsletter *The Downtown East* and fighting City Hall.

1983: When Solidarity erupts, Jean is a researcher at the Hospital Employees' Union and it seconds her to the Solidarity Coalition. "Well, the bills were horrendous. I switched offices from the HEU office over to the BCFED office on Boundary Road." Jean sees the Socred bills as the work of the right-wing think tanks that formed just as she was becoming active in the early 1970s—"1972 was when the Council on National Issues got together and that's about the same time the Fraser Institute got together. So these two corporate think tanks lobby for policies that will reduce taxes on the rich and cut services and programs for the poor. The Solidarity stuff was part of it, right. Cut back on stuff that people need. Cut back on welfare. Cut back on human rights. Cut back on education." Jean gave her all to the Solidarity Coalition. "Printing all kinds of leaflets and getting them distributed. Organizing different events. And we had meetings. There would be twenty or thirty of us around the table." Jean's old organization was speaking out, too, its *DERA Newsletter* assailing "the Socreds' anti-human budget, which attacks damn near every person in the province who is already struggling to find a job, keep their home and raise their family."[4]

At Solidarity Coalition meetings, Jean found union organizers mingling with community activists focused on human rights, tenants, women, students, gays, poverty and seniors. As well as raising public awareness, the coalition and its weekly meetings were an education for the participants. "It's where I learned about discrimination against people who were gays and lesbians. I knew nothing about that before. We had quite a few people who were gay and who were fighting HIV and AIDS, which was new then." The Solidarity Coalition's environmental representative Cliff Stainsby and gay rep Stuart Alcock recall the intense interaction and learning among activists at the Steering Committee table. "It was that cross-fertilization," Cliff says. "People would talk, another group talked, another perspective came, and everybody was open to the perspectives, including myself. Like you said for Jean, it changed my life after that because when I think of the world now I can relate to those [varied] people. I didn't know any of the other people, really. . . . It was just a wonderful experience." Before encountering environmentalists at Solidarity Coalition meetings, says Stuart, he was largely unaware of groups like Greenpeace and the Society Promoting Environmental Conservation (SPEC). "Unless you were drawn to those groups, you were not terribly aware of them," says Stuart. "That was not a place I had any particular consciousness of at the time, other than what was appearing in the media. So it's that personal contact across boundaries that you're normally not crossing that I think is important. Putting a name and a face to an issue is really valuable."

Raj Chouhan was one of the few active in both Operation Solidarity and the Solidarity Coalition. As president of the Canadian Farmworkers Union, Raj knew many inside the labour movement and he attended Vancouver's annual peace walk. "There was not any shortage of progressive-thinking people [in the Lower Mainland]. There were lots of people who were involved in the anti-war movement, in the peace marches, but I had never heard about environmentalists in those days. And gay movement—gays and lesbians were also something totally new. My involvement was from the labour side." These movements' issues were not discussed in his usual circles but now, as the Solidarity Coalition rep for anti-racist organizations, he was introduced to the magnitude of the B.C. resistance. "Very broad-based. Discussions about women's rights, workers' rights, and all those kind of things. People were really concerned that we got to do it now. We got to stand up, otherwise the attacks by the Socreds were so severe that people said we will lose everything. People were genuinely, sincerely, seriously concerned about it. That brought all those people together in such a short period of time. And it was quite a phenomenon, you know, like when you saw people from the faith groups, socialist types, or women's rights, suddenly together."

———

B.C. had a reputation across Canada as a rambunctious province— "the Left Coast"—and its not-so-loyal opposition to the powers-that-were included every stripe of political radical and cultural rebel. So, alongside this Solidarity Coalition, another, even larger solidarity coalition was rising across the province. It wasn't so much an organization as an anti-Socred frame of mind and it had a long, diverse history that included folk songs and punk rock, peaceful occupations (the Raymur mothers of 1971) and occupations gone wild (the post office of 1938), Stanley Park Be-Ins and Oakalla Prison Be-Outs, volunteers for Spain and volunteers for Nicaragua, anti-nuclear pacifists and anti-nuclear guerrillas, beat readings and Beatles concerts, political pie-throwing and bakery co-ops, May Day parades and women's Take Back The Night marches, strikes for an eight-hour day and student walkouts, Wobbly free speech fights and Lenny Bruce's free speech comedy, Greenpeace whaling blockades and First Nations' logging blockades. Anyone who had been active in any of this, and much more, over the past half century now seemed to be enlisting in the uprising against the Socred government. And beyond all these political and cultural activists, there were thousands upon thousands of British Columbians who had never been active but were now simply fed up with the Socreds and their injustice budget.

―◦◦◦―

Born in Yorkshire as the Second World War was ending, Stuart Alcock grew up in working-class England of the 1950s. "As a teenager my personal political awareness was informed by two significant events. One was the shooting of people in Sharpeville in South Africa and the other was the Soviet invasion in Hungary, which left me with a view of the world that says regardless of whether a regime is right-wing or left-wing it can do some pretty ugly things to people. I think that, plus my family background, led me to a place of fundamentally social democracy and a sort of attitude which R.D. Laing once referred to as benign skepticism. I'm a person who's not ready to believe anything that people want to spoon-feed me."

By the 1960s, Stuart was living in London, working with young offenders in a remand home, observing jazz and art, campaigning against apartheid and nukes, a member of the Labour Party. "I decided to leave the Labour Party because I didn't like some of the positioning that then–prime minister Harold Wilson was doing on the Vietnam issue. He was saying that his government would give the Americans 'conditional support' around Vietnam, and I frankly didn't understand what the difference was between support and conditional support." An ad he saw recruiting U.K. residents to work in Quebec changed everything for Stuart. He wound up in suburban Montreal, then in Vancouver in 1973. Returning to the activism he left in Britain was a prolonged process beginning in the late 1970s, when he joined the board of the Vancouver Gay and Lesbian Community Centre and co-founded the B.C. Human Rights Coalition. "I represented the VGLCC at the hearings held by the Human Rights Commission on sexual orientation," he says.

1983: When the legislation comes down, Stuart is appalled by the attack on the B.C. human rights system and, as a BCGEU member working at Burnaby's Maples Adolescent Treatment Centre, he's directly impacted by the labour bills. As a founder of the Human Rights Coalition he had spent time with Renate Shearer of the Human Rights Commission. "So Renate approached me and asked if I would be interested in serving in the Steering Committee of the Solidarity Coalition. Renate was committed to having that [gay] community referenced and engaged as part of the Solidarity movement." Stuart thinks the presence of gays and lesbians in the Solidarity Coalition helped bring their concerns to a "higher consciousness" in the union movement. The coalition passed a motion at its October 31 meeting "that Steering Committee recommend to local coalitions, to constituent groups, and Operation Solidarity to adopt an education policy on Lesbians and Gay men; to open their doors to this educational process and the resources available through the Solidarity Coalition."[5] Stuart says the disparate nature of the coalition created challenges. "It was very obvious very quickly to me that we had a collection of people who had different decision-making structures. For instance, we had people from the women's movement who made decisions by consensus within their own organizations. Whoever was representing the women's movement at that table was not able to say, yes, we will vote in favour of this. They would have to go back and consult. At the same time, you've people from the labour movement where there is a long history of electing officers and basically providing them with the authority to make decisions. . . . [This] presented some interesting dynamic issues."

—◊◊◊—

The Solidarity Coalition structure included a Coalition Assembly (large public meetings), Administrative Committee (Shearer, Roberts and Kube), Steering Committee (the member groups' reps who attended the weekly meetings) and subcommittees (formed to address a specific matter). Barrie Morrison, of the UBC Faculty Association, described an assembly of the Solidarity Coalition.

> On behalf of the universities and colleges I attended a meeting of the Solidarity Coalition Assembly (Aug. 30) as a voting participant and as a member of the Steering Committee of the Provincial Solidarity Coalition. . . . The Steering Committee is very large, anticipated twenty-seven members, of which there will only be three members concerned with education. . . . In spite of its size, I expect that the Steering Committee will be the most important body guiding the policies and action of the Coalition. . . . There was an amendment introduced by the BCGEU that no member group of the Solidarity Coalition should enter into any consultation with the Provincial Government. Clearly they were apprehensive that some groups might be mollified by changes in the proposed legislation which would still leave the BCGEU exposed. . . . The sub-committee on local coalitions recommended guidelines to ensure that actions conform with accepted Solidarity principles. The specific recommendation that created divisions was that "no actions to be at MLA's houses." The women's groups which had sponsored the "lunch with Gracie" at Grace McCarthy's house in Shaughnessy were upset at the implied criticism of their actions. However, after much discussion the recommendation of the sub-committee was approved by a substantial majority. I estimate that there were about one hundred and fifty representatives and observers present.[6]

There was division within the Solidarity Coalition over the idea of a general strike. "The community groups all wanted this and the unions mostly didn't," Jean Swanson says. The debates over general strike were occurring within Operation Solidarity, too. Some members, like CCU president Jess Succamore, favoured a general strike, while others were opposed, including Jack Munro of the powerful International Woodworkers of America (IWA). At a meeting, Succamore recalls: "Munro said, 'Goddamn it, man, we could bring the government down!' Like, we're all looking at one another—'Well, yeah, isn't that the idea?'"

Jess says Art Kube "was more in tune with us in getting the other social activists, the various groups, involved in it, whereas a lot in the labour movement, like the Munros and all that, didn't want anything to do with any of the social activists. That was the big push and pull there. They didn't want the rabble to be influencing what was happening. I could see the way Kube had respect for the various groups in society and wanted to build a movement. I was impressed with him. I just liked the guy." Like Succamore, Kube was born in Europe between the wars. When you're brought up in Austria and Poland in the 1940s by left-wing parents, as Kube was, you know what socialism is. You also know what fascism is. Kube had done what he had to do to climb the labour movement hierarchy but he was farther left than the BCFED's right-wing social democrats knew when they made him their president in early 1983. ("Yes he was," says Patsy George. "A nice man, a lovely man.") Like Larry Kuehn and Raj Chouhan, Kube was active in the Solidarity Coalition as well as Operation Solidarity, and unlike some labour leaders seemed to actually care about the social issues. (After retiring from the labour movement he would be a seniors activist.) "Some accuse me of simplicity and idealism," Kube wrote. "Maybe I am simple, and to idealism I plead guilty. I as one man cannot guarantee a happy ending to all the problems of the Trade Union Movement, I can only say that I am not cynical and that I retain my full confidence in our Movement's ability to achieve the triumph of decency, compassion and progress."[7]

During the Solidarity months, I interviewed Kube a number of times. One morning, coming out of a meeting at New Westminster's Royal Towers Hotel, he stopped a moment to chat. He gave me his usual BCFED talking point about social issues being non-negotiable. (Why the Fed leadership insisted upon this was never entirely clear. After all, those issues were in the Socred legislation just like the union issues.) Talk of a general strike was spreading, and we discussed the concept. He was concerned that it would "alienate the public," but I was surprised at how interested he was in the idea of a general strike where workers provide services—such as free bus rides—to the public.

"Inside the Solidarity Coalition," says Stuart Alcock, "there was no question, I think, that some of the key people were deeply committed, and I'm thinking particularly of people like Renate and Father Jim Roberts and Art Kube as the trio who were senior people in the coalition. They were very clearly committed to the full bank of issues." The problem was, some unions "took a rather narrow view of, we're here only to represent our members' interests. IWA was one such union. They had a, let's say, a constrained view of their role. And their role, as they saw it, was to defeat the anti-union parts of the package that the Bennett government introduced."

—⁓—

Cliff Stainsby's father designed chainsaws for a living. "It's a bit ironic because I was in the forest wars." Well before Cliff joined environmentalist wars to save the woods, he spent many a peaceful day exploring the bush near the family home in South Burnaby. "I grew up playing sports with the kids in the neighbourhood but I was sort of the odd one there that loved animals. Dogs, salamanders, frogs, you name it. The survival of those animals for some reason was very deeply important to me, even in that conservative day. Still to this day."

After high school, Cliff was drawn to the impassioned campus debates on Burnaby Mountain. "There were lots of discussions [at SFU]. Women's movement was strong up there. Same with talks about lesbian and gay rights and the lives they led. There was rock and roll. I just ended up with a group of friends into the hippie stuff, which I was, too, but I also was attracted for some reason to the politics. . . . I just listened to all of the discussions and so on. They seemed really serious, especially when you're talking with people who had left their country to avoid a war in Vietnam. It was exciting, too."

Cliff switched to UBC to study agriculture and, after graduating in 1976, landed a government summer job inspecting plant nurseries. That summer, he met Terry Chantler of SPEC at a party and was hired on. "I just was incredibly excited about being able to work and try and save the environment. My first work there was on the Fraser Estuary. We started the Fraser River Coalition with various other groups to defend Fraser." Cliff soon was executive director of SPEC. "It wasn't something I sought, but it kept me awake for a few nights. In those days, it was $500 a month and no benefits and long hours. Lots of good working together with people, though, running old Gestetner machines." SPEC's office was in *environmental central*, a building at 1603 West Fourth that also housed Greenpeace. "Greenpeace was able to reach out to an international audience. Probably the genius behind that was Bob Hunter and Paul Watson," Cliff says. "And we shared an office for quite a while there." While Greenpeace direct action drew most of the headlines, Cliff and SPEC spent long days "doing research, writing briefs, making presentations, participating in hearings." The 1970s and early '80s were formative years for environmental action in B.C. Cliff organized to save farmland in the Fraser Valley and fought Roberts Bank super-port expansion, uranium mining in the Okanagan, the Site C dam in the Peace River and pipeline proposals. Cliff enjoyed making the case so much that he considered law school. "Did a lot of cross-examining and evidence presentation at Site C, for instance. They were trying to flood a whole valley—farmland, forest land and wildlife habitat. Outrageous. I was engaged in it and I wasn't going to give that up to go to law school. We would go around speaking to whoever would listen—small audiences in a church somewhere, in a school somewhere, union hall."

1983: Cliff has stepped down as SPEC executive director to focus on the fight against Site C. "I came back from Site C and I was burned out. Then Solidarity came along." For Cliff, the notion of solidarity went back to his student radical days at SFU. Unlike many environmentalists, Cliff had a background in the left and saw the link between ecological issues and other systemic injustice. "For a period there I considered myself a Murray Bookchin anarchist," says Cliff. "I've read several of his books. It was that combination of this idea of direct democracy and, it seemed to me, his deep understanding and concern for the environment." So, it was clear to Cliff that the environmental movement should be part of this Solidarity Coalition. "The government was terrible on the environment. They were terrible on all these other issues. This terrible sense of unfairness pervaded at the time. I thought environment should be there. You got all these other parts of society there. I'd spent the previous years of my life trying to make environment a big part of social consideration."

Cliff became the environmentalist on the Solidarity Coalition's Steering Committee after persuading the SPEC board to "join this Solidarity movement, that it's important for the environment movement to be in there." His work was voluntary at first, then he became a Solidarity staffer. So, Cliff moved from a coalition of issues surrounding Site C to the Solidarity Coalition. "One of the reasons I was able to get involved in activist stuff at Solidarity is that at Site C we had different phases. We had an environmental phase, we had a what-it-means-for-the-community phase, what it means for seniors, a cost–benefit phase, and a big First Nations phase, which was maybe the most impactful. I think that exposure to a whole range of serious issues from a single project sort of made it easy for me to go [to Solidarity]."

Cliff's environmentalism drew a mixed response from others at Solidarity Coalition meetings. "They could listen and talk but it was more me supporting them than vice versa, but Renate Shearer, for instance, was very pro-environment. Could talk to some of the others but I could see they just weren't going to get it. . . . Didn't know what ecology was." Still, it was exciting to be in a room with so many activists with so many passions. "I can picture the people and the feeling. What was to me incredible, actually, was that you could have fifty people around big rectangular tables in a room and get stuff to happen." The diversity of debate at those tables reminded him of impassioned discussions at SFU in the late 1960s. "You had people from every sector—visible minorities, anti-poverty groups, gays, lesbians, women's groups, unions, the lone environmentalist, religious groups. It was invigorating for sure to see all these people working together for a common goal. And just to see how committed they were, how ordered they were and how willing everybody was to listen to everybody else. It was just marvellous. It was a great experience. You run into people that tell you if you're going to have a meeting or a group, you can't have more than thirty or forty people at the table. I said, 'I think we did that in the Solidarity Coalition. It worked great.'"

Cliff took to Solidarity like he had to SPEC, working long days and speaking at events across the province. "The final one was at Queen Charlotte City. I would talk about Solidarity but I would always include some environmental stuff. There were the disputes in the forests, there was stuff we heard from the community in the hearings about toxic chemicals. The Socreds were a disaster on environment." The Solidarity Coalition made a point of raising public consciousness about the issues of each of its member groups. So, it released an environmental statement—"Government Budget/Legislative Package Threatens the Environment"—that outlined the Socreds' ongoing cutbacks on regulations concerning pesticides, wildlife protection and reforestation, and it linked environmental activism to Socred human-rights legislation. "The attack on human rights," it said, "means that individuals who speak out can be discriminated against by employers and landlords—that is a very real threat to the freedom of speech, organization and political action. Without these freedoms, environmentalists, like others, will be less likely to speak out."[8]

BCGEU members keep management out during Solidarity's occupation of the Tranquille facility in Kamloops, July 1983. (COURTESY: BCGEU)

Lower Mainland Budget Coalition assembles at Vancouver's Thornton Park, July 23. (COURTESY: GEOFF PETERS)

Kim Zander addresses the LMBC rally, July 23. (COURTESY: PACIFIC
TRIBUNE PHOTO COLLECTION-SFU, SEAN GRIFFIN PHOTOGRAPH)

Protesters marching on the B.C. Legislature in Victoria, July 27.
(COURTESY: GEOFF PETERS)

▲ Rallying at the Legislature in Victoria, July 27. (COURTESY: PACIFIC TRIBUNE PHOTO COLLECTION-SFU, SEAN GRIFFIN PHOTOGRAPH)

◄ The Legislature protest was Victoria's largest rally ever, July 27. (COURTESY: BCTF)

▲ The massive Solidarity crowd viewed from the B.C. Legislature entrance, July 27. (COURTESY: PACIFIC TRIBUNE PHOTO COLLECTION-SFU, SEAN GRIFFIN PHOTOGRAPH)

◄ Larry Kuhen speaks at the Victoria protest, July 27. (COURTESY: PACIFIC TRIBUNE PHOTO COLLECTION-SFU)

Solidarity rally at Empire Stadium, August 10.
(COURTESY: PACIFIC TRIBUNE PHOTO COLLECTION-SFU)

Raising the Operation Solidarity banner at Empire Stadium. (COURTESY:
PACIFIC TRIBUNE PHOTO COLLECTION-SFU, DAN KEETON PHOTOGRAPH)

Women Against the Budget's Stone Soup Rally at Grace McCarthy's home,
August 27. (COURTESY: PACIFIC TRIBUNE PHOTO COLLECTION-SFU)

Signs of the times at the occupation of the premier's Vancouver office,
September 16. (COURTESY: PACIFIC TRIBUNE PHOTO COLLECTION-SFU)

Many of the coalition's member groups that had operated in semi-isolation now linked their issues with others around the Solidarity table. The coalition organized a series of "weeks," each focused on a different issue or community impacted by the legislation—Human Rights Week, Workers Week, Women & Children Week, Tenants & Co-ops Week, Consumers & Small Business Week, Social Services/Education/Health Week and Seniors & Disabled Week. For Tenants & Co-ops Week, the B.C. Tenants Rights Coalition staged a "tent-in" at Vancouver's Vanier Park to protest the new Residential Tenancy Act. Tents were erected to demonstrate that tenants could be driven out "with no place to live except a tent."[9] A troupe called the Generic Theatre Players performed *Bill Bennett Towers or Apocalypse Now*, a skit about an unscrupulous landlord evicting Jane and John Public. "The Socred move is clearly a savage attack on the tenants of British Columbia, and a massive gift to big, corporate landlords," wrote Tenants Rights Coalition chair Jim Quail, the tenants rep on the Solidarity Coalition Steering Committee. "Unless we can unite to stop it, we will find ourselves plunged into the Dark Ages of landlord-tenant relations. Let's evict Bill Bennett!"[10]

During the Solidarity Coalition's Human Rights Week, silent vigils were organized across the province. On September 9, Doug Ibbotson sat holding candles on the stairs of Vancouver's Robson Square. He had come because of the "assassination of human rights." Nearby, Maxie and Don Abbott said their grandchildren—the eldest had just started grade one—were foremost on their minds as they drove in from Surrey for the vigil. "You work all your life to try and make things better, and then in one fell swoop you see it wiped away," Maxie said.[11]

There were Solidarity Coalition protests, workshops and teach-ins. Between September 15 and September 24 in the Vancouver area, there was a coalition-organized People's Law School panel at John Oliver high school (Sept. 15), an Unemployed Week protest downtown (Sept. 17), a forum at Capilano College (Sept. 20), an information meeting at Surrey's Newton Community Centre (Sept. 20), a meeting with public school parents at Mount Pleasant Elementary School (Sept. 20) and a Women Against the Budget petition drive in Champlain Heights (Sept. 24). There was so much activity that at times two Solidarity protests were scheduled at the same time—minutes from the September 13 Solidarity Coalition meeting note that the Tenants & Co-ops Week tent-in at Vanier Park was in "possible conflict with Oct. 1 Day of Protest Pro-Choice on Abortion rally to be held same day."[12]

Roisin Sheehy-Culhane was born shortly after the Second World War ended and her Catholic atheist Dublin-born father, Barry Culhane, and Jewish atheist Montreal-born mother, Claire Culhane, moved to Vancouver. "My parents were Communist Party in Montreal in the '30s and union organizers. My memories of Vancouver are red-diaper baby memories—the summer camps and the party meetings and all of that. My dad was thirty years in the party. My mom was less than that." Roisin's childhood memories of Vancouver were pretty good "apart from my parents' very, very rocky marriage with major fights and dramas."

In the early 1950s, Claire left Barry and Vancouver, taking Roisin and her younger sister Dara back to Montreal. Barry followed Claire to Quebec, where they reunited and then moved to Ireland. Barry's family declared his mixed marriage unacceptable. "My dad had a sister a nun, a brother a priest and another sister who should have been a nun. They were horrible to my mom. According to that side of the family, they weren't married in the eyes of the church so they treated her terribly. . . . I didn't know anything about any religions at that time apart from the Communist Party, which was kind of a religion unto itself at times."

Claire wanted her daughters to return to Canada with her, and Dara did, but fourteen-year-old Roisin refused. This would leave long-lasting hurt feelings between Claire and Roisin. "I really loved being in Ireland. After my mom left, my dad put me in convent boarding school. I was considered incorrigible. Rebelling." Roisin married at eighteen, returned to Montreal, then settled in Vancouver. By this time, Claire was immersed in the anti-war movement, travelling to Vietnam and writing extensively about the war, and she no longer tolerated misogyny—from a husband or from fellow leftists. Roisin, though, didn't attend a single demonstration during the Vietnam era. "I was trying really hard to disassociate from that. My ex-husband was pretty reactionary, and I was trying to make a go of this traditional marriage thing. My parents' marriage was an absolute disaster and I kind of, at that age, figured it was all about the politics they were involved in, so I tried not to be that." Soon Roisin was a single mom of three children, working as a tugboat cook. "I was the first woman to go on the tugs," she says. Some of the men didn't want to sail with a woman, but she stood up for herself. "Basically fighting for the job." Shortly after Roisin's seafaring ended in 1979, Irish republican prisoners began a hunger strike to press the Thatcher government to recognize their political status. Roisin joined Vancouver's Irish Solidarity Committee.

1983: After a lengthy detour, Roisin has returned to the politics of her childhood home. On July 7, she is "horrified and appalled along with everybody else" and attends the earliest anti-budget rallies in Vancouver. The most powerful aspect of Solidarity for her is its way of inspiring people who ordinarily had nothing to do with the left or unions. Roisin is elected treasurer of the Lower Mainland Solidarity Coalition's Steering Committee. The Solidarity Coalition brings daughter Roisin, representing national liberation movements, and mother Claire, representing prisoners' rights, to the same political table. Now, Roisin understands better the mother of her childhood. "I think she was frustrated all to hell with the limitations of her life just in terms of being a woman with a brilliant mind in her time." By this time, Claire Culhane is a legendary Canadian activist, renowned for her writings and her prison abolitionist and anti-war activities.

When I emailed Roisin an article I'd written about the Solidarity uprising, she responded very quickly. It had evoked a mix of emotions left over from 1983. "The Solidarity Coalition meetings were exciting, and I felt a connection to my parents and what they had gone through in the heyday of their political life," she says. "It felt like we were—this sounds kind of corny, I guess—but it felt like we were kind of winning or we could win though the protests and the coalition of people that was coming together. I noticed people saying, in reading your article, about it being euphoric. It was—*totally*. I don't know who said it, but 'revolution is the carnival of the oppressed.' It was definitely carnival. It definitely *felt* like carnival."

CHAPTER 4

The Socialist Coalition:
Left Field of Dreams

BOB SARTI AND MUGGS SIGURGEIRSON were a coalition. Before they began a hectic lifetime together in the early 1980s, they had
equally interesting lifetimes separately. Together they were seemingly
tireless, exceedingly effective organizers in their Downtown Eastside
neighbourhood. Before that, between the two of them, Muggs and
Bob represented practically every left-wing ideology of the twentieth
century. Muggs grew up in North Vancouver under the influence of
her mother, Winnie, a Trotskyist and CCF activist. "She dragged me to
picket lines and demonstrations." Bob grew up in Greenwich Village's
Italian milieu, his father Paul a veteran of the Communist Party–
organized Abraham Lincoln Battalion, which fought the fascists in
Spain. Later, Muggs was active in the Vancouver City College Wom-
en's Caucus, then the feminist union the Service, Office, and Retail

Workers Union of Canada (SORWUC) and the social-democratic New Democratic Party. Bob was active in the Youth International Party and *The Georgia Straight* and co-founded *The Open Road*. So, Bob and Muggs were a socialist coalition, having ties with Trotskyism, anarchism, the CCF, the NDP, Yippies, the CP's International Brigades, the underground press, student movements, unions, feminism and counterculture.

———

There is a moment in the noir film *Key Largo* when Johnny Rocco (played by Edward G. Robinson), a gangster holed up with his gang in a Florida Keys hotel, is questioned by hotel guest Frank McCloud (played by Humphrey Bogart), a self-possessed veteran of the wars against fascism, and James Temple (Lionel Barrymore), the frail owner of the hotel.

Frank: "He knows what he wants, don't you Rocco?"

Rocco: "Well, I want uh . . ."

Rocco is baffled, silenced.

Frank: "He wants more, don't you Rocco?"

Rocco is instantly excited, squeals: "That's it. More. That's right. I want more."

James: "Will you ever get enough?"

Like any good noir gangster—and like any number of Socreds and their friends—Rocco wanted more, and he didn't know why. But the audience knew.

———

Socialism was a coalition. In order to understand the Solidarity Coalition, you should know the socialist coalition. Socialist ideas, including the general strike concept, have deep roots in B.C. and played an integral role in shaping the 1983 Solidarity uprising. The S Word became part of the political vocabulary in the early 1800s, when new technology was triggering an industrial revolution, replacing old agricultural and mercantile economies with heavily mechanized urban factories run by a new economic system: industrial capitalism. These capitalists and their system wanted more. In this new system, success meant dominating others. All the profit derived from factory workers' hard labour went to someone else—the owner. For the fast-growing industrial working class, conditions were sweatshop, with child labour, long hours and unlivable wages. Many saw this new state of affairs as unfair. In the first half of the nineteenth century, this resulted in uprisings and bloody strikes and a new idea: socialism. Socialists believed large-scale wealth of major industries was generated by the labour of many and should be socially, not individually, owned—*socialized*—and used for the good of all (education, health care, etc.) rather than the benefit of a handful of millionaires. Much of the working class and many men and women of letters welcomed a movement that put people before profit. British writer William Morris, an early socialist, predicted: "In spite of all the infallible maxims of your day there is yet a time of rest in store for the world, when mastery has changed into fellowship."[1]

In attracting virtually every faction of the left, Solidarity in 1983 was a throwback to the first major worldwide socialist organization, the First International. Formed in 1864, it was a big-tent coalition, bringing together in their early stages the three defining branches of socialism: democratic socialism (also known as social democracy), Marxist socialism (also known as communism) and anarchist socialism (also known as anarchism). Not everyone completely separates these branches of socialism. Activist historian Howard Zinn, for example, liked elements of anarchism and democratic socialism and his politics were a mix of the two. Said Zinn:

Socialism basically said, hey, let's have a kinder, gentler society. Let's share things. Let's have an economic system that produces things not because they're profitable for some corporation, but produces things that people need. People should not be retreating from the word socialism because you have to go beyond capitalism.[2]

And activists often partake in more than one movement. Many members of Women Against the Budget, for instance, were part of the Solidarity Coalition and the socialist coalition as well as the feminist movement.

The twentieth-century clash of ideas reached its apex during the Spanish Civil War—1936–39—when anarchists, Communists, democratic socialists and Trotskyists each had their own army in the fight against Franco's fascists and their Nazi Germany benefactors. The world was watching Spain, and International Brigades came from many countries to join the "good fight," believing that if they could defeat fascism in the civil war, they could stop a world war. The Canadian government passed the Foreign Enlistment Act, which called for two years in jail and a $2,000 fine for Canadians who fought in Spain. Regardless, the Canadians continued to leave for Spain.

Len Norris said goodbye to his parents in their home along the New Westminster–Burnaby boundary and made his way to Spain in 1937. He had ridden the rails across Canada, taking what work he could find, before returning to B.C. in time to be at Ballantyne Pier when police on horseback charged into strikers. By 1937, Len was a committed leftist due to the Depression conditions he witnessed and an Upton Sinclair book he read (*The Brass Check*). Like other volunteers for Spain, Len had warily watched the rise of fascism in Europe and in the streets of America and Canada, too, so he was determined to do something about it. In Spain, Len fought in battle after battle for almost eighteen months, but after two years the socialist republic was losing this civil war and sent the International Brigades home. Len told me of the thousands of Spaniards lining the Barcelona streets to give an emotional goodbye to the internationals as they paraded by on their way home. La Pasionaria, the charismatic Communist orator who served in the Republican government, silenced the massive crowd as she said her farewell to Len and his heroic friends. "Communists, Socialists, Anarchists, Republicans—men of different colours, differing ideology, antagonistic religions—yet all profoundly loving liberty and justice, they came and offered themselves to us unconditionally. . . . Comrades of the International Brigades. . . . You can go proudly. You are history. You are legend. You are the heroic example of democracy's solidarity." Len's eyes teared as he recalled that day in Barcelona. "We shall not forget you," La Pasionaria continued, "and, when the olive tree of peace is in flower, entwined with the victory laurels of the Republic of Spain—return! Return to our side for here you will find a homeland—those who have no country or friends, who must live deprived of friendship—all, all will have the affection and gratitude of the Spanish people who today and tomorrow will shout with enthusiasm—*Long live the heroes of the International Brigades!*"[3]

—◦◦◦—

Jess Succamore grew up in a working-class family in England during the Depression and war years. His parents supported the Labour Party and his earliest memory of politicking was, as a small child, banging a dusting lid, "marching and chanting, campaigning for the Labour Party's Alfie Barnes."

In 1952, Jess was a twenty-year-old apprentice sheet metal worker in Lancashire, England, when a friend talked him into a short vacation in Canada. It ended up being a lifetime. First, Jess found work in Montreal. On pay day, he got comfortable at a pub and looked up to see a Canadiens–Rangers game on the black-and-white television hanging behind the bar. "I'm sitting there. What's that? Hockey. Pulled my chair up. Never knew there was ice hockey. Richard comes flying down the wing and goes boom, scores this goal." Face-off, and a Ranger races up the rink and scores. "And I thought, man, what a game." Jess moved on to building transmission towers at B.C.'s Kitimat–Kemano Project. Arriving at the Vancouver airport, he got his first glimpse of the city and a bite to eat at the old White Spot restaurant on Seventieth and Granville. "I ate my first White Spot hamburger in the spring of 1954. I'll never forget." The first North Americans Jess fell for, Rocket Richard and White Spot hamburgers, were madly popular on the West Coast of the 1950s. By the 1980s, Jess was living on the West Coast and had helped to organize White Spot workers into the Confederation of Canadian Unions. And he was still watching hockey. "To this day, I've only dreamed about one sport: me between Richard and Howe." Two right-wingers and a lefty. ("I've been a socialist for as long as I can remember," says Jess.)

The day Jess was glued to hockey in that Montreal bar, he did not yet know that the Rocket was, especially in Quebec, as mythological an athlete as Babe Ruth had been and Muhammad Ali would be. Much later, I would see Richard play in an old-timers game at the Vancouver Forum. He was one of two players making end-to-end rushes that night. The other, Hy Buller, was one of the NHL's exceptional defencemen of the early 1950s, a dazzling skater with a bullet shot. At the time, I did not know that Hy's aunt was legendary radical Annie Buller, who had faced actual bullets at a 1931 riot in Estevan, Saskatchewan. A dazzling public speaker widely known across the country, she was convicted for inciting the Estevan rioting, which pitted striking miners against police. Later, Annie Buller helped to organize the On-to-Ottawa Trek.

Margaret Black grew up in Regina, and was a volunteer making sandwiches for the many arrested at the 1935 On-to-Ottawa Trek riot. As she walked into a cellblock carrying her sandwich tray, one of the political prisoners reached out his foot to pretend-trip her. "I'm going to marry you," he said. That would be George Black who, like Annie Buller, was arrested at a Saskatchewan riot. He was arrested on the speakers' platform at the Regina On-to-Ottawa rally and charged with being a member of an illegal organization, the Relief Camp Workers' Union. Margaret and George's daughter-in-law Dawn would, much later, become NDP opposition leader in the B.C. Legislature.

In 1986, at the fiftieth anniversary reunion of veterans of the International Brigades in Spain, I met Margaret and Dawn Black. In Vancouver during the civil war, Margaret did support work for the Spanish Republic and the volunteers. She did everything from sending medical supplies to organizing public meetings. Fifty years later in Madrid, Margaret told me she'd come to honour the memory of lost friends. "I'm not getting the feeling one ordinarily gets visiting a foreign city. There's a kind of sadness about it, like returning to the tomb of a martyr of something."

—◦◦◦—

The Idea—the term by which socialist adherents referred to socialism—is often passed down from a parent or an aunt. Others, like Larry Kuehn, find their socialism in books. The 1950s were Cold War years. Once a week, Larry's father took his turn at the Elgin, Oregon observatory to watch for oncoming Russian bombers. His mother was a school teacher. Born in nearby Tacoma, Washington in 1944, Larry grew up in the closed environs of small-town Oregon ("We didn't even get television until I was sixteen") but found a way to satiate his intellectual curiosity. "I developed an interest in reading. You could order things through the school library. And I ran across John Dos Passos. The *U.S.A.* trilogy was the book that really, for one thing, let me know that there was a socialist tradition in the United States. So, that made me critical of everything at that stage that I was reading or thinking about, hearing about, and so on." In the trilogy, Dos Passos quotes democratic socialist Eugene Debs: "While there is a lower class I am of it, while there is a criminal class I am of it, while there is a soul in prison I am not free."[4]

So, young Larry left Elgin filled with ideals of what America might be, searching for souls to set free. In his first year of political science at Portland's Reed College, he joined the first protest he encountered—against a red-baiting Senate committee holding hearings in town. "Against the Senate version of HUAC [House Un-American Activities Committee]. So, it was very much a milieu where the activism of the '60s was an important part of the climate." (Larry and fellow Solidarity activist Jean Swanson have discussed whether his first protest rally was her first protest rally, but they aren't certain.)

That first year at Reed, Larry met students preparing to go south for the Freedom Rides against American apartheid. The following year, at Christmas break, he bought a bus ticket to see Deep South segregation for himself. "I wanted to understand that situation." That trip solidified his commitment to fighting racism. Back in Portland, he attended the first mass rally against the Vietnam War—the 1965 Students for a Democratic Society (SDS)–organized March on Washington, featuring Joan Baez, Phil Ochs and Judy Collins.

Graduating in 1966, Larry joined VISTA, a federal anti-poverty program known as "the domestic Peace Corps." Dispatched to Florida's Dade County, he met Sadie, from Georgia. They fell in love but couldn't marry in Florida because she was black and he was white and there were miscegenation laws forbidding interracial romance. "That prevented us from getting married in Florida and eighteen other states. . . . The ["coloured" and "white"] signs were gone, but the day-to-day reality was still very much what it had been before the '60s."

At this point, Larry was thinking law school but his experiences in Florida opened his eyes to teaching. His job entailed interviewing people awaiting trial and "the most important thing I saw was a father and son there who were both illiterate—genuinely good people who simply were so marginalized because of their lack of education." It was true of so many he interviewed. "So I decided that really education—if you're going to make a difference in terms of some kind of social activity—more than law was actually what was important to do." While attending Reed College's teaching program, he taught American history in a working-class high school. "I tried to get the students to understand the Vietnam War indirectly—look at human rights history, look at the Revolutionary War in the context of what if the British had won." The day the principal happened by Larry's class to observe, Buffy Sainte-Marie was on the turntable. "The principal wrote a reference letter for me that said, 'He would do well teaching Negroes or Indians but will not fit into the American public schools.'" After that, Larry couldn't get a school interview in Portland. Some friends who had fled to Canada because of the draft sent him a newspaper listing of job openings. "I applied. And a week later I had a teaching job in Kitimat." By this time, Larry and Sadie had married and they moved to Canada.

Larry has the manner of an attentive teacher who—when he's not absorbed in a Dos Passos passage or Leonard Cohen lyric—actually listens to his students and might even change his opinion if an argument is convincing. These are also the qualities of a grassroots union activist. By 1976, he was president of the Kamloops local of the B.C. Teachers' Federation. By the Solidarity summer of 1983, Larry was president of the entire union.

1983: Larry has just become BCTF president. He is one of a handful who became active in the Solidarity Coalition as well as Operation Solidarity. Had Larry stayed in the U.S., he might have become a "radical Democrat" like Jesse Jackson or Tom Hayden. In Canada, he found a place in the left caucus of his union ("Teachers Viewpoint") and joined the activist wing of Dave Barrett's New Democrats. "The democratic socialist part of the party. On the left of the party."

Democratic-socialist governments are not unusual in other parts of the world. Sweden has had nine socialist prime ministers. The B.C. CCF/NDP has been a cornerstone of these politics in North America. While democratic socialists believe in social change through the ballot box and operate within the existing legislative structures, there are wide variances among its adherents. In 1983, right-wing social democrats inside the BCFED were planning Solidarity's anti-climactic demise while left-wing social democrats like Larry Kuehn, Raj Chouhan and VDLC president Frank Kennedy were preparing for a general strike. Tommy Douglas, the heart and soul of Canadian left-wing democratic socialism, enacted North America's first free health care system when he was premier of Saskatchewan in the 1940s. "We are all in this world together," said Douglas, "and the only test of our character that matters is how we look after the least fortunate among us."[5]

David Lester's politics have always been left of the electoral left, but he maintains a fondness for the NDP, which was extremely popular in the working-class East Vancouver neighbourhood where he grew up. "I was really aware that I lived in a CCF/NDP stronghold. I really had that identity, and I felt very proud that I lived in that area and my parents voted for the NDP. [Marxist alderman] Harry Rankin was significant, too. My parents always voted for him. They really liked him. And it's a small thing in the world, but to me it meant a lot—growing up in the East End and having progressive-voting parents. Back then, I was inspired by it."

David was born in East Vancouver in 1958, grandson of a Wobbly, brother of a Yippie. Along with its Marxism and democratic socialism, the B.C. left has an anarchic tradition that includes members of the Industrial Workers of the World (Wobblies) and the Youth International Party (Yippies). It was the rebel side of the evening news with Walter Cronkite, however, that David credits for prompting his early interest in politics. "Even though I was only seven or eight, I was aware of social struggles. I know it seems bizarre. It was all through the CBS News with Walter Cronkite. That became my education." Like so many young Canadians of the era, David was influenced by the civil rights movement, Vietnam and the Chicago Eight ("the Chicago conspiracy trial . . . I followed religiously"). His older brother, Ken, was a writer at the then-underground *Georgia Straight* newspaper and would bring home the underground press. "*The East Village Other*. Papers from L.A. and Chicago. And *The Black Panther* newspaper as well. *The Oracle*—I was transfixed by the amount of psychedelic colours. I had access to them because they were just lying there. They seemed exciting, and I was interested in art and graphic design and drawing and that's what I was looking at. They had cartoons. They had great, beautiful coloured covers." And there was music to love, too. "I discovered Phil Ochs and the Fugs and the Grateful Dead, not just the Rolling Stones and the Beatles."

In the late 1800s, David's grandfather Frederick Lester came from England and worked his way across the U.S. In Spokane, he paved sidewalks and joined the Wobblies, playing the horn in a Wobbly marching band. The Wobblies were a musical bunch, with their own songbook and minstrel Joe Hill. (While visiting B.C., Hill wrote the classic protest song "Where the Fraser River Flows.") Borders weren't enforced so rigorously in the early 1900s and, following work into Canada, Frederick participated in the Vancouver Wobblies' 1912 Free Speech Fight in opposition to the city fathers' ban on outdoor gatherings. Despite the ban, large crowds continued to assemble in parks and speak out until city council finally backed down. Frederick was in the IWW hall when right-wing militiamen attacked it in the aftermath of the First World War. "My grandfather was in the hall defending it." He became a longshoreman in the 1920s and was at Ballantyne Pier when war broke out between union members and scabs/police during the great waterfront strike of June 1935. (A *Vancouver News-Herald* subhead noted: "Stones, Paving Blocks, Bottles, and Roofing Materials Used as Missiles From Housetops By Mob.")[6] Adds David: "My grandfather was a tough guy. He was very nice to me. He was great. But he was a tough character. We discovered afterwards in his closet he had brass knuckles and a blackjack."

When David was eleven years old, he organized a demonstration at Sir Wilfred Grenfell Elementary School. "I wrote out a bunch of grievances, like we were complaining about a teacher who would throw chalk at us and stuff like that." The principal brought students into his office one by one to question them about the protest. "Somehow, they knew it was me." David's radicalization continued through high school. "I didn't like high school and I wanted to get out of there as quickly as possible but I was involved in some student papers." He produced art for *Youth Liberation*, a magazine out of Ann Arbor, Michigan, and devoured Jerry Rubin's *Do It!* and Abbie Hoffman's *Revolution for the Hell of It*. "Opened up the whole idea of what politics was and could be. What Hoffman and Rubin seemed to be doing in the [Chicago] courtroom was like theatre. So, the whole thing of performance. I was a guitar player and I wanted to make posters and art and comics and be a musician. And that all tied into the whole idea of art and politics together. They were manifested in the Chicago trial is the way I looked at it. You had Phil Ochs and Judy Collins sing at the trial. And you realized, wow. This is a world they didn't teach me in school."

After high school, David worked on *The Open Road*, a well-read international anarchist journal founded by Vancouver Yippies. "I embraced the whole idea of anarchism as the way to go . . . the concept of a free people. I did a lot of reading about anarchism and it was the ideology that appealed to me the most." Anarchists strive for the most freedom possible in any given situation, combining the economic equality prescribed by the Marxists with the emphasis on personal freedom of the democratic socialists. To many anarchists, joy and fun are essential ingredients in constructing a socially owned society. As anarchist Emma Goldman said: "If I can't dance, I don't want to be part of your revolution." David moved to London, England, where he squatted and worked on a publication called *Zero*. "At that time, I really believed what we were saying. I thought there is a possibility of a social revolution. It could happen, right, and so I operated with that instinct in mind for everything I was doing, but then you realize you have to carry on. So I can only do so much—within a band, being on a newspaper and just getting by."

1983: David is back in Vancouver after his sojourn in England. He is watching a lot of punk, playing his own music, designing posters. Then Bill's bills are unveiled. "It seemed an insane moment—a classic case of government oppression in an electoral democracy. It was a complete shock but it was well in keeping with the type of people who were in the Socreds. And so that wasn't a shock on that level. I recall the sense of emotion about it because it seemed to attack society as a whole." David is asked to join the staff of the resistance's newspaper, *Solidarity Times*.

—⁓—

The branches of socialism have had their differences since the First International broke up in the 1870s. Extra-parliamentary radicals (including revolutionary anarchists and Marxists), who believe the established state apparatus is irredeemably corrupt and must be dismantled, say democratic-socialist governments don't go far enough, noting that even largely progressive ones like Dave Barrett's do things like legislate striking ferry workers back to work. (It should be noted that there were left-wing democratic socialists in the Legislature who voted against this.) Democratic-socialist and anarchist critics of Marxism say there has always been a streak of authoritarianism in this branch of socialism, pointing for example to the Eastern Bloc governments. (It should be noted that there were anti-Stalinist Marxists appalled at some of the things done in Marx's name.) While these socialisms—Marxism, anarchism and democratic socialism—differ significantly from one another, they all reject the prevailing capitalist system. As democratic socialist Martin Luther King said: "We are saying that something is wrong with capitalism."[7] In the first half of the twentieth century, rank-and-file activists from each of these persuasions of the anti-capitalist left played vital roles in building labour unions and fighting fascism and racism. They all have deep roots in B.C.

The Canadian socialist movement, so active during the Depression, never disappeared—the CP and the CCF/NDP soldiered on in the postwar decades. It gained a new vitality, though, in the New Left movement of the late 1960s and early '70s. While some Solidarity activists, like Renate Shearer and Jess Succamore, were born between the wars, there were also baby boomers, like Marcy Toms, who had their political coming-of-age in this latter movement. On Canada's West Coast, the New Left featured organizations such as Students for a Democratic University (SDU), Vancouver Women's Caucus, Gay Liberation Front, Youth International Party, Native Alliance for Red Power and Vancouver Liberation Front.

—⁓—

Marcy Toms was born in Vancouver in 1949, and her teen years weren't so different from many others in the postwar middle-class Lower Mainland. (She lived on the west side of Vancouver, then

Surrey.) Marcy dined in the family car at White Spot drive-ins ("loved the butter horns") and was completely taken by the British Invasion. "Everybody who came, I saw—from the Beatles, to the Rolling Stones, to Gerry and the Pacemakers, to anybody else who showed up. Got really interested in Bob Dylan as well." Her generation was the first to grow up watching television news and there is one prevailing image, occurring far from Vancouver, that has stayed with her since she saw it as an eight-year-old. "Do remember seeing on our little tiny fuzzy old black-and-white TV the integration of the schools in Little Rock, Arkansas. You didn't really understand exactly what was going on. You just knew that something was really wrong when all these white people were holding revolting signs and spitting at little kids."

Having closely watched every kind of 1960s activism on the evening news, Marcy had more than her classes in mind when she enrolled at Burnaby Mountain's spanking new, Arthur Erickson-designed SFU in the fall of 1967. "I showed up at Simon Fraser University as a first-year student, seventeen years old, eager to become a student radical, and it didn't take me long to find people on campus who I found agreeable, way out there in left field." That October, Marcy journeyed into downtown Vancouver to attend her first anti-Vietnam War march. "There were probably about 600 people there, and it might as well have been 600,000. I was delighted and it seemed like I, personally, was on the cusp of something really big." The Burnaby North campus had an emerging reputation as Berkeley North. Marcy took to the new student radicalism, becoming a socialist, a feminist and an ardent organizer of the SFU Women's Caucus and the campus chapter of Students for a Democratic University. SFU students rallied against the inequities at the university and in support of a Political Science, Sociology and Anthropology (PSA) faculty at odds with the administration. In 1968, Marcy was active in SDU's occupation of the administration building, which resulted in 114 arrests. After SFU, Marcy co-founded the non-sectarian left-wing Spartacus Books. The bookstore became a Vancouver institution, opening on the second floor above a pool hall on East Hastings and then moving slightly farther west on the same street, with an inventory as diversely left as the Solidarity movement would be. She also became a school teacher.

1983: Marcy is on the Vancouver Secondary Teachers' Association executive when the July 7 bills come on the heels of a provincial election that practically everyone expected Dave Barrett and the NDP to win. "To everybody's surprise," says Marcy, "the NDP did not win, and the Socreds won in that era when what people today call neoliberalism—I just call it capitalism—was going to be implemented with a vengeance. And it was. Bill Bennett's government made the decision to attempt not only to put the kibosh on any further gains that the labour movement might make, but to roll things back, so rolling back social legislation, going so far as to try to roll back wages, roll back any gains to maybe, I don't know, 1939." No matter what you call it—Reaganism-Thatcherism-Bennettism, neo-liberalism, restraint, austerity or just plain capitalism—it's a profits-before-people ethos that Marcy has fought since her earliest days at SFU. "Everybody who knows anything about capitalism knows that it never, ever gives up anything," she notes. "It exists for one reason—to maximize capital. It claims no responsibility for any social responsibility at all, and it will do anything and everything to prevent that from happening. So, any gains working people have ever made have been by forcing capital to kneel down and do something, really."

Returning to school in September, Marcy finds the fear of uncertainty. "People are just kind of freaked out. They don't know what this means. They were worried about their jobs because people were going to be laid off in the interests of austerity. The contract was brutal in terms of its attack on groups of people in the province who teachers—teaching being a noble profession—felt some responsibility for. Marginalized people, poor people. Not only considering our own skins at that time."

—⁓—

As a Toronto high school student, Gary Cristall joined the Student Union for Peace Action. Born into the Communist Party in 1950, Gary was a teenage New Leftist, beginning with a protest in support of Alabama civil rights marchers, then anti-Vietnam War demos, then selling the *Yorkville Yawn* underground paper on street corners. "I grew up on the left. I'm very conservative—I never left the left. I switched horses at a certain point."

Gary dropped out of high school and into the counterculture. "I read a lot and was involved in nefarious things," he says. It was a time when revolution seemed just around the corner, and in Canada organizations such as Toronto's Red Morning and Vancouver's Youngblood were modelled on Weatherman, a militant U.S. group which set out to organize "lumpen youth" and stage street confrontations. "We used to help out the Weather Underground and stuff like that because I lived in London, Ontario for a while and we had connections in the States through Detroit," recalls Gary. "We put out a little underground paper there." The radical New Left groups of the era were critical of old-style left organizing, saying the working class had turned conservative. They turned instead to others they thought were more receptive to their ideas, such as youth or racial minorities or women. "We published the FLQ manifesto. We felt like it was like living in Nazi Germany. People were not going to change. The working class had been bought off. And the only thing you could do was to help the Vietnamese militarily by destroying as much of the war machine as was possible." Returning to Toronto, Gary was torn between Red Morning and the Waffle (a left democratic-socialist faction inside the NDP). "And finally I had to make a decision, which was either go break the windows [with Red Morning] in Eaton's on the anniversary of the War Measure Act, or go and help the women immigrant textile workers at the Texpack strike by going out on the picket line and getting roughed up by the cops. I went and got roughed up by the cops. So, I was moving politically to a more orthodox Marxist point of view."

Orthodox, yes, in the sense of identifying with working-class struggle. Orthodox, no, in that he was about to go beyond the ideological pale for a red-diaper baby. "Well, I had gone to hear Ernest Mandel, who was one of the leaders of the [Trotskyist] Fourth International in the fall of 1971, and he got me thinking." A short time later, on an extended stay in Allende's Chile, Gary began devouring Leon Trotsky's writings about the Spanish Civil War and permanent revolution. "My girlfriend came back up to Toronto because her father was sick, and she said, 'Hey, what do you want me to bring [down to Chile]?' I said, 'Bring down a kosher salami, a dozen bagels and everything by Trotsky you can find.' Then, at a certain point, I said, 'Okay, so it turns out I'm a Trotskyist.' My parents were horrified. My mother said, '*A Trotskyite.*' But in the end they, too, came around. Later on, when we founded the Revolutionary Marxist Group, a Trotskyist organization, my parents made a donation." Gary was visiting Vancouver when the military coup overthrew the Salvador Allende government. "I was here and couldn't go back there, so I stayed here and became active politically and eventually went to university. Just when I was going to become an academic, I got involved with an old friend in starting the Vancouver Folk Music Festival."

1983: Gary is director of the Vancouver Folk Music Festival. "I had a day job, if you like, organizing a musical event, which is a big to-do in one of the parks in the West Side of Vancouver, and we did concerts and were making records. Essentially, I was running a cultural organization that was doing a lot of stuff and it was quite openly political. We would do Solidarity events for various groups, one thing or another." Gary draws upon every kind of progressive to produce his highly regarded folk festival. He had a particular affinity with Latin American solidarity work, having spent considerable time in Chile, Nicaragua and El Salvador. "I was happy with the work, and with the activist work I did in trying to build this little organization, Socialist Challenge, and that's when the Solidarity events took place. . . . All of a sudden there was this draconian right-wing kind of prefigured neo-liberalism legislation." He immediately thought general strike.

"If you come from the revolutionary Marxist left and you've read a little bit of Marx, and you read some Lenin, you read a little bit of Rosa Luxemburg on the mass strike, you always think this is the way you need to go."

—⁓—

Kim Zander was thirteen when her father, Bill, took her to see the movie *Joe Hill*. "I remember being absolutely shocked at seeing the story of this man's life and how horrible it was that he was killed by the police," says Kim. A couple of years later, her father took her to another stunning film. "A movie about the Vietnam War called *Hearts and Minds*. I had never had an experience of walking out of a movie theatre in absolute utter silence. No one spoke, no one clapped at the movie, no one said anything. It was absolute silence as people moved out of the movie theatre because it was a shocking film, and it was amazing."

At fifteen, Kim had already gone to demonstrations against the Vietnam War. Born in New Westminster in 1959, she grew up exploring a North Delta filled with small farms, orchards and wild bush. She also grew up passionate about the injustice she was observing, not just in *Hearts and Minds* or *Joe Hill*, but everywhere. There were, for starters, the stories her father would bring home from his carpentry work. "One story in particular—he came home totally in shock and we pushed him to tell us what was going on. Eventually, he told us that one of his co-workers had fallen off the building that day and they had to go and get him, and he was hanging by his neck off of one of the balconies they were building. My dad was a political lefty. He was involved in his union, he was involved in the Communist Party." There was a party side to the Party, and the Zander family often joined in gatherings at community halls. Her mother was on the left, too. "She was with the Communist Party for a while but didn't stay with it."

In Kim's mid-teens, she worked at getting signatures on the anti-nuclear Stockholm Appeal. (Signatories included Leonard Bernstein, Pablo Picasso and Charlie Parker.) She also joined the Young Communist League (YCL). "I was curious about the world and I was disgusted by the things that I had already learned, as a young person, were going on, and I couldn't countenance that people were allowing this to happen." YCL members were taught about the failings of capitalism and the history of working-class activism. "We were going to classes. We were having discussions." Meanwhile, Kim was on the volleyball team at North Delta Secondary School. It was a dual existence, with a YCL social life and socialist studies alongside a high school sporting life and social studies. The two would clash on occasion. "I had a teacher who I used to have debates with in social studies class all the time. His name was Mr. Bennett." Kim dropped out of North Delta athletics and rebelled against high school. "I had been a bit of a wild child. Not only did I have no interest in high school but I was involved in politics. I was in a folk rock choir." Post-high school, Kim continued to sing in the touring lefty choir Bargain at Half the Price. "We used to sing at all sorts of rallies and events and political fundraisers. We even did some of them for the NDP, ironically." She also started working at the Quality Fish plant, by the Knight Street Bridge, which she came close to unionizing. "It took me three years, but I was almost there.... They knew I was up to something when I was working there." They laid Kim off in 1982.

1983: Kim is recognized in CP circles for her organizational acumen and impassioned public speaking. The party plays a significant role in the formation of the Lower Mainland Budget Coalition and she is a speaker at the first big anti-budget rally in July. After Quality Fish, she becomes coordinator of the new Vancouver Unemployed Action Centre. Located at the Fisherman's Hall, it's a place where the unemployed can drop by for information and support. "Some of the stories were heartbreaking, about how people's lives had just fallen apart." Organized by the Vancouver and District Labour Council, with heavy Communist Party participation, the Unemployed Action

Centre is a throwback to Depression-era CP activism, which often focused on the unemployed. Soon, more than thirty action centres were established across the province. Kim is a headstrong young activist who knows exactly what is in her heart and mind, and believes it, and is determined. These can be extremely admirable qualities, especially when you're fighting Socreds in the Solidarity months of 1983. "The Action Centre had been in play for many months prior to the Solidarity Coalition and because of our work. With our tentacles out into the community, we had a lot of connections already. I'd go out and speak to community groups and to local unions and to labour conventions about what was going on and we would gather support."

—◆—

The communist movement emerged from the Marxist faction of the First International. Karl Marx knew that no one wants to be second class. He saw history as a series of class conflicts—oppressed classes rebelling against ruling classes—culminating in the working-class overthrow of the capitalist class. This, he believed, would eventually usher in a classless society rooted in economic equality. Through the nineteenth century and the first two-thirds of the twentieth century, it wasn't just Marxists who saw unions and "the workers" as the engine for fundamental social change. While they differ with Marxism in other ways, many anarchists and democratic socialists drew on Marx's historical class analysis and critique of profit ("surplus value"). The left would, on occasion, organize around race or peace or women's rights, but the underlying focus was class. This focus was not surprising, considering that the socialist movement emerged as a response to capitalism's brutal treatment of workers.

The First International of the 1860s and '70s was a coalition of socialist ideologies. What made the Solidarity Coalition of 1983 so distinct from this earlier socialist coalition was that its diversity lay more in identity than ideology. In the 1960s and '70s, radical new social movements had suddenly appeared that regarded their issues as no less revolutionary than class. Emerging from the New Left, these movements were organized around gender, race, sexual orientation, environment and counterculture. It is the division between unions and these new social movements that would largely come to define the Solidarity movement.

———

1983: On page two of Issue No. 1 of *Solidarity Times*, there is an ad that reads: "CRAIG PATTERSON, Barrister & Solicitor, 1400 Dominion Building."[8] Craig Patterson was an activist lawyer at the meeting that launched the Lower Mainland Budget Coalition. "This was a line in the sand. This was something that could not be brooked. This had to be stand up and get up off your haunches time for everybody." Craig also has vivid memories of another, much earlier confrontation with Bill and his fellow Bennetts, at North Vancouver's Presentation House.

Before he was battling Bennetts, though, Craig was growing up as a son of wealth in working-class Welland, Ontario, a town full of steel and associated metal-manufacturing businesses. "My grandfather ran a business with fifty employees and the union was Communist. United Electrical Workers. This was in the '40s and the '50s." In 1964 and '65, when Craig was eighteen and nineteen, he worked summers at his grandfather's plant. "This factory was barbaric. The noise and the heat were unbelievable. This was before there was anything like worker health-and-safety protection." He especially remembers the hammersmiths. "These were men who were once six-foot-three, and by the time they finished twenty years of being a hammersmith they were like five-foot-eight and sinewy because they were holding heavy metal that was white-hot. It would bounce up and down. A bang! A bang! A bang! You could hear it all across town, fifteen miles away. So there was some class consciousness. You couldn't avoid it. It hit you right in the face." Craig became self-conscious about the family business. "I was quite conscious of the fact that I was a privileged kid who had two grandparents who were prominent citizens in business and we lived on the right side of the canal. We were white and spoke

English at home. Half the town, at least, did not speak English at home. They spoke a variety of European languages."

Neighbouring Buffalo, N.Y., helped to shape Craig's notion of race. Craig loved sports and his father took him across the border to watch Negro League legend Luke Easter play for the Triple A Buffalo Bisons. Craig sat cheering in a stadium filled with black baseball fans cheering Easter on. "And there are no black people in my small town." In the 1950s, residents of Welland actually regarded nearby Buffalo as more of a "world-class city" than nearby Toronto. Buffalo was to young Craig what Seattle was to young Vancouverites of the time—"radio programs from Buffalo, television programs from Buffalo." Not long before Craig was born in 1946, his parents saw an unknown Tony Bennett sing at a Buffalo nightclub. "My mother always told the story about how Tony Bennett drew attention to my father and mother in the audience because [father] was wearing a war uniform. Tony Bennett was giving him the attention so that the crowd would applaud this couple who were fighting fascism."

After high school, Craig attended Western University in London, Ontario. He became president of the Student Law Society, advocating, like student movements across North America, for student participation in course content and the hiring and firing of professors—"anything that affected the curriculum." His fledgling activism intensified in 1969 when he went on to graduate school at Harvard. The Cambridge campus was a cultural/political revelation for Craig, with Vietnam the galvanizing issue. "Every day was intense. There were strikes and rallies all the time on the Harvard campus. Educational sit-ins were a big feature of the time. There would be flash gatherings with posters slapped around and people talking to each other—Meet at the building at 5." Along with being swept up by an American New Left at its height, Craig was immersed in subcultural offerings and attended an off-campus film school run by Jake Mostel, son of blacklisted actor Zero Mostel. "And there were tons of French and Italian films playing. Double headers. Triple headers. I was soaking it up. I came from sterile Southwestern Ontario, with its rigidities and nothingness, to this incredibly rich, intellectual, cultural ferment. Everybody was buzzing in what they wore, the way they spoke, the books they read. I had a friend at the time who was in Africa on a Canadian peace mission. Both the U.S. and Canada had their overseas youth service programs. And he [the friend] wanted me to find him a book—a Swahili–English dictionary." So Craig went into a Harvard Square bookstore. "It had four different Swahili–English dictionaries available. I couldn't believe it."

After Harvard, Craig taught law at the University of Windsor. In 1972, he heard talk of the electoral goings-on in B.C. Socred W.A.C. Bennett was a durable demagogue, premier for twenty years, but rumour was this time Dave Barrett's NDP had a fighting chance. Craig headed west "to participate in the election . . . to defeat the right wing." Shortly after arriving, he recalls, "I was the subject of one of the most famous political quotes in B.C. history. When W.A.C. Bennett screamed in the meeting hall in North Vancouver, '*The socialists are at the gates*,' he was pointing at me."

Craig explains: "I never joined the NDP but I've mostly supported them for lack of something else. Anyway, I came out here with a couple of other guys on a mission to take part, and the first month of the election nothing happened. Like, there were no demonstrations, there were no parades, there were no speeches, there were no debates. Nothing." An entire month had passed when Craig learned of a Socred event. "It was held in a theatre that's still there in North Vancouver, just off Lonsdale." Presentation House. "We decided that we would sneak in there and do some nastiness. And it worked like a charm. It was so easy. It was like a hot knife through butter. They were so taken by surprise, they had no way of dealing with it. It wasn't within their experience that there would be opposition to any of their social events, to what they saw as an in-party team event, building solidarity."

Craig arrived outside Presentation House to find a gay group holding pro-Socred placards. "It was beautiful theatre, right. They were being ironic but they were trying to look serious. They were dressed like Socreds." Meanwhile, actual Socreds were arriving dressed like Socreds. "They had suits on and dresses and purses and hats and things like that." The place was packed. "We had to sneak in and we strategically placed ourselves. Three of us." This was the moment when Craig first caught sight of Bill Bennett. "I'll never forget—the two Bennett brothers were at the front of the room. One on each side [of the stage], standing facing the crowd. There was Bill and then there was his brother, Russell." Craig and friends started heckling the evening's first speakers. "You know, just a phrase here and there." The early, relatively undemonstrative heckling intensified when a Socred named Jim took the stage. "He was blond, had a suit on. He was giving a rousing, positive speech and he had a huge smile on his face. He couldn't have been smiling any more than he was. So the phrase was '*Smile, Jim, smile!*' And it was like the gas was going out of a balloon when Jim heard this. His face just sunk. People were starting to shift. They were looking at us because nobody else was making any noise of any kind. It was like a ceremony of the dead.

"Then, finally, W.A.C. came on and he started pointing at us," says Craig, "*and he's talking about the socialist hordes.* People ridicule him for that remark, but he was dead on. He was absolutely right. We were the socialist hordes. And we were coming to Vancouver."

CHAPTER 5

From Grace to Grace:
Rising Up Feminist

THERE WERE ELEVEN fireplaces in Grace Manor. The estate extended over two acres in King's Point, the opulent slice of Greater New York City that inspired F. Scott Fitzgerald's *The Great Gatsby*. William Russell Grace built this Long Island mansion and the conglomerate W.R. Grace and Company, both of which would remain in the Grace family long after his death in 1904. Grace was the first Irish mayor of New York. In 1886, he personally accepted a special gift from France: the Statue of Liberty.

Gail Meredith's grandparents came to New York from Ireland, too. Arriving in the late 1800s, they found work at Grace Manor as a chauffeur and a maid. When Gail was born on Long Island in 1942, her father was overseas in the navy. After the war, Gail's parents established a home in Mineola, a village twenty-two miles from King's

Point. "My parents were typical working-class people," Gail says. "We never had a lot of money." Gail thought her corner of Long Island was wonderful, though, "near enough to New York that there was interesting stuff going on. My mother was very taken with dance. She would take me to dance things in New York." Her parents were lifelong, rock-ribbed Republicans. "They were sad that I went in a different direction."

That direction was northwest and left. By 1983, Gail was a long-time Vancouver resident and feminist activist. On July 20, she attended the first mass meeting of Women Against the Budget. Nora Randall was at that meeting, too. Nora had been active in the feminist movement almost from its start, but when she stepped into the First United Church at Gore and Hastings on July 20, she could barely believe her eyes. "It was huge . . . tons of women involved." Canadian Union of Postal Workers organizer Marion Pollack was there, too. "It was a unique and moving experience to have meetings with activists from the women's movement and trade unionist women in the same room," she says. "That's what I remember, like, holy shit, I'm in a room with all these people, and we're all talking, and we're all on the same page." That WAB meeting was attended by more than 200 women representing, according to a press release, "minority, labour, feminist, church, welfare, civic and professional groups."[1]

WAB's opening press release—SOCRED BUDGET UNITES WOMEN'S OPPOSITION—was appropriately blunt. "The Socred budget assaults women, wiping out twenty years' hard-won gains in the struggle for women's equality. This was the consensus of representatives of twenty-eight women's organizations from labour, ethnic and community groups meeting on Wednesday July 13 to discuss the budget's effect on their constituents. . . . The budget, if implemented, will entrench women in poverty, and reestablish widespread discrimination. . . . The meeting of Women Against the Budget agreed that the government is concerned not with restraint, but with curtailing the democratic, economic and human rights of the people of British Columbia." The release promised "a varied programme of action which will inform British Columbians of the devastating effects on women of the Socred proposals."[2]

Women Against the Budget more than lived up to that promise, becoming the key component within the Solidarity Coalition. During the Solidarity months of 1983, WAB was always on the front line —organizing its own imaginative protests, bolstering union picket lines, backing militant resistance "up to and including" a general strike.

———

In 1968, Marcy Toms and Doreen ("Dodie") Weppler were Students for a Democratic University radicals enrolled in SFU professor Martin Nicolaus's Political Science, Sociology and Anthropology class. As a class project, the two rewrote *The Communist Manifesto* as a "women's liberation manifesto." Their resulting document called for an SFU women's organization. "Women of the world unite," the manifesto closed. "You have nothing to lose but your apron strings and a world to win." In July 1968, Marcy and Dodie called SFU's women activists to a meeting to found a new student club called the Feminine Action League. A few weeks later, its name was changed to the SFU Women's Caucus. In 1969, some members established the Vancouver Women's Caucus.

The feminist movement arrived as a cultural/political earthquake in the late 1960s, challenging everything from gender stereotypes to abortion laws to the artificial division between the personal and the political. After Canadian suffragettes ("first wave" feminists) won their long fight for the vote in 1919, feminism was largely dormant for almost fifty years. By 1968, emboldened by groundbreaking writers and a passion to right ancient wrongs, a second wave was emerging, with a newly coined word—"sexism"—and a handful of unconnected collectives across North America. Feminism did for sex what Marx had done for class. Shulamith Firestone's *The Dialectic of Sex*, for example, put gender oppression into detailed historical context. "For feminist revolution," Firestone wrote, "we shall need an analysis of the dynamics of sex war as comprehensive as the Marx-Engels analysis of class antagonism was for the economic revolution. More comprehensive. For we are dealing with a larger problem, with an oppression that goes back beyond recorded history."[3]

When the SFU Women's Caucus formed in 1968, it was not only the first feminist organization in Western Canada—it was one of the first in the world. By the following year, the Vancouver Women's Caucus had its own newspaper (*The Pedestal*) and a dozen action committees (abortion, teachers, newsletter, SFU, VCC, UBC, book workshop, *Pedestal*, orientation, legal, finance, artists). A front-page item in Issue No. 1 of *The Pedestal* headlined "JOIN WOMEN'S CAUCUS" said the caucus was an organization of women students, workers and housewives. "As women, we recognized that we too have little control over the forces that shape our lives in this society, that we face specific problems because we are women, and that women must be organized independently to struggle for solutions to these problems."[4] Says Marcy Toms: "We were working on issues that at the time were not only extremely important but pretty much challenges to the state. The biggest one would be reproductive rights. We did things that were illegal. We counselled women about where to get terminations of their pregnancy." In 1971, the Women's Caucus helped organize one of the early international feminist conferences. The Vancouver Indo-Chinese Women's Conference was a vital melding of the anti-war and feminist movements, bringing together nearly 1,000 feminists from Canada, the U.S., North Vietnam, South Vietnam, Laos and Cambodia.

—◦◦◦—

The old Vancouver City College (VCC)—first at Twelfth and Oak, then at its Langara campus—had its own lively New Left, and Muggs Sigurgeirson joined the VCC Women's Caucus. Muggs grew up in a North Vancouver of the 1950s and '60s that was rural and working class. Her father, "a small-l liberal," worked as a bookkeeper at Imperial Oil. Her mother was a socialist and Muggs' childhood summers were spent at the Co-operative Commonwealth Federation's camp on Gabriola Island. "They would run socialist summer school, and my mom would pack up all her kids and drag us over there. We'd all live in cabins and people looked after all the kids collectively. Everybody had to do chores. It was like living in a commune. It was a big, beautiful camp." The CCF sold the land when she was twelve. For Muggs, this move epitomizes the political divide among social democrats. "My mom told me the left was all out on the back porch having a smoke and the right-wing passed a motion to sell it. I said, 'That's a metaphor for life.'"

After high school, Muggs continued her activism. Besides the VCC Women's Caucus, she participated in anti-war and anti-poverty protests. She found work at the Transition House women's shelter, which had been certified by the Service, Office and Retail Workers Union of Canada, a union with deep New Left feminist roots. "Everything was decided collectively. Somebody like [SORWUC activist-writer] Helen Potrebenko would write a letter to the Labour Board. She'd put it on the table and for the next three days everybody had to read it and improve on it and correct it. It was pretty amazing. We elected one paid person." Muggs was up at five a.m. to begin her SORWUC activism. "We used to be downtown at Burrard and Hastings, where all those big buildings were and where all the buses came in with office workers from the suburbs. At seven, seven-thirty in the morning, we'd be down there and we would leaflet till nine and then all go to work."

The leaflets asked, *Do you know what a union can do for you?* The democratic feminist union had considerable success in the 1970s, daring to organize where unions seldom went, including banks. "It was a tough fight," says Muggs. "SORWUC did all the work and then those unions went in and raided it. [By 1983] our numbers were down." Still, SORWUC did its bit during the Solidarity uprising. "SORWUC was trying to get out all of the people and we actually took women from Transition House to Empire Stadium."

—⁓—

No component of Solidarity exemplified the movement's transformative nature more than Women Against the Budget. Like much of the Solidarity Coalition, second-wave feminism was rooted in the new radical movements of the 1960s and '70s, and WAB knew that fundamental social change in 1983 had to go beyond the labour movement's conventional economism. WAB met Thursday nights at First United Church. Meeting minutes from July 20 paraphrase Sara Diamond outlining WAB's first days:

> [WAB] came out of women getting together at the first LM Budget Coalition meeting. 60–70 women came representing approximately 30 organizations. Women discussed the necessity of unity, how we can mobilize large number of women, how to join with others, that we need a clear voice for women inside the coalition, that we do leafleting of shopping plazas, etc. To date WAB has participated in the LMBC, issued a press release and discussed the possibility of a public meeting detailing the effects of the budget on women's lives and producing a fact sheet concerning the same. WAB plans to continue to meet.[5]

At that July 20 meeting, a wonderful voice for justice—Frances Wasserlein—was voted to be the WAB speaker at the upcoming rally of the Lower Mainland Budget Coalition. A committee was formed to write the speech—Frances, Deb Bradley, Sara Diamond and Esther Shannon. So, barely more than a week after WAB's first meeting, co-founder Frances Wasserlein addressed the massive July 23 LMBC rally. Frances told the protesters:

> Women are fighting [the budget] because we CANNOT survive and, as importantly, we will not advance under the terms it seeks to impose on our lives. Women have a long experience of being blamed for what goes wrong. If we are raped, it's our fault. If we are beaten, it's our fault and if we lose our jobs, it's our fault. These are lies. They are part and parcel of the ways that women are denied equality in our society.

Now not only women, but all of us have been fed a pack of lies. Women have learned to be very good at spotting lies. All of our rights are under attack but it's not because it's our fault and it's not because of "restraint," rather it's because we have in Victoria, a government that is a disgrace to the ideal of a democratic society. But and this is by far the most important truth for us to remember. Today we have here the commitment of British Columbians. We are women, men, trade unionists, minority church groups, gays and lesbians, tenants and many more. This government will learn that our fundamental social, political and economic rights are not dependent on their whims or even their "master designs." Rather those rights are dependent on our will, the will of the people.[6]

Sara Diamond recalls Frances's fierce stage presence at the rally. "Frances was a very powerful, big woman, passionate speaker," says Sara, "and one of the labour guys—I think they didn't like what she was saying, and a woman talking that long, that powerfully—he began to move in on her and she blocked his body with her body and kind of danced backwards and body-blocked him and I think stomped his foot, and got him out of the way and just kept going with her speech. I had to do that once in a situation. It was many years later, and I just remember at the time when I had to do it, just remembering Frances, watching Frances do it on the stage and just cracking up about it afterwards. But she was an amazing spokesperson."

—◦◦◦—

Speaking of riveting stage presences, there is an opening scene in *The Way We Were* where 1930s radical Katie Morosky (Barbra Streisand) goes off script and, for a moment, speaks with an emotional power that grabs hold of her mostly apolitical campus audience. Watching 1970s radical Sara Diamond speak at a crowded Fisherman's Hall (she was introducing Dennis Banks of the American Indian Movement) I knew that she, like Katie Morosky and Frances Wasserlein, instinctively knew how to hold an audience.

Sara was born in New York City in 1954, but the family left for Toronto after run-ins with McCarthyism. As they settled into their new city, Sara became a precocious activist. At fourteen, she attended protests and co-founded Seed, the first free school in Canada. When Sara was twenty-two, she moved to the West Coast. She loved the beauty of the place, but there was more to her move than mountains and seawalls. "It was progressive. It had these big movements. It was an exciting place to be. There was this phenomenal history of left-wing activism." Soon, she was active in the Revolutionary Marxist Group and an Association of University and College Employees (AUCE) organizer.

In 1970, the Vancouver Women's Caucus had formed the Working Women's Workshop, which in October 1972 helped to found SORWUC. A year later, it was active in the founding of AUCE. Like SORWUC, AUCE was focused on organizing women who had been unorganized by the labour movement. Sara was part of the AUCE organizing group at UBC. "I remember getting up and speaking to a room full of—it felt like 5,000 people, it was probably about a thousand, talking about why we needed to have a union."

Sara went on to SFU to study and helped organize its staff into AUCE. "We really were looking at the experience of work from a woman's perspective and what was needed to look at these jobs and improve the quality of work. And we did get very good labour agreements."

1983: Sara is at the first meeting of WAB. "It was a sort of network of women's organizations who all stepped forward and individual women who began to meet to put together an organization that would be able to really defend the rights of women, including vulnerable women."

Women Against the Budget joined the Lower Mainland Solidarity Coalition when it formed on August 3. Like other coalition members, WAB's specific issues were highlighted in Solidarity literature. An early Solidarity leaflet (endorsed by WAB, Operation Solidarity and the BCFED) noted that the Socreds had cut funding to the Women's Health Collective, Planned Parenthood, postpartum counselling, Serena, Woomb, Vancouver Transition House, Vancouver Rape Relief, B.C. Coalition of Rape Crisis Centres, family support workers and child care centres. It also noted cuts in rural communities—the Fort Nelson Women's Emergency Shelter for battered women was closed. "The Socreds are attacking Women," the leaflet said. "We demand the withdrawal of the 26 bills taking away what legal rights we have as workers and women. . . . Demand reinstatement of funds to services, including those developed by feminists."[7]

—⁓—

Nora Randall was born in 1947 in Minnesota—land of lakes, Bob Dylan and Jessica Lange. Like Nora, Jessica lived in Little Falls, although the Langes were relative newcomers. "In a town like Little Falls, you're from away unless you've been there forty years," Nora says. (Jessica Lange went on to be a student radical at the University of Minnesota, then starred in *Frances* and *King Kong*.) Young Nora was athletic and loved baseball, but the feeling wasn't reciprocated by the town's sporting authorities. "I got sent home from Little League baseball for being a girl." As a University of Minnesota student in Minneapolis, Nora frequented the Scholar coffeehouse where Dylan had often performed before he moved on to Greenwich Village. "He wasn't singing there anymore but he recently had been. It was kind of the place to go." Nora abruptly left the university to join a convent. "I only lasted six months. There was a moment in which I realized that if I stayed I would lose myself."

Having in short order left Little Falls, the University of Minnesota and a convent, Nora was wide open to new ideas and experiences. Her next sea change would last a lifetime. In 1967, while at Webster College in St. Louis to study theatre and social sciences, she joined protests against the Vietnam War. "I went to Washington. I can remember seeing the trucks full of national guardsmen, and they would flash us the peace sign." When she graduated in the spring of 1970, students were shutting down campuses in forty-three states to protest Richard Nixon's invasion of Cambodia and the shooting of students at Kent State, Ohio. "Everybody was pretty much in shock, right, because the national guard had killed college students for God's sake." At the graduation ceremony, Nora was among a group of students that pulled the plug on the loudspeaker system. To the assembled students and their families, she read aloud from *Waiting for Godot*— "The tears of the world are a constant quality. For each one who begins to weep somewhere else another stops. The same is true of the laugh."[8] Then, along with other protesting graduates, Nora walked out.

Nora kept walking. Finally, after a couple starts and stops, she followed friends who had moved to Canada. "The bus that goes through Little Falls, going south it said 'Minneapolis,' going north it said 'Winnipeg.' But I had never been." She arrived in Vancouver in August 1971, when the talk of the town was the Gastown Smoke-In that had turned riotous. "I missed the Gastown Riot. I arrived just shortly afterward," she says. "Vancouver was pretty spectacular because it had mountains and ocean in the same place, in a city. You could swim in the beaches right off of downtown. And it was beautiful, though I have to say that the first winter in Vancouver was the hardest winter of my life because it was gunmetal grey for six months." The international borders of 1971 weren't so difficult to navigate. "Canada was wide open. I was a college-educated American. I spoke English. I spoke some French. I had a bit of money. They were happy to have us. I registered at Manpower as a poet." Nora was drawn into the city's expansive counterculture. "West Fourth Avenue. There were people living in communal houses, there were health-food stores, tie-dyed T-shirt shops. I didn't have a lot of money and I had no connections here. Also, I was anti-war. And I was getting into feminism."

While settling into Vancouver, Nora read Germaine Greer and Simone de Beauvoir, Kate Millett and Jane Rule. These and other feminist writers were inventing concepts that would endure and change political language. To Simone de Beauvoir, woman had become "the Second Sex" as man defined himself the essential one and woman "the other." Nora's fellow Minnesotan, Kate Millett, deconstructed patriarchy in her *Sexual Politics*. She writes, "If a critical attitude toward the sexual politics of patriarchy precedes reform, reform itself precedes revolution."[9] All of this and much more was an insurrection inside Nora's head. "It was like a gong went off when I read feminism." So, Nora offered her services at the office of *The Pedestal*, Canada's first feminist newspaper, at 307 West Broadway.

"I wrote some articles and I helped typeset it and helped lay it out, helped print it, distribute it." *The Pedestal*, like any twentieth-century newspaper, was a hands-on, labour-intensive production. "All this stuff is gone now," Nora says. "I mean, we had to typeset it into these machines, and then get these little rolls of tape, and then feed them into this bigger machine, and then get printouts that we then had to wax the back of, and then cut them, and then lay them out on layout sheets, and then roll them all down and then send them to the printer. *And that entire thing disappeared.* It all became computerized and a whole graphic arts industry disappeared. But we were doing it. I can remember the very first time somebody said, about eleven o'clock at night, 'Call the taxi. It's ready.' I thought, 'Oh my God, we're done.' Like, I thought it was going to go on forever. I just thought we're going to be just laying it out and laying it out." Nora was part of the group that in 1973 established the Vancouver Women's Bookstore downtown in an old clapboard house.

1983: When the Socred legislation comes down, Nora joins Women Against the Budget. "We were doing stuff. We passed resolutions, we wrote letters, we showed up at marches. There were five of us who started Budget University. We basically decided to do a bunch of public lectures and invite people to learn about the economic principles behind what was happening."

In the 1960s and '70s, the high school I went to—Winston Churchill in Vancouver's Oakridge neighbourhood—graduated a notable number of soon-to-be activists including, among others, Clyde Hertzman, Sharman Kanee, Jackie Weller and Larry Stoffman. Mike Harcourt, too. None were more admirable, though, than Marion Pollack.

Marion has a way of taking each thing life throws at her—from callous bosses to schoolyard bullies—and not allowing any of it to slow her down. Instead, she became a bold champion of anyone treated unjustly. She was an organizer for the Canadian Union of Postal Workers with an instinct for synthesizing the day-to-day concerns of her members with large social justice issues. Before Solidarity, she was active in the socialist-feminist organization Bread and Roses and the Women's Committee in her union. The committee was instrumental in the union striking for maternity leave in contracts. "It really gave you a sense that unions could be in that critical struggle for justice and fairness for women," she says.

1983: On August 10, Marion is a shop steward urging co-workers to leave work to attend the Empire Stadium rally. "For the Victoria rally, they fired the president and vice-president of the local for leading people out," she notes. She represented WAB on the Solidarity Coalition's Steering Committee. Marion was so moved by the massive Solidarity resistance building through the summer of 1983 that she made the life-changing decision to abandon her personal plans and stay in Vancouver to fight the budget. "I was very excited. On a personal level, I had been admitted to grad school in Ontario and I decided not to go because of Solidarity." Marion went on to become president of the Vancouver local of the Canadian Union of Postal Workers.

———

Beth Hutchinson grew up in Telfordville, a poor Alberta farming community where her father was the United Church minister. "There were lots of community connections. Farmers and definitely my parents were involved in organizing a co-operative phone company." Her parents were to the left of most in "a community that was conservative politically and theologically." After graduating high school in 1965, Beth attended the University of Alberta in Edmonton, wanting nothing more than to "fit in with the mainstream." It was her father who, in a roundabout way, changed that. "The boyfriend of one of my roommates came for dinner, and he said that he had been at a United Church meeting that day in which my father was putting forward the suggestion that the church should push the Canadian government to accept American draft dodgers, and I thought, why am I thinking that I should think this war is a good thing? I realized in that moment the extent to which I was just still reacting to trying to not be my parents. And I didn't have to do that anymore."

Like most anywhere in late 1960s North America, the University of Alberta had a student movement and Beth soon embraced student/anti-war activism. "Both of those. I went to meetings. I definitely was not in the leadership of that at all. I was a quiet member. It was also at that time that I first heard about sexism and first heard about women's liberation, and it was such a momentous moment because I always thought that the reason I sat quietly and whenever there was a chance to say something I did not say a word was because of my own inadequacies. So to hear the idea that, in fact, this was influenced by a society-wide oppression was a massive insight for me, personally. It was the beginning of my involvement in the women's movement."

A decade later, she was a veteran of the Canadian New Left—"a feminist and socialist"—influenced by an autonomous Marxist group called the New Tendency, which opposed hierarchy and favoured direct democracy. The group also believed that activists should connect with the working class by getting working-class jobs. "I must say, my partner had this idea more strongly than I did." In Edmonton, partner Michael worked in a steel plant and Beth worked as a typist in a hospital. In 1975, they left Edmonton for Vancouver. "Michael said,

'I want to go see what it's like to live somewhere where the left is more active.' And so we decided to come. It was just, yeah, sure, we can go live there for a while." Beth was working as a unit clerk at St. Paul's Hospital when she encountered the Women's Health Collective, which provided women with everything from an information phone line and pregnancy testing to abortion counselling and workplace health. Beth started as a volunteer and became a staff member.

1983: Beth is outraged by the budget, but exhilarated by the rising of Solidarity. "I do remember the thrill of the building movement as it developed. The excitement that all these groups were organized and working together. So I remember following the development of the Solidarity movement with some involvement and a lot of excitement." The Women's Health Collective is the focus of Beth's political activity and she's familiar with Socred cuts. "Once, we took a position about housing and Grace McCarthy—at that point the minister that had responsibility for housing—made sure we got cut." Now, the collective's funding is among the women's services cut in the budget.

Gail Meredith was in her teens when rock 'n' roll arrived on Long Island. She was a regular at DJ Alan Freed's shows starring Chuck Berry and Buddy Holly at the Brooklyn Paramount. "I remember just hordes of kids my age being riveted. The rock 'n' roll thing was so fascinating. It really changed things. It got the focus of younger people on something that was entirely different." After finishing high school in 1960, Gail received a scholarship to Washington University in St. Louis, then attended the University of Wisconsin, then moved to upstate New York. "I was madly involved with some guy in Buffalo." Introduced to the '60s in Buffalo, Gail found new things to be madly involved with—housing issues and marching against the war.

Gail moved to the San Francisco Bay Area, the heart of the era's activism and counterculture, where she counselled draft resisters and became involved with the United Farm Workers (UFW). With the UFW on strike against California growers in 1973, she was asked to visit Vancouver to raise support for the union's grape boycott. Support for the boycott was immediate in Vancouver, with grapes removed from Safeway shelves. "There were a lot of people [in Vancouver] who were involved in a lot of things, including food-based stuff. It was a time. It definitely was a time." Gail decided to stay, quickly finding work and friends. "By that time, I had figured out that I was gay and my partner was chairing the NDP Women's Committee. I was working for the Federation of Labour, doing women's programs."

1983: Gail is working in a Safeway warehouse. Her reaction to the July 7 bills: "Absolute fury." She attended Women Against the Budget meetings and in late August joyfully participated in WAB's Stone Soup Rally at the plush home of Socred politician Grace McCarthy, who had recently presided over deep "restraint" cuts to social services as Minister of Human Resources.

—◦◦◦—

For Gail Meredith, there wasn't much distance between the Grace mansion of Long Island and Grace's mansion in Shaughnessy.

"PROTEST at Grace McCarthy's," announced the Women Against the Budget leaflet.[10] It gave the place and time—4610 Beverly Crescent in Shaughnessy, twelve noon, August 27—and explained how the Socred budget had disproportionately adverse effects on women. "Thousands of women in the public sector are laid off. Seventy per cent of laid-off teachers are women. Two-thirds of Ministry of Human Resources workers are women. . . . When Grace McCarthy says the family will provide the social service the government is cutting, she means women will provide the services with no pay and no support."

Gail spoke to the joyful crowd from a makeshift stage. "I was actually MC on one of the trucks. People came from all over. . . . It was kind of a shock to the neighbourhood. It was great." Says Marcy Toms: "We got a flatbed truck, we got some music, we got some loud-speakers, and we got stones because, you know, the old legend, with moral lessons, about stone soup. A smashing success. Speaking truth to power where it lived to bring home the realities of the budget and the harm it was already doing to women and children in particular."

Through September, Women Against the Budget continued to rally the province. A WAB Solidarity Coalition picnic drew 500 to East Van's Grandview Park. WAB's Nancy Jackson said the focus of this "cultural celebration" was to alert the public to the bills' impact on women and children.[11] Similar picnics were held in Gibsons and Chilliwack.

At a crowded Women Against the Budget public meeting September 7 at Vancouver's Mount Pleasant Community Centre, WAB's Ruth Annis, a childcare worker, decried the budget as an "attack on feminist services . . . a political attack."[12] Then, she proposed a way forward that drew resounding applause. "The only way to stop the determined policy of the Social Credit to destroy what we have won in past years," she said, "is to fight back in an equally determined way, organizing to use our ultimate weapon—a general strike."

CHAPTER 6

Cultural Combustion:
Beats, Hippies, Punks & Lenny

ONE OF THE MORE pleasurable five hours of my life was spent at L.A.'s Nate 'n Al's deli talking with the remarkable Norma Barzman. Norma has lived life fully. She told me of the barriers she faced as a female screenwriter in 1940s Hollywood, her close encounters with Einstein, Picasso and Marilyn, the warm comradeship inside the old Hollywood left, being forced into European exile by the blacklist, witnessing the streets of France during the general strike of 1968. (Her son, Aaron, was heavily involved in the strike.)

Norma told me something about her husband, the equally black-listed screenwriter Ben Barzman, that I did not know—he was from Vancouver. Ben's family immigrated from Russia to Canada and he was raised in the Strathcona district. He scripted some classic films (*The Boy with Green Hair*, *El Cid*) after he moved south, but his values were shaped in Vancouver. There was the night, for instance, when his lefty father gave young Ben a lesson in human solidarity by taking him along when he drove his truck to a dark, desolate beach. They were there to pick up a woman and her daughter being smuggled by boat into Canada to circumvent a federal law banning Chinese immigration. Ben and his father drove the two—the wife and daughter of a Chinese vegetable vendor in the neighbourhood—to a designated meeting place where their family was reunited. As the overjoyed vendor and his wife and daughter embraced, Ben saw a tear run down his father's face.

After the Second World War, the blacklisters insisted that the youthful Depression-era lefties had wanted to create a Stalinist tyranny, but that was the furthest thing from Norma and Ben and their friends' minds. The Communist Party was a mass movement and young idealists joined to build labour unions and fight racism and fascism. Like Rose Barrett, Norma and Ben quit the CP in the late 1960s. They did not, however, quit the left. While they rejected Eastern Bloc-style Communism, Norma and Ben remained socialists.

When the Hollywood blacklist waned, Norma and Ben moved back to L.A. They drove up the coast to Vancouver once and he showed her the old neighbourhood.

More than eighty years after Ben Barzman left Vancouver, I sat down with Fred Wah at a new coffee place in Ben's old Strathcona neighbourhood. Fred says he got his first good look at Vancouver in spring 1958 when he was down from Nelson for the provincial high school basketball championship held at the University of British Columbia. Coming into Vancouver, he was taken aback by the sight of its lit-up glass tower. "We showed up at night," says Fred, "and the first thing we could see were all these bright lights in the city, and it was the B.C. Electric Building." Twenty-two storeys of brand-new, blue-and-green modernist glass, porcelain and aluminum illuminated the city. This was so different from the brick-and-stone main street back in

Nelson. There, the low-rise downtown buildings were miniature versions of the constructions that dominated the Vancouver skyline before the Electric Building went up on Burrard Street in 1957. Soon, it seemed, all of downtown would be slim, tall glass. So different, too, than the older-fashioned edifice, with its green copper rooftop, that had previously been the dominant building in Vancouver's skyline— the Hotel Vancouver.

That school year, Fred was starting guard on a good basketball team and played horn in the school band. His love of music, inspired by teacher Edward Baravalle, brought him to UBC in the fall. Along with his first-year music studies classes, Fred took an English course. After a few weeks of English professor Warren Tallman, a major proponent of the New American Poetry burgeoning across North America, Fred was hooked and switched from music to writing. Over the next few years at UBC, Fred partook in Vancouver's emergence as an influential player in the new poetry/beat world. "In North America, not just Vancouver, there had been a very sudden turn in poetry, and it was a kind of resistance against the traditional British European influences," Fred says. "So North America was discovering itself in a way, and had been for a number of years. Vancouver was finally getting on the scene."

From Ben Barzman to the twenty-first century, Vancouver has consistently produced talented artists committed to challenging the status quo. In the postwar decades, there was a rising of subterranean, youthful cultures expressing a widening alienation with the plastic aesthetic of everyday life. Vancouver became renowned for its creative, vibrant subcultural life, first with its beat-infused writers, then its hippie counterculture, then its punk scene, all highly regarded in their international underground worlds, although many people in their Canadian home-city didn't know they existed. Sharing a culture can be a deeper bond than sharing an ideology, and these resistance cultures often reached middle-class youths who were beyond the reach of leafletting lefties. Many Solidarity supporters of 1983 had been influenced by the melding of alternative culture and politics. Solidarity's ranks included writers, musicians, actors, filmmakers and a folk festival director.

———

When the beats morphed into the much larger counterculture in the last half of the 1960s, the new SFU became known as Canada's radical campus. UBC, however, had its own, less-known subcultural moment in the first half of the 1960s. In 1961, Fred Wah co-founded a UBC-based publication called *TISH* that became renowned across the continent. "Robert Duncan, the San Francisco poet, had been doing lectures in Vancouver, and then Robert Creeley did some lectures in Vancouver, and they told us about all these small magazines in the United States," Fred says. "There was a snail-mail community of poetry going on in North America. There weren't many publishers in Canada at the time, and most were down east and weren't particularly interested in West Coast Canadian stuff. So, we ended up publishing a little mimeo magazine that has become a kind of touchstone of modern Canadian poetry."

TISH drew inspiration from the beats and the New American Poetry and featured such young Vancouver literary lights as Fred, George Bowering, Daphne Marlatt, Jamie Reid and Carol Bolt. "The beat culture was fairly influential for a number of poets," says Fred. "For those of us involved in *TISH*, it was mostly what was called the Black Mountain poetry group. But we were interested in all of it— Kerouac, Ginsberg, Gary Snyder and so forth. Vancouver was a kind of West Coast centre for jazz and poetry." There were Vancouver jazzy clubs like The Cellar, coffeehouses like the Black Spot, and parties at Warren and Ellen Tallman's place on West Thirty-Seventh.

Fred and friends printed *TISH* at UBC offices in a barracks left over from the Second World War. "We asked LeRoi Jones and Diane di Prima in New York, who were then editing a magazine called *Floating Bear*, if we could use their mailing list. And they graciously sent us their mailing list, which was about 200 poets and writers all over North America, Britain and Australia. And we just printed this thing, put a two-cent stamp on it and mailed it out." The response was overwhelming. "It was fantastic. The great thing was that it opened up the poetry community to us." The Vancouver *TISH* group was now in touch with poets across North America and beyond. Fred and his wife, writer Pauline Butling, helped with the international writing conference Warren Tallman and Robert Creeley organized at UBC. That Vancouver conference of 1963 has become legend in the new poetry/beat world, featuring, among others, Creeley, Allen Ginsberg, Robert Duncan, Charles Olson and Margaret Avison. Fred's recordings of the Vancouver Poetry Conference have become important documents of the era. "It was the first time a lot of these poets had got together. So it was a totally new thing," Fred says. "At the time it was just a lot of fun and it opened up connections with, particularly, young American writers, but in hindsight now, it turned out to be one of the major conferences of North American poetry and poetics in the modern age."

Quebec's groundbreaking independent filmmaker Jean Pierre Lefebvre told me that culture runs more north–south than east–west. "All my friends in Vancouver," he said, "were more influenced by Seattle and California than by the East Coast." The influence runs both ways. Vancouver's Greenpeace and the city's punk rockers, for instance, had impact down the coast. There are many ways in which Vancouver—from its casual dress code to its cultural politics—is more California than it is Toronto or Montreal (just as Toronto is more New York and Alberta more Texas than they are each other). The California beat writers had a considerable influence on Fred Wah and company. "Yeah, I think that there was a movement from San Francisco up to Vancouver," Fred says.

—⁓—

Stan Persky, who moved from San Francisco to Vancouver, says Fred Wah and his *TISH* circle, "were the real beginning—the intellectual beginning—of the '60s in Vancouver. "Just a complete world of people totally hip to what was going on, the intellectual foundations for the challenges that the '60s raised with respect to normal bourgeois society." In Chicago, still in high school, Stan heard about the beat movement, which was just starting. "I was, early on, attracted to the literary world, and in 1957 there was a guy named Jack Kerouac who published a book called *On the Road*. And I had read a review of it in a magazine called *Saturday Review of Literature* in which the reviewer just hated it. But he made the big mistake of quoting lots of passages from it. So I rushed down to the bookstore and got a copy and read it." Stan was enthused enough with *On the Road* to send a package of his writings to Kerouac's literary agent, whose name was in the book. "I was sixteen years old and, of all things, soon there was a response from Jack Kerouac telling me how much he was interested and he would tell Allen Ginsberg about this. So, soon I was in correspondence with all these people at a very early age."

Stan found inspiring characters in his family, which had fled Eastern European pogroms and settled in the midwestern metropolis. "My father's family was pretty bohemian and women in the family were the first fully independent women I met. They read books and had opinions about things and weren't afraid to announce what those opinions were." His father had been "a kind of activist" who rode rails during the Depression. ("Told me about the IWW, things like that.") After high school, Stan went on the road himself—on the sea. "I served a hitch in the American Navy in the late 1950s, early 1960s." The navy took him to San Francisco. "There was the entire beat world. Ginsberg was there. A whole bunch of writers that I became close to." By this time, beats were drawing considerable attention. "People wearing berets and little beards and black turtlenecks. It was a kind of style and attracted the attention of *Life* magazine, *Time* magazine. It was becoming a cultural phenomenon."

Stan was a link between the 1950s beat movement and the 1960s counterculture and counter-politics. In Berkeley in 1965, Stan went with Allen Ginsberg to a Vietnam Day Committee organizing meeting for an early anti-war march. The following year, poet Robin

Blaser, with whom Stan lived, was hired at the new SFU. "Since I had to do something with myself, I registered as a student. He was going to be a prof at Simon Fraser. So I went to UBC." Stan didn't just go to UBC. He made a lasting impression on the place—he became the school's best-known radical of the era, organizing every kind of challenge to campus authorities. "It's not a single item. It's all of the items. It's everything about life, and so I tend to think of the '60s as a moment when there were practical utopian experiments under way—and that had to do with music, it had to do with how to live, it had to do with how to do sex, it had to do with how you represented yourself in terms of identity, of how you thought public health, medicine, education and everything else ought to be organized. And of course there was a kind of anti-capitalist ethos. Yet, at the same time, we already knew that there was authoritarian communism. We didn't want that. So, there were these practical utopian experiments in how to live. Again, there was a set of conditions which made it possible to fool around with those possibilities. And that was enormously un-usual. There has been nothing really like that since then. And of course, for conservatives and reactionaries, the '60s is the site of hell itself, when everything went wrong. . . . I took to it all like a duck to water and soon I was involved in student politics, but student politics also meant being involved in all sorts of underground city politics."

Like many student radicals, Stan moved from campus to commu-nity. "I became one of the founders of the *Georgia Straight* newspaper and was involved with a whole group of people in the city who were doing all kinds of alternative things." Communes, gestalt therapy, protests and many an evening spent talking radical politics over drinks at the Ambassador or Castle hotels. He was also involved in the first gay activism in the city, joining the Gay Liberation Front and writing for *Gay Tide* magazine. "We saw gay as a way of reinventing human sexual relationships that wouldn't be centred around nuclear families, around heterosexual norms or any of those things. We saw ourselves as radicals connected to a general political world of issues." Many on the left weren't exactly overjoyed at the arrival of a gay liberation movement. "The various standard leftists were very awkward about a lot of this," Stan says. "Just in the way that males were very awkward about the feminist movement, they were equally uncomfortable with gays, as I recall." For Stan, the notion of gay liberation wasn't as novel as it was to others in late 1960s Vancouver. "I was friends with Ginsberg, and Ginsberg was maybe the only openly gay public intellectual in North America in 1955. I entered into what was a kind of literary gay world very early on before there was a gay movement, and as far as I can tell I didn't have a huge identity crisis of some sort at any point."

As Stan became increasingly active in the city, he kept involved in student politics. Stan was a perennial candidate for student office at UBC (sometimes winning) and was instrumental in everything from campus tent-ins to teach-ins, with a succession of demos in between. SFU wasn't the only B.C. campus acting up in the late 1960s and early '70s. UBC students occupied the lounge of the arts building, transforming it into a countercultural hangout they called the John Stuart Mill Lounge. Chicago Eight defendant Jerry Rubin spoke on campus, then led a student occupation of the faculty lounge. "When I was at UBC, I met all of the versions of the left that were available," Stan says.

"The Movement" of the 1960s was a coalition—a movement of movements—albeit an unharmonious one at times. To Stan, the most impressive movement of that era of movements was feminism. "The built-in assumed limitations of what it was to be a female was extraordinary when you look at it retrospectively. And that change is probably a more dramatic change than almost anything else I've seen of all the movements, it seems to me. The very simple notion that a woman is an equal human being is really what underlies it in many ways."

1983: After the '60s, Stan was a college prof and a prolific writer—newspaper columns and books about everything from Vancouver's civic politics (*The House That Jack Built*) to Poland's Solidarity movement (*The Solidarity Sourcebook*). "I actually had, ironically enough, experience with the real Solidarność movement in Poland. So, when

1983 came along and we suddenly had B.C. Solidarity, I was kind of familiar, at least with the terms." After the Empire Stadium rally, Stan presents his proposal for a movement newspaper to the Solidarity Coalition. "The Solidarity Coalition meeting I went to said, 'Oh yeah, that's a great idea. We should do that. And we'll pass this on to Operation Solidarity.'" So, Stan presents his proposal to Operation Solidarity. "I duly appeared at one of those BCFED–run meetings and made this proposal, and they agreed with this. This would be late August, early September '83. That's how I got to meet Art Kube. So I was then given the mandate to start this newspaper, which was called *Solidarity Times*, and my job was to assemble a staff and find a place and find a printer and produce a newspaper." The plan was to have the first issue out in time for the big October 15 march in the streets of Vancouver.

———⌇∿⌇———

Stan was already hip when the hippie counterculture became a universally known phenomenon during its "Summer of Love" in 1967. Before that, in the early '60s, there were the stirrings of a pre-hippie hip—a new generation that liked folk music, the civil rights movement, Brando and James Dean, the French New Wave, Lenny Bruce and beat writings. Young men who looked like Leonard Cohen, women like Jeanne Moreau. No one in Vancouver was more pre-hippie hip than Carol Pastinsky.

Carol remembers her Kerrisdale block being jam-packed with Beatles fanatics after her next-door neighbour, concert promoter Hugh Pickett, leaked that the band would be staying at his home while in town for their Empire Stadium concert. It was a diversionary stunt to keep fans away from the hotel the band was booked into. "I never saw them at Empire Stadium," says Carol, "but I saw them at the Hollywood Bowl."

The soundtrack of the Pastinsky household was more Weavers than Beatles. Carol fondly recalls gatherings there of the left-wing United

Jewish People's Order. "We used to have meetings at our house. It was a cool time. It was a sense of belonging. . . . My whole life I've always been on the left. I found a comfort in it." She found joy in acting, and after co-starring turns at Vancouver's Magee High, she was accepted into Southern California's Pasadena Playhouse acting school. Hugh Pickett, who had seen Carol perform at Magee, talked her parents into letting her attend the Pasadena school. "Thanks to Hugh Pickett, I got to go."

After Pasadena, Carol returned to Vancouver and continued acting. She co-starred in Larry Kent's 1964 movie *Sweet Substitute*, one of Canada's first independent films. "Larry was very enthusiastic about this sort of thing, and he really worked hard on it. It was a great deal of fun making it." Several of Vancouver's early independent filmmakers—Larry, Sandy Wilson, Jack Darcus—had activist backgrounds. Larry, like Carol, was a red-diaper baby turned artist. "Carol," says Larry, "was a *very* talented actress." She travelled to L.A. to promote *Sweet Substitute*, which became a classic of early English-language Canadian cinema. "I don't know what Larry expected it to do but the film went to the States, made money, and Larry stayed with it," Carol says. Larry and his movies helped to inspire the innovative indie film scene that would, in subsequent decades, be a vital part of alternative Vancouver.

The edgy, new culture of early '60s Vancouver was pressing up against a staid city establishment determined to keep up a culturally repressive front. Larry Kent's movies were regularly harassed and censored. In those years, there was a new taboo-busting reality in every art form. Comedy was no exception. A year before Larry Kent's first feature *The Bitter Ash* (1963) was banned in B.C., he was at Isy's Supper Club to see oft-censored comedian Lenny Bruce a day or two before his week-long engagement was cut short by a civic censor. "We knew he was busted all over North America, so we weren't surprised," Larry says. Lenny brilliantly pilloried all things phony and used words no one else dared speak in public in 1962. "He was destroyed by being the first and saying things that were considered uncouth, especially in Vancouver," Larry says. "If they couldn't take *The Bitter Ash*, they really couldn't tolerate Lenny Bruce. Wonderfully on edge. He didn't care what the audience thought. He looked and sounded so brave and so modern. When Lenny Bruce came to Vancouver, it was like the end of the '50s."

Not long after *Sweet Substitute*'s release, the '60s were well under way. Many who had acted in Vancouver's earliest indie films fell heavily into the counterculture, with some—like Carol Pastinsky and Lanny Beckman—also becoming New Left activists who would later support Solidarity. Carol protested the war, assisted draft resisters and lived in Kitsilano.

—⌇∿⌇—

In the early 1960s, a smattering of beats lived in the clapboard houses in what came to be known as Coal Harbour. This is also where writers and UBC theatre students lived out a classic beat party—complete with bongo drums, sunglasses at night, and then-racy sexuality—for Larry Kent's movie *The Bitter Ash*. This compelling bit of circa-1963 Vancouver was captured on film as the steamy summer night wore on at writer Jamie Reid's house, and the movie party became a real party.

By 1967, this small hip scene was morphing into a burgeoning countercultural community in Kitsilano. Its main street was Fourth Avenue, dotted with head shops and healthy food. Plymouths and Chevies would crawl along the street so entire families could ogle the freaks who convened on the slight hill at Fourth and Arbutus. The city's bohemians have been a wandering lot. By the late 1970s, Kitsilano was facing gentrification and alternative Vancouver relocated to the old Italian quarters off Commercial Drive. In 1983, the Commercial Drive neighbourhood was a bastion of Solidarity support. Not long after that, much of alternative Vancouver was on the move again, this time to Main Street.

—⌇∿⌇—

"Ed Sullivan."

Melanie Ray says the name affectionately. To her, it means more than the host of a television variety program, more than a song in *Bye Bye Birdie*. Coming of age in postwar Vancouver, Melanie "didn't have a whole lot of cultural input" from family elders. She did, however, find momentous influence some Sunday nights in front of *The Ed Sullivan Show*. One particular *Ed Sullivan* night especially affected young Melanie. It wasn't, unlike the rest of her generation, the ones with the Beatles or Elvis that moved her. "I was sitting on the floor, the grown-ups were behind me on the couch, and Marlene Dietrich came on. And she was absolutely in darkness except for a light that was supposed to be coming from a street lamp. And she sang: 'It's the wrong time and the wrong place, though your face is charming . . .' Anyway, I was transfixed . . . mostly by the acting involved, the heart that was coming through the song. Behind me, my grandmother said, 'Ugh, that woman has a terrible voice.' And I didn't say anything but I smiled to myself and thought, *It doesn't matter, she's amazing*. Not so much what she said, but how she said it. A song about a sad woman."

Melanie got out of high school as the finishing touches were being put on SFU, and she enrolled in its inaugural semester. It was the fall of 1965 and she wanted to be a librarian. Everything on campus was new and exciting. Almost immediately, Melanie fell in with students "who thought differently than I did or than my family did—people who brought up subjects like what was going on in the States with black people. I think we all felt we were starting something new and fresh and that there was something exciting going on." Melanie, like Cliff Stainsby and Marcy Toms, was politicised at SFU. "Not getting very active particularly, but just finding assumptions that I didn't even know I had being overturned by what was going on on campus, and friends of mine who were involved in things. My first-ever rally of any sort was because the university had decided to turn what was supposed to be green space into a parking lot and we went and protested. My father saw it on TV and he got really mad at me." Melanie dropped her plans to become a librarian. "I went into theatre and that was extremely wonderful for me."

While at SFU, Melanie learned how to hitchhike, saw Jefferson Airplane play the SFU cafeteria and Country Joe and the Fish at Stanley Park and marched against the Vietnam War. "My mind opened up to a lot of stuff I hadn't thought about before, just questioning a whole lot of stuff." By the time she left Simon Fraser, Melanie was fully immersed in the counterculture. "I loved it. I thought it was beautiful. The whole sexual part of it was something that suited me very much. The freer sexuality. That people could be who they were. Well, it was right in the period between easy access to birth control and no AIDS. It was like, if you felt like it, you could go do it. I was living in a co-op. I was in Kits, several different places there." She moved to Toronto for a year and came back a single mother. That was when feminism discovered her. "When Erin was about three, I read *The Female Eunuch*, and it was so exciting I had to leap on my bike every once in a while and ride around the block and come back and sit down and read some more. And I was trying to be in theatre. It was very difficult to be a single mother and work as an actor." She was involved in alternative theatre, working with the Tamahnous theatre company and appearing in the Net City version of Bertolt Brecht's *Rise and Fall of the City of Mahagonny*. She also worked at the Ridge Theatre when it opened as a great revival movie house that mixed classic old Hollywood and new wave Europe—Abbott and Costello and Fellini.

—◊◊◊—

In the late 1960s and early '70s, North America's West Coast was the world capital of the counterculture, with vibrant scenes from San Diego's Ocean Beach to Vancouver's Kitsilano. Vancouver was home to one of the largest counterculture communities anywhere, just behind L.A. and San Francisco. Some New Left hippies saw the progressive potential in all this and tried to synthesize counterculture and counterpolitics. At one point, Yippies contemplated calling a press conference to announce that Kitsilano had seceded from Canada to form a communal New Nation. It was as if young people were inventing their own ethnic group, complete with neighbourhoods, delis (health food stores), drug stores (psychedelic), fashion (informal), language ("That's groovy but it's not far out"), lifestyle (communal), politics (anti-war), movies (*Easy Rider*), newspapers (underground), hair (long), nightclubs (Vancouver's Retinal Circus) and music.

The heart of counterculture music was L.A.'s Laurel Canyon, and there were great San Francisco bands, too. Vancouver also had its hippie music scene with bands such as Mother Tucker's Yellow Duck, the Seeds of Time and the Collectors. A young Californian, Shari Ulrich, saw the Collectors play San Francisco's legendary Fillmore West. As a teen in suburban San Francisco, Shari was irresistibly drawn to the countercultural goings-on in the city—anti-war marches, concerts, the first Be-In. ("I had a little dog named Roach who got run over by Janis Joplin's equipment truck.") A first-year college protester in California when anti-war students were shot at Kent State in 1970, Shari was so devastated that she had to get out. So, independent young Shari jumped in a car by herself and drove up the coast to the wilds of Vancouver. (She didn't know there were cities in Canada. "Very shocked.") In B.C., Shari lived communally and—with Joe Mock and Rick Scott—formed one of the later Vancouver counterculture bands, the exceedingly popular Pied Pumkin. They performed at the first Vancouver Folk Music Festival and the Stanley Park Be-In. "It was just such an indescribably unique time, although when you're immersed in it that's just what's happening," Shari says. "It just had that spirit of hope and optimism." The band toured as far as Ontario. "The hotbed for us was the Kootenays. Funky little community halls. That was our most common kind of venue. Somebody local would put up some posters and the hippies would flock to us. . . . It would be a frenzy of dancing."

Like Solidarity, the counterculture wasn't confined to urban areas. While it was fading in West Coast cities by the mid-1970s, it was more durable in the countryside and continued to flourish in the Kootenays,

Gulf Islands and central B.C. communities like Barkerville–Wells. After Fred Wah's UBC adventure, he went to graduate school in the U.S. He returned to teach at Selkirk College in the Kootenays, where he saw that political refugees were still coming up from California, only now they were fleeing the Vietnam War rather than the Hollywood blacklist. "During the late '60s and through the '70s, one of the major structural dynamics in counterculture is the commune. So, of course, up in the Kootenays we had lots of communes out in the country . . . the whole back-to-the-land movement. But first came the York Street Commune here [in Vancouver]. We had that commune going, and several other communes in the city."

Ken Mather says those who settled in Wells and found work at Barkerville in the 1970s formed a tight community. "It was an interesting life because we were all fairly young—in our twenties, early thirties—and we had a really wonderful group of people. I think Wells had a population of 300 in those days." Before settling in Wells, Ken had hitchhiked through Europe and travelled overland to India. "That's one of the journeys you took if you were a hard-core hippie. That whole element was part of the culture of Wells in the day, so most of the people I worked with who had been there for any length of time came out of that culture. Mostly city kids, really. Mostly British Columbians who had come up from the Lower Mainland."

Ken had worked in Fort Edmonton Park, a tourist attraction in his Alberta hometown, researching the reconstruction of an 1885 street. This brought him to a 1979 job at the Barkerville heritage site. In 1861, Billy Barker discovered gold and veterans of the California gold rush poured north to Barkerville, which transformed overnight into a bustling town of 5,000 residents. It was said to be the largest city north of San Francisco and west of Chicago. "That's why the Colony of British Columbia was established," notes Ken, "because the British government was a little bit nervous with all these Americans arriving." As the 1870s faded, so did Barkerville. It had a comeback in the 1930s when Fred Wells discovered gold nearby and a town was established in his name. My father, Jack, was one of the young British Columbians who worked the Wells mines during the Depression. The boom was short-lived, and in 1957 the provincial government designated Barkerville a touristy historic site.

Vivid images of Old West towns, with their unholy saloons filled with gambling men and dancing women, were everywhere when Ken was growing up in 1950s Edmonton—on TV and at Saturday matinees, in drugstore novels and comic books. "I was totally enthralled by that. Roy Rogers and Gene Autry and Hopalong Cassidy. I mean, they were my heroes when I was a kid." So, Ken was happy to work at the Barkerville historic site, something akin to a northern version of Disneyland's Frontierland. Although Barkerville was the closest thing to a Canadian Old West town in the late 1800s, with its saloons, prospectors and stagecoaches, the Canadian West was never so wild as the American one of Wyatt Earp and Ken Maynard. "We don't see shootings in the street and all that sort of stuff," Ken says. "There certainly was enough wildness that goes on, but there was an element of control."

Susan Safyan was a young counterculturist from L.A. when she arrived in Wells in 1978 to find that the last of the mines had closed, but a new community was remaking the town. "Hippies move in and sometimes find houses with linen in the cupboards and cutlery in the drawers, and they just either squat the house or somebody pretends to own it and sells it to them. My friend Judy bought her house for $300." Susan was part of the first graduating class at Crossroads, a well-regarded alternative high school in Santa Monica, while immersing herself in the L.A. counterculture of the early 1970s. "We lived right next to the L.A. County Art Museum, which was surrounded by beautiful parkland. The hippies used to congregate there and dance and smoke pot and do events. And I was completely taken with all of that, with their freedom and their look and everything. And politics were important to me: leftist politics. The Vietnam War was the big issue then." Her alternative L.A. background made the Wells–Barkerville area an inviting place, with its mix of 1970s West Coast counterculture and 1870s Wild West. Nineteenth-century cowboys, in their Levis and boots and coonskin jackets, had pioneered the hippie look of the next century, so Barkerville's young workers' usual dress wasn't much different than the period costumes they wore for the tourists. "You got to dress in a fringe vest, grow your hair long and a grow a moustache and a beard if you were a man," Susan says. "Wear a long skirt and little granny glasses and grow your hair long and put it up in a beautiful bun if you were a woman. What a fabulous job. You got to dress in the coolest clothes of that era and get paid for it."

These Barkerville workers were members of the B.C. Government and Service Employees' Union. Their jobs entailed guiding tours of the town, staging shows at the Royal Theatre and researching the manner of nineteenth-century British Columbians to recreate an accurate experience for visitors to the site. Susan found work at Barkerville doing inventory of historic artifacts. The counterculture and the old-timers of Barkerville leaned left. "It was pretty strongly NDP at the time," says Ken. "A lot of us disliked the Socreds."

Susan's family would have disliked Socreds, too, but they had their hands full with Republicans and McCarthyism. She was born in late 1950s L.A., her mother in the Communist Party, her father a fellow traveller. "It was just part of the fabric of our lives. We didn't watch television without my parents deconstructing the capitalist angles of it." The blacklist that had Ed Baravalle packing for Nelson touched many Safyan family friends. Her mother was harassed, too, which brings us to Susan's origin story. It happened the day her father had two wisdom teeth removed and was put on strong painkillers. Returning home, he decided to make himself a martini, and then another. "And my mother made minestrone soup. There was a knock on the door, and it was the G-men and they wanted to talk to her. My father was a teeny-tiny person, and I think the painkillers and the martini emboldened him. He told them to 'shove it where the sun don't shine. The lady doesn't want to talk to you.' My mother was so amused by my father's sudden burst of chivalrous protectiveness that here I am."

1983: During the May election campaign, Ken drives to Quesnel to hear Dave Barrett speak, and when the election is lost there is disappointment in Wells. When Bill Bennett brings down his twenty-six bills in July, Wells feels something stronger. "There was a general outrage in terms of what was going on," Ken says. Information wasn't instantaneous in the pre-Internet age, but every corner of B.C. was aware of the bills and the responding tumult. "Of course we had television. We had two stations that, occasionally, you could get."

———

Alan Zisman grew up in suburban Newark, New Jersey. His father worked for the state government, and his mother was the travel agent for, among others, William Kunstler, radical lawyer of Chicago Eight fame. By high school, Alan was frequenting the short route into New York City for anti-war protests. He went on to Montreal's McGill University, majoring in revolution and counterculture. Alan was also a musician and presided over the McGill Folk Music Society. When the campus Students for a Democratic University staged an occupation, he organized cultural events for the occupiers. "So I'm hustling rock bands, poets to come and perform in the occupied buildings. The connection between left politics and rock 'n' roll."

In 1971, Alan returned to the U.S. to partake in May Day protests that promised, "If the government won't stop the war, we'll stop the government." The plan was to shut down the Vietnam War machine by occupying bridges and intersections across Washington, D.C. "While the event theoretically defined itself as non-violent direct action, the people in our affinity group decided our goal was to set people free from the police." So, finding opportunity in chaos, Alan grabbed hold of a riot cop's billy club, prompting his fellow riot cops to pull their guns on Alan. "When they say, 'Drop the club motherfucker, or we'll blow your brains out,' I comply." Thus, Alan became one of 14,000 arrested over three days, a still-standing record for arrests at an American protest. He was back in Montreal the following year when Quebec had its general strike.

At a Montreal party in 1976, Alan met Bob Sarti, a friendly West Coast anarcho-Yippie in town to spread word about a new journal being published in Vancouver. "I was feeling kind of dead-end in Montreal. The early '70s were way more exciting than the mid-'70s, and I meet Bob Sarti right after issue number one of *Open Road*. He's travelling Canada to preach the gospel of *Open Road*. I was this young, smart-ass Yippie. He says, 'Come out to Vancouver and work on *Open Road*.'" (While Bob went out east, I travelled down the West Coast talking up the new publication.) Soon, in Vancouver, Alan was a political/cultural activist working on *The Open Road*, piano player/vocalist in the benefit band Ad Hoc, and MC of the Anarchist Party of Canada (Groucho Marxist) "May Day Carnival" in Stanley Park. To that May Day crowd in 1978, Alan introduced Joe Keithley and his brand-new band D.O.A.

⟶ɯɯ⟝

Growing up in Burnaby, Joe Keithley was acutely aware of the radical goings-on up the mountain at SFU. In grade ten at Burnaby North Secondary School, Joe finally got a protest of his own. Greenpeace announced plans for a series of rotating high school marches protesting nuclear tests on the Aleutian Islands, off of Alaska. "That was the first thing that I did. I was sixteen," Joe says. The day of the walkout, the Burnaby North principal stepped outside to order departing students back to class. "And about 300 kids—we all left. It was a great thing because we left Burnaby North, and then went to Alpha [Secondary School], and then we marched down to Tech and got a bunch of kids, and then we marched up to Britannia. And it kept growing. By the time we got to the American Consulate, we probably had six or seven hundred." Joe's buddy Ken Montgomery led the parade, pounding his bass drum—"hitting the drum with great volume as everybody's chanting." The next day's *Vancouver Sun* had a front-page picture of Joe and Ken at the rally. Joe knew that not everyone at home would be impressed by his moment in *The Sun*. "My dad thought that the hippies should be rounded up and shot. He was like a Canadian Archie Bunker." Joe hid the newspaper before his dad got home from work. "Of course he came home and yelled about the paper and I said, 'Ah, it must be the paper boy screwed up again.' I threw him under the bus for that because I knew, it was like, I probably would have been kicked out of the house, living in the bush or living in Dimwit's garage."

Dimwit, by the way, was the punk name Ken Montgomery selected for himself. Joe's was Joey Shithead. Joe (in D.O.A.) and Ken (in the Subhumans and Pointed Sticks) and their Burnaby pals—including Brian Goble, Gerry Hannah, Sid Houniet and Ken's brothers Chuck and Bob Montgomery—became the heartbeat of an extraordinarily talented Vancouver punk scene that would soon be legend across the punk world. After high school, Joe and friends had a brief foray into countercultural country living in the B.C. Interior before he caught a glimpse of punk rock in 1976 and knew he had seen his future. It wasn't like he wanted to be a punk. It was more like there finally was a label, *punk*, for what these Burnaby friends already were—a mix of raw rebel rock and raw rebel politics, served up with a dash of hilarity. Authentic cultural artists and movements, like punk and the counterculture, express things that people are already feeling and doing. Bob Dylan, for instance, had such a deep connection with his generation because he articulated what millions were already feeling but hadn't heard expressed in songs. There are moments when a political organization or movement arises as an expression of popular feelings, too. In 1983, Solidarity was such a movement.

The counterculture that was so prevalent in Vancouver and other West Coast cities in the late 1960s and early '70s was supplanted, as the rebel youth culture, by punk in the late 1970s. I knew the counterculture was no longer on the cutting edge when high school rebels started calling themselves punks instead of hippies. So, the Retinal Circus was displaced by the Smilin' Buddha. The Vancouver punk scene soon grew beyond Joe and friends, its small core producing such stellar bands as D.O.A., the Subhumans, the Pointed Sticks, UJ3RK5 and the Young Canadians. "There was no music industry in Vancouver," says Joe. "There's a big one now. But then you couldn't get a record contract, so the only thing to do was travel. So, Subhumans did. D.O.A. did. Pointed Sticks did. And people, to this day, still remember all three of those bands really fondly. . . . We were very isolated. The world was a much more isolating place without the Internet, obviously, so information didn't travel, but it made for a pretty fun community-unique thing when I think about how we organized shows and what daily life was like."

More than any other North American punk rockers, the Burnaby contingent instantly identified with this phenomenon coming out of the U.K. They got the Clash's socialism, having grown up at the foot of SFU's mountain (and with a Canadian "labour party"), and they got the Sex Pistols' "God Save the Queen," having had her enlarged photograph on the school gymnasium wall. So, Joe gave himself a memorable punk handle and sang "Anarchy in B.C." By the early 1980s, the centre of punk had shifted from London to L.A. and D.O.A. and the Subhumans became honorary members of that scene, often sharing bills with Black Flag, X and Circle Jerks. While the local scene appreciated L.A. and London punk rock, Vancouver punk was about its own roots. As the Subhumans sang: "Oh Canaduh, what's wrong with you?"

1983: Like every right-minded lefty in B.C., Joe is offended by the Socred legislation. "I thought it was crazy," he says. "It was a big blow against anybody who wasn't rich. Let's put it that way." (There were other musicians actively supporting Solidarity, like Kitty Byrne of art band UJ3RK5, who was an activist at UBC.) Joe's band D.O.A. was known for its musical activism, playing Rock Against Racism (or Radiation or Reagan) concerts, so when their manager Ken Lester suggested they express solidarity with Solidarity by releasing a sing-along single called "General Strike," Joe and bandmate Dave Gregg huddle in their Gore Street abode and begin to write:

Come on, stand up for your rights,
stand up, stand and unite.
It's time for a general strike.[1]

"We took a real basic chord structure and, okay, it's 'General Strike,' we want people to sing along with this, so it's got to be anthemic," Joe recalls. "When you're a songwriter, if you have the sentiment, then you can write the music to fit that sentiment, because if you play the wrong kind of music it doesn't fit the words." The song had an unusual tempo for a D.O.A. tune. "Most of the songs we play are faster, right, but we went, we want punk rockers to get this and we think they will. But we want people who are not punk rockers to join in and see the point of what's going on, this anti-Bennett thing, pro-people thing with Solidarity. So we want regular people to be able to sing along with this song, too." Vancouver punk had a do-it-yourself ethos, so it didn't take long for D.O.A. to record the instant crisis single "General Strike" as an anthem for Solidarity. "We had it written in about an hour. We practiced it maybe two or three days in a row. . . . Three weeks later we had the seven-inch single. It was like boom, boom, boom. It was really fast. We got on the CBC News— 'D.O.A., that punk rock band, joins in Solidarity movement.' And they played the song."

—⁓—

My three favourite Vancouver concerts: the Beatles at Empire Stadium, the Clash at the Commodore, Bruce Springsteen at the Queen Elizabeth. Springsteen was new to his Vancouver audience in 1978. The first half of the show was strong, but something magical happened during the second half that made it phenomenal. Nettie Wild was at that concert, too, and decades later would tell me what happened to that show during intermission. Nettie saw a lot of concerts growing up and, like Carol Pastinsky, this had to do with Hugh Pickett. Her aunt, Pat Proud, worked with Pickett at his Famous Artists productions and would regularly provide Nettie with concert tickets. Her biggest memory: Bruce Springsteen at the Queen Elizabeth shortly before he broke out big. Because she was Pat Proud's niece, Nettie got backstage at the intermission. "I'm all getting ready to meet Bruce Springsteen, except for he's in a huddle with his band. He's pulled

Clarence [Clemons] and everybody else together and he's giving them this pep talk. And he's going, 'They're not on their feet. Why aren't they on their feet. Look, we're here for one reason and one reason only. We're here to give people something money can't buy. So when we go back out there, we're getting them on their feet.' So they go out on stage and we go back to our seats. And the second set was—I thought the first one was extraordinary—the second one was mind-blowing. And everybody was on their feet."

Nettie grew up in West Vancouver, her mother a pianist, father a newspaperman. The Wild home was near Barnston Bay ("It was heaven"), but much of Nettie's teen experimentation occurred at the family home of her best friend. "A fantastic family. My mother thought that nothing could go wrong in the house of a Presbyterian minister. I was allowed to hang out there. The boys all had their girlfriends down in the basement, everybody smoked dope, and it was amazing. And so I got away with murder because I was allowed to hang out with this family."

At UBC, Nettie wrote for *The Ubyssey* newspaper while studying theatre, film and creative writing. Afterward, she became an actor/writer at the Touchstone and Tamahnous theatre companies. Severe Socred cuts to arts funding in 1981 triggered a meeting of artists from different disciplines in the lobby of the Arts Club on Seymour Street. "The formation of Headlines Theatre came out of it." At the meeting were several founders of this theatre troupe, including Nettie and David Diamond. "David and I kind of clicked, and then we decided to make a play about what was going down." The result—*Buy, Buy, Vancouver*—was a musical about the city's affordable housing crisis. "*Buy, Buy, Vancouver* really took off," notes Nettie, who co-wrote and co-starred in the production. "This was just straight agitprop. And it was funny. The Socreds were in power, so we had a lot of material to play with." In 1982, Nettie directed her first of many film documentaries, *Right to Fight*, set at the housing co-op where she lived. Residents had been evicted by a slumlord but refused to leave, resulting in the longest squat in Vancouver history.

1983: Nettie was sharing a house on West Tenth with the Presbyterian minister's daughter, her best friend since high school. "But she
was, in her way of moving through the world, more conservative than
I was." As the two rang in the new year of 1983 they were, however,
in agreement on one thing: their home was for partying. "One of
those wonderful old Kitsilano houses all on one floor and we spruced
it up and we threw parties. There was a hell of a lot of people that
went through it, right, because we were two young women who were
having a very, very good time in life. We would have gatherings of all
these people from different walks of life. So it would be all my lefty
friends and all of her childcare worker people, some of whom were
going to walk out—all of whom, actually, except for her." Nettie's
friend was a childcare worker opposed to Solidarity activism at her
government-run workplace. "I'm living in this house with my good
friend coming down on the other side. It had an absolute impact on
my house and how we lived and how we spoke to each other. It was a
very heavy time in the house." This was not unique during B.C.'s
uncivil war of 1983. The July 7 legislation made the province's old
left/right split more pronounced than ever. "All this stuff that was
happening with these bits of legislation," says Nettie, "had lines into
houses and dinner tables and families and relationships all over the
province."

CHAPTER 7

Racism: It Just Doesn't
Seem to Stop

IN 1914, THE *KOMAGATA MARU* was filled with Indian passengers coming to Canada. Instead of successfully immigrating, though, they were held in their ship for two months in Vancouver harbour, then they were sent back to face violence and imprisonment. Said the enlightened Canadian immigration official in charge of the harbour: "The Hindu never did one thing for humanity." At one point, a right-wing militia group attempted to storm the docked ship. Said the enlightened *Vancouver Sun*: "We do not want these people here."[1]

Some of the passengers on this ship were inspired by their Vancouver experience to help overthrow British colonialism when they returned to India. In Ali Kazimi's documentary about the *Komagata Maru, Continuous Journey*, there is archival footage of "White Canada Forever," a beer-parlour sing-along song circa 1914. Ali added subtitles. "That sequence, to this day, just makes everybody in the audience squirm," Ali told me, adding that he wanted audiences to "question how Canadian history had been constructed and what had been left out."[2]

There are Canadians who like to believe such racism is confined to the American Deep South or South Africa. Racism, however, and the resistance to it are a big part of Canadian history. Virtually anyone who faced discrimination elsewhere found some of the same when they disembarked in Canada, from anti-Asian riots in 1907 Vancouver, to the *Komagata Maru* in 1914, to rioting between anti-Semites and Jewish youths in 1933 Toronto, to the Japanese internment camps of the 1940s, to a black university student uprising in 1960s Montreal, to Islamophobic murders in twenty-first century Quebec, to the continuing Indigenous sovereignty struggles.

The first time Fred Wah was called "chink" in Nelson, he was in grade four and didn't know what it meant. "So I had to find out what that was all about." By the time he graduated high school, he was well acquainted with the meaning of that schoolyard slur. "I was going with this girl in grade twelve and her father basically said, 'I don't want you to see my daughter anymore because I don't want my daughter marrying a Chinaman.' He said he knew my dad was a good businessman and all that, but 'I don't want my daughter going out with a Chinaman. . . . I don't want to see you around here anymore and no more phone calls either.' I was pissed off but I guess it was kind of the norm in a way. I was, okay, well, screw you. We went behind his back and made out for a little while, and eventually she was sent off to live with her sister in Seattle and I was going to UBC anyway so we sort of split up."

While the focus for many in 1983 was class war between the Socreds and the unions, sexism—as Women Against the Budget so boldly showed—was intrinsic to Social Credit and its legislation. So was racism, with the budget's all-out assault on human rights. Beth Hutchinson was at the Solidarity rallies in 1983. "I do remember the thrill of just the building movement as it developed," says Beth, "the excitement that all these groups were organized and working together. I think that what always gets us is divisions. The only way we're going to be able to create a better world is if we do get through these [divisions] and learn how to face up to and understand and move beyond these ancient oppressions like class and racism and sexism—the big three—and understand their effects on all of us and work to change everything at once."

Raj Chouhan and Charan Gill of the B.C. Organization to Fight Racism (BCOFR) represented anti-racism groups at Solidarity Coalition Steering Committee meetings. The Socreds' elimination of the Human Rights Commission and the Human Rights Branch, which combatted prejudice in the province, was the main focus of the coalition's anti-racism component. In late July, a Human Rights Coalition formed within Solidarity. "Call the Human Rights Coalition representation in your area," urged a Solidarity Coalition leaflet, noting that the dismissal of human rights commissioners meant little recourse if "a restaurant won't serve you because you are black or native ... an employer or a landlord treats you differently and puts you down because of your sex, race, religion, sexual preference, age and so on."[3] The B.C. Civil Liberties Association released a fact sheet about Bill 27's elimination of enforcement agencies (Human Rights Commission, Human Rights Branch). "It is hard to avoid the conclusion that the bill is designed to make it much more difficult to bring a human rights complaint and to strictly limit the function of human rights agencies," the association's director Bill Black said. "Taken together, the changes mean that only clear cases brought by people with financial resources, enough to take a case forward on their own, are likely to succeed."[4]

Anti-racism was at the forefront of budget opposition at the first mass rally. BCOFR president Charan Gill reminded the large crowd at B.C. Place on July 23 that a hundred years earlier, Chinese workers died building B.C.'s railroads. "The minority people helped to build this province. We're going to fight this legislation every inch of the way."[5] Alongside their work in the BCOFR, Chouhan and Gill founded the Canadian Farmworkers Union. "Some of the human rights commissioners, before they were gotten rid of, actually worked with the farmworkers organizers to find out what their needs are and what can the government do," Patsy George says. "Renate Shearer did some work with the farmworkers." In September 1983, a half-dozen Sikh temples united to form the Sikh Solidarity Coalition. In announcing the new group's formation, Gill said the legislation was a "profound" attack on religions and ethnic minorities. "Objectives of the Sikh Solidarity Coalition are the withdrawal of Bill 27, the new Human Rights Act, full reinstatement of the Human Rights Commission, the Human Rights Branch and two human rights commissions that have been scrapped by the government."[6]

—◦◦◦—

B.C. joined the Confederation in 1871, and a year later its newly formed government denied the vote to Chinese and First Nations. Asians weren't allowed to vote until 1949, Indigenous people 1960. For a time in the late nineteenth century, Indigenous people comprised the majority of the province's labourers, often working sawmills, mines, docks, canneries and farms.[7] As a colonized people, with all the indignities that come with that, B.C.'s First Nations workers were often stuck in the lowest-paid positions by employers. They were active in the International Longshoremen's Association and the Wobblies, but many trade unions of the early twentieth century were bent on "protecting the interest of the white workers, and excluding the Indian workers."[8] Asian workers also faced the dual assault from employers and white workers. When Chinese railroad workers braved terrible conditions to construct a pathway to the coast in the late 1800s, they were paid far less than white workers and hundreds died from accidents and illness. In 1883, white miners, who would not allow Chinese workers in their union, went on strike at Wellington on Vancouver Island. One of their demands was that Chinese workers be fired. In 1900, the *Victoria Daily Colonist* asked if B.C. should be a white colony "or must it be given over entirely to the yellow and brown hordes of China and Japan."[9] With this mood in the province, in 1907 three days of anti-Asian rioting swept through Vancouver's Chinatown and Japanese neighbourhoods, as well as Steveston. Well into the 1920s, Asians were racially segregated in many B.C. public schools, from Vancouver Island's Cumberland to Vancouver's Marpole. In 1914, the B.C. Federation of Labour newspaper, *The B.C. Federationist*, proclaimed: "The organized labour movement is opposed to Asiatic immigration because Asiatic labour is cheap labour."[10]

Fred Wah's grandfather came from China to build Canadian railroads in the late 1800s. Fred's parents moved from Saskatchewan to B.C.'s Kootenays when Fred was six years old. "After the war and after the Depression, a lot of the Prairie people moved out to British Columbia." They settled in Nelson, where his half-Chinese father opened the Diamond Grill restaurant. "Chinese and Canadian Food" was common signage in B.C. restaurant windows of the time, although Fred notes: "Most of the Chinese-Canadian cafes in the '50s were pretty much just white food, and they would have half a dozen items on the menu that were Chinese food like egg foo young and chicken chop suey and sweet-and-sour spareribs. But it was mostly just western food." Hamburgers and beef stew and chocolate sundaes. "I was a soda jerk. I cleaned up. I was waiting on tables and making milk shakes and sundaes and things." After UBC, Fred went on to graduate school in Buffalo and witnessed another racism. The "Summer of Love" of 1967 didn't reach into black neighbourhoods and in Buffalo, like Detroit and Newark, race rioting raged that year. "Buffalo was a real eye-opener, because it was a segregated city."

Muggs Sigurgeirson was thirteen when the principal at North Vancouver High School phoned her mother. "He said, 'Winnie, I know you've got a house full of kids and you don't have any room, but I got this student coming from Toronto. He's black and he's an athlete and we really want him in North Van because Harry's here. I have tried every single place in North Vancouver to see if I can get him billeted and not one home will take him because he's black.' So my mother said, 'Oh, of course.'" The student was track star Paul Winn, who became best friends with North Van classmate Harry Jerome, who became one of the world's great sprinters. Muggs and Harry's sister Carolyn Jerome were also best friends. Muggs says the Jerome family was a constant target of racism in the 1950s. "Harry got beat up all the time." As for Carolyn: "People didn't call Carolyn names. She was the toughest."

Harry and Carolyn's father, Harry Senior, was a railway worker active in the black porters union. "He was very politically aware and was a member of the CCF. He got fired one time, or suspended, because some passenger called him a 'nigger' too many times in the drinking car and he punched him. And his union got him reinstated." In the first half of the twentieth century, railway porter was one of the few steady jobs available to black men in North America. The Brotherhood of Railway Employees was, in its constitution, a whites-only union, so a group of Winnipeg-based black porters organized the Order of Sleeping Car Porters, which signed contracts with the major Canadian railways. In 1939, Canadian porters joined the integrated, American-based Brotherhood of Sleeping Car Employees. They signed a collective agreement with Canadian Pacific Railway, achieving better wages and conditions and a sign in sleeping cars stating the name of the porter who was tending to passengers' needs. *Harry Jerome.*

Reading through newspaper clippings from the 1930s, I'm stopped short by a headline on a *Vancouver Sun* report of the Bloody Sunday police riot that ended the relief workers' occupation of the post office —*"Chief Foster's a White Man" Says Steve Brodie in Hospital Interview.* After being beaten badly by police, relief workers spokesperson Steve

Brodie lauded Vancouver police chief William Foster as a white man who tried to ease tensions between police and protesters. "That was pretty white," Brodie concluded.[11] These kind of racist utterances were such common "compliments" in the North America of 1938 that Brodie, a charismatic Communist Party organizer, could say this so casually and a daily newspaper could quote it so acceptingly. There were others on the left of this era who engaged in similarly despicable nonsense. Many unions had racist practices, and the B.C. CCF supported the internment of Japanese Canadians during the Second World War. It is not that the left was any worse on race than the rest of the country. Problem was, too often it was the same. At its best, however, it was far better. Many rank-and-file CPers were anti-racist. It was, after all, the party that organized the Mackenzie–Papineau Battalion of "premature anti-fascists" who fought in Spain. Many rank-and-file CCFers were also anti-racist and the conscience of the party, Tommy Douglas of Saskatchewan, vehemently opposed the internment of Japanese Canadians. It was the CCF's call for universal voting rights that inspired this Liberal Party campaign slogan of 1935: "A Vote for ANY CCF Candidate is a VOTE TO GIVE the CHINAMAN and the JAPANESE the same Voting Right that you have!"[12]

So, racism was not casually accepted by everyone in the early twentieth century's left wing. While some unions excluded Chinese, Indigenous and black workers, others pointed out that divisions among workers only served the interests of employers. From its founding in 1905, the Industrial Workers of the World was committed to fighting racism—organizing Mexican workers in the Southwest, Italian immigrants in the Northeast and everyone in between. On the Philadelphia waterfront, Wobblies integrated previously segregated work gangs, social gatherings and union leadership. Black IWW leader Ben Fletcher said: "No genuine attempt by Organized Labor to wrest any worthwhile and lasting concessions from the Employing Class can succeed as long as Organized Labor for the most part is indifferent and in opposition to the fate of Negro Labor."[13]

In B.C., IWW Local 526 was mostly composed of Indigenous workers when it was founded in 1907. This longshoring local was proudly known as "Bows and Arrows."[14] It has been said that the IWW was given its "Wobbly" nickname in Vancouver. American Wobbly organizer Mortimer Downing wrote:

> In Vancouver, in 1911, we had a number of Chinese members, and one restaurant keeper would trust any member for meals. He could not pronounce the letter 'w', but called it 'wobble', and would ask: 'You I Wobble Wobble?' and when the card was shown credit was unlimited. Thereafter the laughing term amongst us was 'I Wobbly Wobbly,' and when [Wobbly] Herman Suhr, during the Wheatfield strikes, wired for all footloose Wobblies to hurry there, of course the prosecution made a mountain of mystery out of it, and the term has stuck to us ever since. Considering its origin, I rather like the nickname. It hints of a fine practical internationalism, a human brotherhood based on a community of interests and understanding.[15]

Beyond Wobblies and other anti-racist leftists, there were Chinese and Indigenous workers who knew instinctively that the discrimination so rife in B.C. was wrong, and the groups developed intimate cross-cultural bonds. On the banks of the Fraser River in the nineteenth century, Chinese built gold mines in Indigenous communities. Still, the relationship was respectful and the two cultures intermingled and intermarried. "The Chinese dealt in reciprocal ways with First Nations. They didn't take, they asked. They brought gifts, they shared foods," noted historian Henry Yu.[16] NDP politician Jenny Kwan added: "It is a beautiful story we need to know and to honour. . . . I feel so fortunate that the Chinese community, faced with extreme discrimination at that time, found friendship and support from the aboriginal communities."[17]

1983: It should be no surprise that a modern-day Wobbly, Tom Wayman, is moved by the discussion of race at Solidarity public meetings. "It was at the community meetings that I was most impressed. I was there, where guys would stand up and say things like, 'I'm of Chinese descent, why should I support the unions when their traditions have been racist?' And I just loved the fact that everything was up for grabs. People were rethinking, you know, what is a government for, what is a union for, and it just seemed for those weeks, especially in the fall, that everything was on the table . . . people were questioning everything."

The postwar decades marked a turn against racism as a result of the horrors of American apartheid, the Second World War and Vietnam. There was still a long way to go, as we know in the twenty-first century, but it was the beginning of a fundamental shift.

Many children of the 1950s came home from school one day to find something new in their living room. Television. There was magic in this TV set—from Little Richard on *American Bandstand* to the Canadian comedy of Wayne and Shuster. There was also, on the evening news, images of civil rights protesters, so obviously on the right side of humanity, being set upon by spitting, punching southern mobs and police with dogs, clubs and water cannons. Frequently mentioned by the Canadians interviewed for this book, these scenes were broadcast the world over, and the civil rights movement became a template for the New Left activism that came in its aftermath. The youthful civil rights activists' moral courage inspired millions of young people to engage—in Canada and everywhere—and Marcy Toms and Tom Wayman and others would draw on lessons of that resistance as they went on to march and sit-in and create new movements. I was also deeply affected by images of the civil rights movement, so much so that in elementary school I wrote a poem about events in Selma, Alabama. A few days later, the teacher told the class she'd be reading aloud something I'd written. Expecting to hear my anti-racist poem, which she'd given an A-plus, I was surprised when she read something else I'd written. Even then, I knew why she'd not read the Selma poem. "Controversial" subjects were to be avoided in public. It was my first lesson in censorship. (No doubt, this teacher was a decent person who likely wrestled with whether she could read the Selma poem in her classroom.) I watched Selma on TV, but some young British Columbians, like Carol Pastinsky, had first-hand experience with southern etiquette. After graduating from Magee High, Carol received her scholarship to the Pasadena Playhouse, a renowned acting school whose alumni include Dustin Hoffman and Eleanor Parker. More than any class there, though, the memory that stands out for Carol is an incident involving two fellow students—her first boyfriend, from the American Deep South, and her friend, also from the south. "He was a really smart guy, a really nice guy," she says of her friend. He was also black, and when she walked with him down a stairway between classes, they were confronted by her boyfriend and two of his buddies. "Waiting for me at the bottom of the stairs to say that I couldn't have done anything worse than to be walking with this guy. I was just devastated. They said this in front of him. It was horrible. I said, 'I won't listen to this.'" Carol was, of course, done with the boyfriend. "As soon as I heard that come out of his mouth, that was it. That's one thing I've never come to terms with—having to deal with people that think that way. I mean, it just doesn't seem to stop."

Standing up to prejudice was personal for supporters of Solidarity 1983. Besides growing up on TV newscasts about the civil rights resistance, many had parents who had fought fascism in the Second World War. It was a time when the Remembrance Day assembly meant the principal giving a first-hand account of his experiences overseas during the war. Melanie Ray was in high school the first time she "had any real awareness of the world beyond my own." She got home from school and turned on the television. "The screen came to life, and it was a very strange picture. I couldn't quite make it out. There was no real dialogue or anything. It was just these bulldozers and they were in a field, this kind of terrain, kind of wavy thing, and gradually I realized they were shovelling bodies. This was Auschwitz, or one of those camps." Melanie's voice cracks and she pauses. "My dad," she continues, "did not talk about the war. He talked about his time in India, which he loved, but he had not described in any detail anything about that war. I knew about it, but at arm's length. And this was a show about what happened to the Jews during the war. And I was absolutely horrified and sad and angry. Appalled. And I'm not sure that that started any kind of focused learning, but I did take up history when I went to university."

The high school Remembrance Day assembly might also have included the playing of Barry McGuire's anti-war "Eve of Destruction" or a Phil Ochs tune. Many at Solidarity protests had marched against the war in Vietnam. The anti-imperialism of Vietnam War protest was also intrinsically anti-racist. Vietnam raised awareness about racism everywhere. As Muhammad Ali said, the war was about "white people sending black people to fight yellow people to protect the country they stole from the red people."[18] Parallels between a racist war and racism at home were clear. In Vancouver, for instance, there was Red Power, a First Nations New Left group that marched against the war and organized protests and cultural events in their Indigenous community.

—•ʌʌ•—

Raj Chouhan grew up on a farm in Punjab, but followed friends to Canada in 1973 with plans to attend law school. Back in India, he had been a good student at Arya College but was more engrossed in his work as general secretary of the Punjab Student Union. It was, after all, the late 1960s and early '70s. "It's not a quiet time in India either," he says. "The student movement was quite strong. It was a multitude of things. When you see your education fees were too high, students were not treated well, there was a student strike going on at a nearby college. We supported them."

While settling into the Lower Mainland, waiting to begin college, Raj saw a newspaper ad looking for fruit pickers. "My family did farming, so I said, 'I want to see what they do here.'" At 6:30 the next morning an Econoline van picked Raj up. "People are sitting on the floor or on a bucket in which they would be picking the fruit. I was without any knowledge of farming in Canada. I thought they probably would be doing much better than what I have seen in India." Instead, Raj saw no running water, no toilets. "Conditions were horrible. Around lunch I said to somebody, 'Why are conditions so bad here?' I didn't know that he was the son of the farmer. I didn't get the ride back home." This experience was repeated four times in ten days. "Same thing. Got fired from everything. I thought, something needs to be done." Raj learned there was a union of farmworkers in California. "I spoke with a few friends here, then we got together—'So, why don't we do something about farmworkers in British Columbia?'"

It took years of organizing before the Canadian Farmworkers Union was established. "People were afraid, intimidated. They were not willing to talk to anybody." In September 1978, organizers finally drew twenty-plus farmworkers into a room to talk union. "We said, okay, let's do it." Raj was elected CFU president at the union's founding convention in 1980. By that time, he had contacted Cesar Chavez, the fabled co-founder of the California-based United Farm Workers. Raj had gotten hold of Chavez's phone number and, as people were wont to do in the twentieth century, called him out of the blue. "Oh, he was unbelievably friendly. He said that he was so happy to see that somebody was thinking about organizing farmworkers in British Columbia, and anything he could do, he would be more than happy to assist." Chavez invited Raj to California. "When you have read so much about a person who is like a legend hero and then you personally finally meet with him, and you're like, *wow*, you know, and he was so down-to-earth. Met with his wife Helen and the kids. He guided me so much. He became my mentor." Chavez visited Raj in B.C., too, and they became close friends. Like Chavez, Raj has a gentle manner, but begin to think he's saintly and he'll let out an earthy laugh and a sarcastic quip, and you'll suspect *Mad Magazine* might have been another mentor. "At that time I also came to know about the NDP in British Columbia, met with Dave Barrett, and I joined. I considered myself socialist, so that's where I landed and I was very comfortable with it."

The CFU won its first certifications at two farms in 1980 and soon had some 4,000 members. There were ongoing conflicts between the CFU and Socred notions of justice. When nineteen-year-old farm-worker Jarnail Deol died from pesticide poisoning in October 1982, a committee of farmers and farmworkers proposed new regulations. The Socred Minister of Agriculture threatened the Workers' Compensation Board chair with firing if he annoyed farmers with pesticide regulations. At the time, Raj said: "We believe that the contempt this government has shown for our lives is repulsive to British Columbians. . . . We can only win equality when this government gets that message loud and clear."[19] Raj also co-founded the B.C. Organization to Fight Racism in response to rising racist incidents in the Vancouver area, from assaults to workplace discrimination. He says the BCOFR was "a very broad-based organization which had members from almost every ethnic community—Ethiopians, Chinese, First Nations, you name it."

1983: Raj's union and anti-racist activism introduced him to a range of progressive organizations, so Art Kube calls on him in July 1983. "Given the profile of the Canadian Farmworkers Union, it was decided that we should be there in the leadership." Raj becomes one of a few active in both the Solidarity Coalition and Operation Solidarity. "We just offered ourselves, so we were there," he says. "We thought the time had come to stand up to the Socreds. I, personally, was shocked to see the vastness of their right-wing policies, that kind of broad assault on everything progressive that we have had."

The roaring reception for the Canadian Farmworkers Union when it stepped into Empire Stadium that August, seventy-one years after the *Komagata Maru* arrived in Vancouver harbour, was deeply moving for Raj and his union. "It's like you're not alone when you're standing up against this government. There's so many like-minded people there and it gives you a feeling of belonging, of just being part of something which, really, I found it overwhelming. So we were there with our banner and we took many of our farmworkers, you know, older people in turban and all that. And people were quite happy." That month, the CFU lays out a "FARMWORKERS FIGHTBACK" scenario that includes membership meetings to build support for Solidarity and the formation of teams for leafletting, petitions and actions. The CFU holds public meetings in New Westminster and Abbotsford—"Format-Cultural theatre/song/poetry about the B.C. struggle. Punjabi, English, Laotian."[20]

CHAPTER 8

The Hotel Vancouver Rally:
Prepare the General Strike

IT COULD HAVE BEEN the grand hotel of almost any downtown. It was *the* Vancouver hotel. The Hotel Vancouver, with its expansive lobby and posh rooms, was from an era when railway magnates built massive, ornate hotels across Canada. Victoria had the Empress. Just past the B.C. border, there was the Banff Springs. My mother, Anne, worked in a shop at Toronto's Royal York in the 1940s. In Vancouver, there had been two earlier Hotel Vancouvers (built in 1888 and 1916) before the enduring one opened in 1939 at the corners of Georgia and Burrard and Hornby Streets. Several of Vancouver's visual artists were enlisted to create wall paintings for the hotel's grand opening in May of 1939. Artist James W.G. Macdonald described the work he submitted: "A swing movement in colour, I call it. It is Indian in motif."[1]

The Hotel Vancouver's green copper rooftop dominates any 1940s photograph of the downtown skyline. This green roof had a moment of movie stardom in 1975, when it co-starred with George Segal in the climactic scene of the thriller *Kosygin is Coming* (later renamed *Russian Roulette*). This is also the hotel with racial policies that disgusted Canadians when they watched them on the evening news reports from Mississippi. It was the place where royal families and prime ministers slept, but which for decades barred a parade of celebrated black entertainers passing through Vancouver, including Louis Armstrong and Lena Horne, who instead found rooms across the street at the slightly-less-glitzy Hotel Georgia. The Georgia, by the way, opened in 1927 with segregated washrooms.

By 1983, there were half a dozen taller downtown buildings and the Electric Building, while shorter, was more luminous. Still, the Hotel Vancouver continued to represent the West Side's upper crust at play—from gala receptions to executive luncheons—as much as any building in town and, at the height of unrest that fall, hosted the annual Socred convention. What transpired on October 15 has come to be known as the *Hotel Vancouver rally*, but the protest was called the "March for People's Rights" at the time. At a Solidarity Coalition meeting on September 13, the organization endorsed "a demonstration at the Hotel Vancouver during the Socred Convention."[2] Minutes of that meeting document the debate that occurred. "Such an action," someone suggested, "needs to be carefully organized: a rally outside of the Hotel Vancouver might be a Marshal's Nightmare." Another coalition member voiced concerns about how such a rally might affect Solidarity's anti-budget petition. "We should ensure that such a rally should not distract the Petition Drive, which will be in its last days. . . . The petition should be circulated during the rally." Yet another voice raised a concept that had been percolating within Solidarity ranks since July: "Perhaps a one-day General Strike for the Friday is appropriate."[3]

A lot of this day—Saturday, October 15, 1983—comes down to how you see the world and the concept of the general strike. In October and November, to general strike or not to general strike would be the fundamental debate inside the Solidarity movement.

While others received a Bachelor of Activism at SFU, Vancouver's Tom Wayman left for the University of California and joined Students for a Democratic Society (SDS). It was mid-1960s America and other young activists on campus had experiences he'd only read about. "There were places in the States where there was a white entrance and a black entrance, or white drinking fountains and black drinking fountains. A lot of the energy for the founding of SDS came from people that had gone to the South to do voter registration, to do civil rights work of one kind or another. It was pretty hairy because people got beat up, people got killed." Tom attended the Irvine UC campus, near L.A., just as the city was becoming the subcultural and multicultural place it is today. "It blew my mind because the '60s were in full swing." Within a couple of years, L.A. was home to a famous race riot (Watts), youth riot (Sunset Strip) and anti-war riot (Century City). Wayman was among the 10,000 protest marchers who convened on June 23, 1967, in the Century City area, while President Lyndon Johnson spoke at the Century Plaza Hotel. "The march, at a certain point, was stalled in front of the hotel and it was charged by the police," Tom says. "The guy absolutely to the right of me got a night stick jammed right into his stomach. We fell back across a freeway and dispersed into the neighbourhoods. But lots of people were arrested and beaten up. . . . As this was billed as a peace march, the whole thing was pretty shocking to me."

By 1969, Tom was a seasoned SDS organizer and the increasingly militant group was famed for its anti-war and student activism. At the June 1969 SDS convention in Chicago, Tom met members of the fabled hobo-syndicalist Industrial Workers of the World. "When these guys showed up at the convention and were selling Wob cards, I bought one, almost like a souvenir." It would be more than that for Tom, who became active in the IWW when he returned to Vancouver. Tom found that the Wobblies advanced some compelling notions, including one particularly transformative idea: The General Strike. The idea became popular among socialists of every stripe in the 1800s as the definitive weapon against the newly prevailing capitalist system. General strikes were not uncommon through the nineteenth century and into the twentieth, including Philadelphia (1835), England (1842), New Orleans (1892), Brisbane (1912) and a couple of relatively nearby ones in 1919 (Seattle and Winnipeg). Some saw it as a limited action aimed at forcing concessions from government or employers. Others, like the anarcho-syndicalists and Rosa Luxemburg, saw the general strike as a revolutionary act: instead of walking out, strikers occupy their workplaces in perpetuity and run them collectively for the benefit of all. Syndicalists like writer Stephen Naft called for an insurrectionary general strike—"disorganize the capitalistic society so that after the complete annihilation of the old system, the working people can take possession through its labour unions of all the means of production."[4] In a 1933 pamphlet, Wobbly Ralph Chaplin noted: "There has never been a major labor struggle anywhere in the world in which the General Strike was not discussed. . . . It is Labor's ultimate attitude in the class struggle."[5] Tom Wayman elaborates: "A general strike is a peaceful way of making change. You can withdraw your labour and then you can go back to work and make the working day qualitatively different by taking control of the means of production, all that stuff." Solidarity's Tranquille occupation in Kamloops was a microcosm of what a B.C. general strike might have been in 1983.

1983: Tom is an author and poet teaching at Kwantlen College in Surrey and Richmond. The Wobblies had been a force across much of North America in the first decades of the century. The IWW was, for a moment, the largest union in B.C., organizing the mines, forests and railways as well as notable free speech fights in Vancouver and Victoria. The union was resurrected in the late 1960s in a much smaller form and organized a few work sites in the Lower Mainland. "When there was talk about general strike and so on [in 1983], which began almost right away, then our thing was, hey, well, we know about that." So, Tom and the IWW distributed literature about the general strike idea at community meetings and demonstrations and "did things like bring in the people from Tranquille to talk."

—◦◦◦—

The BCGEU's Gary Steeves said Tranquille workers performed exemplarily during the Solidarity occupation of the mental health facility. "In fact, I think the care was better when there was no bosses around. Workers treated patients like they were their family. This was their life's work. And here was a government in Victoria, trying to downgrade that and say, ah, well, we're just going to fire you all and get rid of you." He says the occupiers were well aware that they were part of something larger than Tranquille. "It was quite exhilarating, really. The workers there were looking at all this stuff breaking out— Operation Solidarity and the Solidarity Coalition and all this stuff was going on and starting up. And they were the first kind of major action of Operation Solidarity, the first major tactical initiation of it. It was all very exciting."

Melanie Ray's life began with an occupation. She was born in 1947 at St. Paul's Hospital, just down the street from the 1916-constructed Hotel Vancouver which, at the time, her father was occupying with other returning vets. That version of the Hotel Vancouver housed military barracks and offices during the Second World War. After the war, its Canadian Pacific Railway owners closed the hotel and planned to sell the property. Meanwhile, the building was empty and returning veterans faced a housing shortage. "They got so angry," says Melanie. "So finally a whole batch of them showed up at the gate. There was one guard there. They said, 'Let us in, we want to occupy this building.' And he said, 'Well, don't tell anybody I did it, but I was in World War One and I know what you guys are dealing with.' He opened the doors and they went in." So, on January 26, 1946, Canadian veterans liberated the old Hotel Vancouver. "Maybe we'll run [the hotel] at a loss, but we'll have apartments at least," organizer Bob McEwen said at the downtown rally preceding the occupation.[6] "To heck with the rent. Once we get in, maybe some organization will want to take it over and run it for us, but this thing has been kicked from pillar to post for the past six months so we're just going to move in."

B.C. occupations are as old as B.C. politics. They were a constant for the relief camp protesters of the 1930s who occupied Vancouver's art gallery, post office and Hudson's Bay department store. The activists of the 1960s and '70s continued this occupational tradition. There were the 114 SFU students arrested during their occupation of the administration building, the Raymur mothers who occupied train tracks to ensure their children could get to school safely, the protesters who occupied welfare offices in 1966. Muggs Sigurgeirson was an anti-poverty activist attending VCC when she got the call from her friend Carolyn Jerome. "She said, 'Muggs, get over here. We're occupying the welfare office.'"

At a house on East Van's Oxford Street, there was a meeting to plan a "people's park" occupation of land at the entrance to Stanley Park, where developers planned a Four Seasons Hotel. "How about calling it All Seasons Park," someone suggested. A few days later, on a brisk early morning, we met again at Lost Lagoon, went under the Stanley Park Causeway and through the fencing around the property, and began to build the park. "It's a sad weekend in Vancouver's history," said the city's conservative mayor, Tom Campbell.[7] The occupation lasted nearly a year, and Four Seasons Hotel Ltd. abandoned its development. The land remained, and remains, parkland.

1983: As organizing gets under way for the Hotel Vancouver rally, there is another occupation in Vancouver. Kim Zander recalls the planning meeting for the occupation of the premier's office. "It had to be a very clandestine organizing body. There could be no leaks, so there was a very small group of people involved in putting that together. Much of that strategizing around that was very CP-influenced." Party members like Kim supported a general strike but felt the widespread consciousness for it had to be built. The occupation was a building action. She says the planning was meticulous. "It wasn't just, let's occupy. There was also discussion about, okay, so you're going to occupy, how are you going to do it—you're going to have a group that stays overnight and then they're going to leave, and leave to what?" The decision was made to have a rally greet the occupiers as they leave. "We're not going to let these people just walk out into nothing." Solidarity activists from other groups were recruited one by one. "A plan was mapped out and people were brought on board for that plan. Are you willing? Yes, I'm willing. How many people can you bring? What can you bring?"

On the morning of September 16, Gail Meredith and other women involved in the action convened at a coffee shop on Robson Street. "And we met [the other occupiers] on a side street along the west side of the mall there. We all looked like refugees. We all had heavy blankets on and stuff like that. We weren't sure whether somebody had blown the cover on this thing, even though we had been so careful about the organizing of it. And we went creeping into the building." They made their way to the premier's office inside the Robson Square complex. "It turned out to be a big shock to the people that were there in the building." When eighty people walked into the office, staff was frightened at first, but the occupation force tried "to convey to them that they didn't need to be afraid. Nobody was going to hurt them. They left pretty quick." Occupiers slapped posters onto office windows—"Tell Grace McCarthy This is the B.C. Spirit" and "Take Back the Legislation"—and the Hospital Employees' Union dropped by with twenty pizzas, cartons of Kentucky Fried Chicken and coffee.

As the occupiers settled in, Gail wasn't pleased that a core group of union men seemed to be running things. "I got very crabby about the whole thing and said that they needed to have some visible participation of women in the group that was calling the shots on this so it wasn't just trade union guys. And it was important to be seen as a community group as well as a trade union group." Gail tried to find another woman who would assume that role, but finally agreed to do it herself, "which I had not planned on doing. So there were three or four guys who were running it, and me." She felt the occupation would motivate people to take action against the budget. "That it was going to have a big impact on them and they had to do something. I wanted to inspire other people around the province to be involved because so much is Vancouver-based." Taking on a spokesperson role meant Gail was doing interviews with the substantial media covering the event. "So I was running around to the women in the group saying, okay, what should we say, what can we say, what would be useful that we say." Gail's message to the public: "'We are your neighbours in here. This is people who care very much about this budget. This is people who care very much about what's going to happen with the community.' It was relatively important in terms of how it was seen by people at large, I think."

Another occupation spokesperson, DERA president Jim Green, described the occupation mood as "joyous. Sure, it's had its hectic moments, but this is an organized occupation. Nobody has been hurt and no damage has been done."[8] After thirty hours they left, singing protest songs as they emerged and entered, as conquering heroes, Robson Square plaza, where an anti-budget protest was under way. They were greeted with resounding cheers at the high-noon rally organized by the Vancouver and District Labour Council's Unemployment Committee. Labour council vice-president George Hewison told the 1,000-strong crowd: "Unless this legislation is repealed, the kind of activity they've just witnessed [at the premier's office] is going to be repeated again and again across the province."[9] At the rally, Gail Meredith told a *Vancouver Sun* reporter: "When the government doesn't listen to people's legitimate concerns, it is time for different action."[10]

Kim Zander saw the occupation as the kind of action that inspires more actions and an eventual general strike. "It sparked people's imagination but it also sparked their confidence. And that was part of the discussion we were having. What is going to take us there and pull as many people with us as possible, because we can't assume that because people are opposed to the budget they're going to feel confident enough and bold enough to get there until they see that they've got solidarity. So that had to be built. And that was the debate on the left. How much of that build do we get into before we get into a general strike."

Days later, Jim Green caught flak from conservative city councillors for his participation in the occupation. When he appeared before city council, which provided an annual grant to DERA, Jim was scolded by Alderman Don Bellamy: "To try and state that he was there as a private citizen just isn't washing, especially when every time his name is on the TV screen there's DERA written right underneath it. I don't think any form of civil disobedience is what we should be supporting with taxpayers' money."[11]

——◦◦◦——

October came around and pressure was mounting for Solidarity to map out a general strike scenario, many seeing it as the endgame for all this resistance. The morning of the Hotel Vancouver rally, at the Queen Elizabeth Theatre's empty plaza, Solidarity organizers waited to see whether their movement, after three months of non-stop activism, had burned out or would draw a decent-sized crowd to the plaza. "I remember because we wanted to choose a location that could hide a small turnout," Jean Swanson says. "We weren't sure we were going to get a big turnout. But in the end, we got a big turnout." By the time the march wound its way through downtown, past the Hotel Vancouver, and Art Kube rose to speak at the plaza, it was bursting with protesters.

Solidarity's scheduled protest for October 15, when the annual Socred convention convened at the Hotel Vancouver, had been cause for consternation inside the NDP and the labour hierarchy. Raj Chouhan, who was on the rally's planning committee, recalls: "I also remember receiving a call from Gerry Stoney, who was the president of the NDP at that time. He wanted to meet with me . . . so I went and met with him. And he was trying to say, 'Raj, are you sure you can handle this?' I said, 'What do you mean?' He said, 'You know,

like this could get out of hand. It could backfire.' I said, 'Are you telling me to call it off? We are not going to do it.'"

Before the rally, Operation Solidarity was—in public at least—
giving the event its full support. In a letter to "all Lower Mainland
Trade Union Organizations," Art Kube wrote: "WE NEED FULL
PARTICIPATION [in the rally] by every trade union in the Lower
Mainland and WE NEED A FULL COMMITMENT in the organizational work leading up to October 15."[12] By now, the Solidarity movement was so widely known that the most prominent image on the
October 15 rally leaflet was the "Solidarity" logo, along with "March
for Your Rights: Social, Economic, Human, Trade Union and Democratic Rights are Threatened in B.C."[13]

On October 7, the Solidarity Coalition adopted—for distribution
at the October 15 Hotel Vancouver rally—a Declaration of Rights of
the People of British Columbia. "We believe that the measure of a
society's humanity is the degree to which it provides rights that protect all," it begins. The document lists which rights, and whose rights,
Solidarity is fighting for. It mentions several groups in the coalition
(seniors, women, the disabled, workers, tenants), education, social
programs (universal medical care, legal assistance), democratic government (local decision-making, consultation on legislative proposals)
and personal protections (freedom of expression, freedom from discrimination).

> This declaration is made in the face of an unprecedented legislative
> assault that seeks to eliminate or subvert existing rights and protec-
> tions. This cannot be allowed. We also assert, therefore, that the peo-
> ple of this province have the right and the responsibility to resist. We
> shall do so with all of our strength.[14]

On October 15, protesters assembled at designated city blocks by
the foot of Robson ("near stadium").[15] Each component of Solidarity
was assigned a block where its supporters were to convene. For instance, CAIMAW, anti-poverty groups, CUPW, Unemployed Action
Centres, DERA, IWA, the Newspaper Guild and tenants were among

the groups assembled on Hamilton Street between Robson and Smithe. At ten a.m., on this unseasonably dry October day, the march began—to Burrard, then along Georgia Street, past the Hotel Vancouver, and on to the closing rally at the Queen Elizabeth Theatre plaza.

—◦◦◦—

Musician-activist Alan Zisman knew his way around a soundboard, so he was asked to do the sound at the Queen Elizabeth Theatre plaza rally. Having moved to Vancouver in the mid-1970s to work on *The Open Road* news journal, Alan was now a teacher at Total Education free school. He was living in Montreal in 1972 when Quebec had its general strike. "The October crisis was just a couple years before that, where Quebec essentially was put under martial law," Alan says. "Even my house got raided. The trade union movement in Quebec was becoming increasingly militant, was under attack, and was discovering a quasi-socialism." There were strikes across the province in the early '70s. In 1971, during a lockout at *La Presse* newspaper, a clash between police and strike supporters left a protester dead and 190 injured. The anger over that was still fresh when the Common Front of unions called a general strike in support of public service workers. The confrontation reached far beyond these unions and the public sector—large rallies and occupations of factories and radio stations spread across Quebec. "Not since the days of the Industrial Workers of the World, since the days of Joe Hill and the battle for the eight-hour day, has a North American union movement been so dedicated to the tradition of revolutionary syndicalism," said Marcel Pepin, one of Quebec's jailed union leaders.[16] The Common Front eventually called for the workers to return to work and the strike ended.

Alan had taken to the streets with much of Quebec, attending mass rallies and supporting the occupations. Now, in B.C., the BCGEU was just two weeks from a legal position to strike. Like many Solidarity supporters at the plaza protest, Alan was excited by talk of Operation

Solidarity transitioning into Operation General Strike. So he worked the soundboard that day fully expecting Art Kube to speak about the growing anticipation of a strike. "Instead, Art holds up a piece of paper and tells us that the next step to broaden this is that, 'Everybody who is here today can get a copy of this petition and go to your neighbours and get people to sign the petition calling on the government, and we will deliver the signed petition to the government in Victoria.' And my sense, I think the sense of the people I knew, was like someone was letting the air out of our balloon. We want militant action. We want to shut down this province. Instead, we're being told, 'Go get a petition signed.'" Alan jokingly fantasizes about what he might have done that day with all of his audio power. "There I was with a microphone in the sound booth and control over the sound levels for Art Kube, and I like to imagine lowering the sound just before Art Kube announces the petition, turning up the sound on my mic, and leading the crowd into the chant for the general strike."

I heard plenty of calls for a general strike that day among the 80,000 or so people marching on the Socred convention. Solidarity felt invincible that day. Waves of protesters filled the streets and poured past the convention, often pausing to shout at the Hotel Vancouver as if exorcising the building of its dreaded Socred curse. The slogan on placards and buttons everywhere: "Prepare the General Strike." In front of the hotel a hospital worker from Coquitlam, Evelyn Farrelly, told me that her co-workers would vote for a general strike. "It's the only thing we have left."[17] Beyond the left or the labour movement, so many people who had never been politically active but were appalled by the Socreds' injustice budget were now ready to make a stand.

The Committee for a General Strike came to the rally armed with "Prepare the General Strike" placards. "We made these things. We couldn't believe it. People were literally ripping them out of our hands," says committee member Gary Cristall. "Guys who two weeks before that had said, 'Ah, you guys are dreaming.' Now, they said, 'Give me one of those things.' The march went past the Hotel Vancouver, and you can see when you look at footage of it all these Prepare the

General Strike signs. It became part of popular consciousness—to prepare the general strike. I wouldn't say that everybody there agreed but it was sort of seen—'Yeah, that's what we need to do.' I saw Art Kube and Renate Shearer, who was a friend of mine on the board of the folk festival, that morning and they said, oh, nobody's going to show up, it's going to be terrible. And then, God knows how many people showed up. I think it was the biggest ever . . . more than you could count. If on that day Art Kube had said, 'We call on the Solidarity Coalition to take over public buildings starting with the schools and community centres,' it would have happened."

The Committee for a General Strike included Gary's Socialist Challenge group and other leftists, and had formed in the fall around two areas of agreement: "A mass mobilization to try to bring down the government and force new elections, and absolutely being convinced that the labour bureaucracy would betray us. It was a committee of far-left militants." That committee, and others on Solidarity's left wing, felt the popular consciousness for a general strike already existed and that people across the province would rise if Solidarity showed the courage to move ahead with it. (The committee's members also included activists from Women Against the Budget, the Surrey and Coquitlam Solidarity Coalitions, the Canadian Federation of Students and CAIMAW.) The anti-capitalist left—Trotskyists and anarchists, militant trade unionists and Maoists, feminists and radical ecologists, Communists and left-wing democratic socialists— can find a lot to disagree on any day. But on October 15, 1983— while they differed on some of the particulars—they were in unison on one thing: the objective was a general strike.

The province of B.C. and the notion of general strike had met a couple of times prior to 1983. Several B.C. organizations of the early twentieth century advanced radical notions of the general strike, particularly the IWW, One Big Union and the Socialist Party of Canada. There had been a one-day general strike across the province in 1918 after union organizer Ginger Goodwin was shot dead by police. Goodwin was a member of the Socialist Party and vice-president of the B.C. Federation of Labour. In 1935, there was more talk of an all-out strike when activists fleetingly advocated combining the Ballantyne Pier and relief camp workers' strikes into a call for a general strike.

In 1983, a Committee for a General Strike leaflet, "UNITE for the GENERAL STRIKE," called for "open forums" in workplaces and neighbourhoods as the backbone of the strike's wide democratic decision-making organization.[18] "The unprecedented, democratic structure of the Solidarity Coalition already provides a framework for this." The committee's slogan, "Prepare the General Strike," captured the spirit of October 15. "We came up with the slogan 'Prepare the General Strike' because we had spent a lot of time in the Fourth International organization, the Trotskyist organization, discussing what an administrative general strike looks like," Gary Cristall says. "You call it a *syndicalist* one, which is, yeah, the bus drivers show up for work, they don't collect the fares. They simply put tape over the fare thing and they drive people around. This is the whole thing. You take over the schools. You have food distribution. You basically start the workers-run society." A Socialist Challenge leaflet urged BCGEU workers to "imagine the impact if the fired Human Rights workers occupied their offices, resumed investigating and following on complaints, only to have their decisions enforced by Operation Solidarity instead of the government and the courts."[19] Besides transforming the workplace, such actions strengthen public support for a general strike. Wobbly syndicalist Ralph Chaplin noted the strikers' self-management efforts during the general strikes of 1919. "The strikes at Seattle and Winnipeg gave some indication of the ability of strikers to organize, picket and police their strike and, at the same time, arrange for the adequate distribution of foodstuffs to the population."[20] In Seattle's five-day strike, workers continued to collect garbage, fight fires and distribute food. Groaned Seattle's conservative mayor Ole Hanson: "The general strike, as practiced in Seattle, is of itself the weapon of revolution. . . . It puts the government out of operation."[21]

Solidarity tent-in at Vancouver's Vanier Park protesting the Residential Tenancy
Act, October 4. (COURTESY: PACIFIC TRIBUNE PHOTO COLLECTION-SFU)

Cultural Workers Against the Budget march on Hotel Vancouver, October 15.
(COURTESY: GEOFF PETERS)

March for Your Rights:

Social, Economic, Human, Trade Union and Democratic Rights are Threatened in B.C.

MARCH

Saturday, October 15 10:30 a.m.

March from the foot of Robson (near stadium) to Burrard, down Georgia St. to Queen Elizabeth Theatre Plaza.

Assemble at 10 a.m. at points listed
on reverse.

Leaflet (front) for the Hotel Vancouver rally. (COURTESY: PATSY GEORGE
SOLIDARITY COLLECTION/BC LABOUR HERITAGE CENTRE)

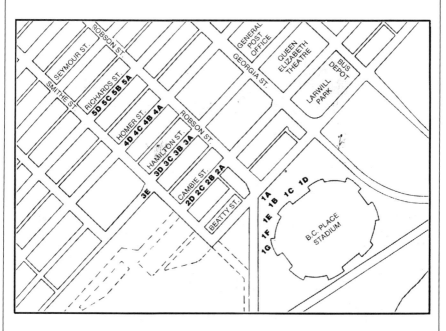

Assembly Points (<u>10:00 a.m.</u>)

Amalgamated Clothing & Textile
  Workers 2D
Anti-Poverty Groups 3B
A T U 4C
Artists and Cultural Workers 5C
AUCE 1E
Bakery Workers 1F
B.C. Federation of Police Officers 1A
B.C. Ferry and Marine Workers
  Union 5D
BCGEU 2A
BCIT Staff Society 1D
B.C. Nurses Union 4A
B.C. Teachers Fed. 1D
BCYT Building Trades Council 1B
BRAC 4D
Brewery Workers 2B
CAIMAW 3D
CALEA 4D
CALFAA 4D
CAMWRU 1F
CBRT 4C
Cement Lime Gypsum 3A
CFU (Farmworkers) 1G
Consumer Organizations 3E
CMSG 5D
CPU 3A
CUPE 5A
CUPTE 2B
CUPW 3C
DERA 3E
Disabled 5A
ECWU 3A
Environmental Groups 1G
ESSA 2B

Ethnic Minorities 1G
Faculty Associations
  University and College 1D
Food and Service Workers 3D
Foundry Workers 3A
Glass & Ceramic 3A
Grainworkers 5D
Graphic Arts 3E
GVRDEU 5B
HEU 4B
Home and School Federation 1C
HREU 2D
HSA 4A
Human Rights Organizations 1G
IAFF 1A
IAM (Machinists) 4C
IATSE 2D
IBEW
  258
  264 .... 2C
ICTU 3D
ILGWU 2D
ILWU 5D
Injured Workers 5A
IWA 3A
LCUC 3C
Marine Workers 5D
Molders 3A
NABET 3E
Native Community 1G
NDP 2D
Neighbourhood Groups 5C
Newspaper Guild 3E
OTEU 2C
PARI 4A

Political Parties 5C
Pottery Workers 3A
PPWC 3D
Printing Pressmen 3E
Professional Employees B.C. 2B
Professional Institute — Public
  Service of Canada 2B
PSAC 3C
Psychiatric Nurses 4A
Railway Unions 4C
Religious Organizations 3B
RWDSU 1F
SEIU 2D
Seniors 5A
SIU 5D
Small Business 2D
Social Service Workers 3E
SORWAC 1E
Students 1C
Tenants 3E
TWU 3E
UAW 3A
UBE 2D
UFAWU 5D
UFCW 1F
UGWA 2D
Unemployment Action Centres 3B
USWA 3B
Vancouver Typographical 3E
VMREU 5B
WCBEU 4D
Westcoast Racetrack Employees 2D
West Van MEA 5B
Women 1E

Leaflet (back) for the Hotel Vancouver rally. (COURTESY: PATSY GEORGE
SOLIDARITY COLLECTION/BC LABOUR HERITAGE CENTRE)

▲ Teachers marching on Hotel
Vancouver, October 15.
(COURTESY: GEOFF PETERS)

◄ Art Kube (centre) and Renate
Shearer (right) at front of the
march on Hotel Vancouver,
October 15. (COURTESY:
PACIFIC TRIBUNE PHOTO
COLLECTION-SFU)

▲ Protesters gather outside Queen Elizabeth Theatre, October 15. (COURTESY: GEOFF PETERS)

◄ Solidarity protesters arrive at Hotel Vancouver as the Socreds stage their convention inside, October 15. (COURTESY: FISHERMAN PUBLISHING SOCIETY COLLECTION-SFU)

Patsy George (left) at Solidarity's Hotel Vancouver protest, October 15.
(COURTESY: PATSY GEORGE SOLIDARITY COLLECTION/
BC LABOUR HERITAGE CENTRE)

B.C. Teachers' Federation activist Marcy Toms.
(COURTESY: GEOFF PETERS)

Port Hardy teachers picketing, November 1983. (COURTESY: GEOFF PETERS)

BCGEU members picket during Solidarity's November strike.
(COURTESY: BCGEU)

Estimates of the crowd size at the October 15 Solidarity rally vary considerably, but it was, at the time, the largest political protest in B.C. history. "It was amazing energy," says Marcy Toms, "and as you probably know yourself, when you're in the middle of that energy, that's all there is. I mean, you're not thinking what kind of anti-your energy might be out there. You're just really thinking about how powerful you feel. Here you are with thousands and thousands of your sisters and brothers. How can this movement that I'm in the middle of right now not succeed in everything that it wants to do. It can't fail. That's the feeling. It's celebratory, really. A celebration."

It was as though the people of B.C. were just waiting for Solidarity to create a moment like this. "It was almost an easy thing to organize because of how everybody was so hyped around it," says Roisin Sheehy-Culhane. "It kind of snowballed. I remember it just being so incredibly exciting to have that many people outside of the Vancouver Hotel, and the Socreds were inside peering out at us and looked really scared and that felt really good. It felt really powerful. Compared to getting people out on the streets for other issues, this one was relatively easy." In spite of some timid naysayers beforehand, the rally was the defining moment of the entire Solidarity uprising. Before that day's march was over, the tone of Solidarity had switched to general strike. "Some unions felt that it was necessary to go into a general strike moment to force the government to back down," says Raj Chouhan, "not only to back down from their policy, but also to set some kind of thinking, some policy, that for years to come the government will not dare to make those kinds of laws that the Socreds tried at that time. So that was the bigger thinking, but at the same time there were some people in the labour movement and outside the labour movement that thought it was not doable."

—∿∿—

Despite the exhilaration in the streets outside the Hotel Vancouver, radical lawyer Craig Patterson knew society's insiders were inside and its outsiders were outside. He wanted to turn that around. So, he spent much of October 15 using his ample vocal chords to rouse an occupation of the hotel. "I was urging that we go into the hotel. We missed an opportunity. We should have gone right into the hotel. I was yelling at the top of my voice."

Craig leans back from the dining room table at his East Side home and shouts like it's 1983: "*Occupy the hotel! Occupy the hotel!*" Quietly he adds: "People said, 'No, no, we're not going to do that.' It was an opportunity. It would have been on the front page of every newspaper."

While the BCTF's Jacquie Boyer was on the outside that day, her brother was on the inside. "My brother was in the convention upstairs. My brother is married to [Socred founder] Bible Bill Aberhart's granddaughter." So, an old family drama played out that day, with Jacquie a protester and her brother a Socred delegate. Although not uncommon in twentieth-century B.C., this family division could be irritating. "Extremely irritating," Jacquie says. "I didn't talk about it if he didn't talk about it. He would always raise it." She has never spoken with her brother about that day in October 1983. "Nope. Did I ever want to? Nope."

The big rally was also a family affair for Muggs Sigurgeirson and her mother Winnie. "My mother was in her mid-seventies by then. She was always at every demonstration. I remember she was pretty bitter because the revolution hadn't come. Anyway, she was at that demo." For Winnie, this massive march on everything Socred was the culmination of a lifetime of protesting, and she happily partook in a moment of spontaneity at the hotel. "People were breaking off and sitting in front of the Hotel Vancouver," Muggs says. "The marshals didn't like that. They were trying to stop that. A marshal had been coming up behind my mother with his boot and was trying to dig it under her to push her over to get her to stand up, just sort of kept kicking her along the cement. She ignored him and finally he stopped, then he turned around and had his back to her. And she's still sitting on the ground. She took off her Solidarity button—she was so mad—and she opened it and rammed it into his butt. And he screamed. What's he going to do? She's this old lady. We got great satisfaction out of that. It was almost a metaphor for Solidarity. The rank-and-file wanted to sit down and the labour bosses wanted to kick them in the butt to move on."

A group calling itself Cultural Workers Against the Budget re-wrote the lyrics to classic protest tunes and passed them out to Solidarity marchers. For instance, "Which Side are You On?" written in 1931 by Florence Reece for mine workers in Harlan County, Kentucky, now had lyrics about B.C. "They say that in old Lotusland you'd better get well quick/They're selling health like real estate—it's enough to make you sick . . . O people can you stand it? O listen to me well—Let's sink this Socred government in the deepest pits of hell."[22]

One song remained unchanged on the lyric sheet passed out on October 15. Ralph Chaplin, the Wobbly who had written so eloquently about the general strike idea a half century earlier, also wrote in 1915 the left-wing anthem "Solidarity Forever." Now, in 1983, the Solidarity protesters marching on the Socreds sang Chaplin's words:

In our hands is placed a power greater than their hoarded gold
Greater than the might of armies multiplied a thousand-fold
We can bring to birth a new world from the ashes of the old
For the union makes us strong
Solidarity forever
Solidarity forever
Solidarity forever

CHAPTER 9

Solidarity on the Line:
We've Taken a Stand

THE OCTOBER 15 RALLY left no doubt about public support for
Solidarity. The following day, Women Against the Budget, at its conference in Vancouver, became the first component of the Solidarity
Coalition to endorse a general strike. WAB organizer Susan Croll
said the Socred government is "pushing the people of B.C. into the
choice between surrendering our democratic rights or standing up in
yet stronger opposition."[1] The day after that, the Lower Mainland
Solidarity Coalition backed action "up to and including a general
strike."[2] Coalition spokesman Al Blakey said: "We had the largest
meeting we've ever had. I guess that came out of the enthusiasm of
Saturday's rally and the possible job action."[3] The Vancouver (October
18) and New Westminster (October 19) labour councils also pledged
support for a general strike. Operation Solidarity planned a series of

strikes that would escalate to a general strike if the government didn't withdraw its bills. The scenario called for the B.C. Government and Service Employees' Union to go out first when its contract expired on October 31, followed a week later by the B.C. Teachers' Federation and many post-secondary faculty and staff. Two days later, crown corporations would join the strike, including workers at B.C. Hydro and the Insurance Corporation of B.C. On November 14, civic and transportation employees—ferry workers, bus drivers—would strike, then hospital workers. Private-sector workers were set to strike, too, as soon as the government took action against public-sector strikers.

"It doesn't look like peace, does it?" Art Kube said, adding that strikers would be asked to defy the law if the Socred government intervened.[4] "If the government wants to make an ass of the law, they'll make an ass out of themselves." As scheduled, the 35,000-member BCGEU went out at midnight October 31. The budget had already decimated BCGEU membership. "We would have lost probably about 10,000 jobs by October," says Diane Wood, who was on the BCGEU strike's Negotiating Committee. "I was called to come down from Prince George. I packed for three days, I think, and we were at the Labour Relations Board for three weeks. We hardly ever left the room." So, Diane hunkered down in Vancouver as BCGEU members struck province-wide. "When we weren't there negotiating, we were on the lines. Wild times."

Just before the BCGEU walked out, Renate Shearer called a Solidarity Coalition meeting to order at its 686 West Broadway office. In a report to the meeting, Art Kube said that representatives of every union in B.C. had met that day and voted to endorse the Operation Solidarity strike scenario. The Coalition's tenants representative, Jim Quail, called for an immediate joint meeting of Operation Solidarity and the Solidarity Coalition. "Art will see what he can do," the minutes say.[5]

By the next day, the BCGEU had struck liquor stores and courthouses, human resources offices and the touristy Barkerville site. Mechanic Jay Northcott joined his first union eighteen months earlier when he became a motor vehicle inspector, thinking a government job meant the security to send his daughter to college. Instead, he found himself declared redundant and his job discarded. "I was un-involved and uninformed," he said, but now the Socred bills were too much to ignore. For the first time, he joined street protests. "When there are 40,000 people out there losing their salaries and standing out in the cold because they agree that the government had done the wrong thing by firing 1,600 people, then that makes you pretty damn humble."[6]

Port Moody family worker Ken Holmes was among the BCGEU members whose jobs were liquidated. A few days into the strike, he described to me his daily routine—starting seven a.m., it was filled with meetings, handing out literature, picket lines. "One night, I was standing at Riverview in twenty-five-mile-an-hour winds with rain coming straight at us. I look back over the past four months and there's been so many marches and protests, and Mr. Bennett has dis-missed everything. . . . People are conditioned to expect corruption from the government and we have a really high boiling point, but when we reach it you have to take sides. My parents and my brother and sister all voted conservative, but this budget has affected all of them to the point where they'd reconsider how they'd vote again." As our conversation wound down, Ken said: "Yesterday, a teacher came up and said he had no problem going out and he'd see me on Tues-day. Whether we win or we lose this, we've taken a stand."[7]

The first weekend of the strike, representatives of 300,000 provin-cial government workers across Canada held an "emergency session" in Vancouver to strategize resource pooling to support the BCGEU.[8] It was the first time all ten provincial government employees' unions convened. "They know that if Premier Bennett wins the right to fire people with no regard to seniority, they could be next," said the BCGEU's John Fryer.[9] The militancy was spreading well beyond any union or leftist organization. Emily Carr School of Art students pro-duced a lively publication called *Class War* with a great comic book cover featuring super-hero EMILY CARR—SOCRED FIGHTER battling

THE DEADLY PERIL FROM VICTORIA. Inside, a general strike time-table notes that the coming Monday, November 14, "civic workers walk off the job. This is it, the dreaded GARBAGE STRIKE."[10] Emily Carr students staged their own Solidarity march on November 8. At SFU, a Solidarity rally was planned for the 14th. "They would like people to wear red and white, the Solidarity colors," noted Solidarity Coalition minutes.[11] Firefighters who left work to join the August Empire Stadium rally had been docked pay by fire chief Norman Harcus. In late October, Harcus phoned the president of the Vancouver Fire Fighters' Union, William Anderson, to discuss "what services would be maintained by your members in the event of a general strike."[12] During a general strike, Harcus was told, the union would take charge of operations and continue to provide needed services.

—⁓—

On November 8, the 30,000-strong B.C. Teachers' Federation became the second union to strike. Deputy Minister of Education Jim Carter sent teachers a warning that if they joined in the Solidarity strike they could be fired, suspended or have their teacher's certificates rescinded. The teachers also had plenty of support, including the United Fishermen and Allied Workers' Union (UFAWU/Fish), which promised to join BCTF picket lines. The president of the Delta Teachers' Association welcomed Fish's support. "They are members of Solidarity and they have told us they will join us on the line. This is a protest against the government, a political protest. They will be walking beside us."[13]

Education was a favourite punching bag of the Socreds. The July bills concentrated power in the government by stripping school boards of budgeting independence. There would be 3,000 fewer jobs when teachers were laid off at the start of 1984. Funding to colleges and universities was decreased. Student loans were cut. A freeze was placed on training at Richmond's Vocational Rehabilitation Services. The B.C. Association for Children and Adults with Learning Disabilities, which provided learning materials for schools, had its contract terminated.

The BCTF rank-and-file was in a precarious position to resist because they did not have the legal right to strike. They weren't even members of the B.C. Federation of Labour. "Along comes the Solidarity movement and then, all of a sudden, we find ourselves on the verge of striking—illegally—so there was this very quick increase in militancy in the teachers' union," says Burnaby teacher Scott Parker. "And of course that reflected the militancy that was going on in society in general in B.C. People were becoming very, very, very, very militant. . . . I think that the community was on the verge of occupying the schools, because the parents had come out before the strike had happened and they were at the schools picketing. It was kind of an occupation in some ways, really."

With the mood of the province and its history of occupation, there's little doubt that a general strike would spark occupations across B.C. as it had in France in 1968 and Quebec in 1972. If early summer's Tranquille occupation in Kamloops showed that workplaces could be "under new management" in a general strike, late summer's premier's office occupation in Vancouver showed that the government itself could be under new management.

———

There had been recent stirrings inside the BCTF. The union was offered bargaining rights by the Barrett government of the early '70s but said no without a membership vote. Larry Kuehn was elected to the union's provincial executive in 1978. The following year, the union's left caucus—Teachers Viewpoint—won an 8–3 majority of the executive, with Alan Blakey as president and Larry the vice-president. At the 1981 annual general meeting, the union executive raised the issue of bargaining beyond salaries and bonuses and called for a referendum on the right to strike. That year, at Larry's first press conference as BCTF president, he said the union would improve working conditions. "And the strange thing that happened was they [Socreds] offered us money." Teachers received an 18 per cent wage increase but in a referendum voted 60–40 against their right to strike, preferring to maintain a system whereby unresolved matters between teachers and school boards were settled by arbitration. The wage increase was the government's way of dissuading membership from voting for the right to strike. Still, the strike matter had been raised. "Everyone had to think about it," Larry says. "They had to think about the right to strike. For fifty years, they had not thought about it." Larry travelled the province talking up the right to strike prior to the referendum vote, so the preconditions for the 1983 Solidarity walkout were established inside the BCTF in the first years of the '80s.

A week after the 1982 referendum vote rejected the right to strike, Socred education minister Bill Vander Zalm introduced an education "restraint" program that reduced teaching jobs, wages and working conditions. "I was devastated by the result of the referendum," Larry says. "You know, now what are we going to do? And a week later, they bring in the restraint program. It just showed that without that power [to strike] we were totally vulnerable and consequently able to say to our members, 'Look at this. It just shows what happens when you give up the potential of the power of withdrawing your labour.'" Larry called on Bennett to remove Vander Zalm from his post "with all possible speed,"[14] later adding:

> The minister is entitled to his personal perspective on education as a narrow, job-oriented activity. He can ignore, if he likes, the student's experience with education, with whether education excites his/her interest, builds his/her self-esteem, or does the opposite. But he cannot be allowed to dictatorially impose his personal prejudices on the public education system.[15]

Some in the BCTF took up the slogan *Stop Vanderism in the schools.* "People were so outraged at Vander Zalm. All [conditions] were the lead-ups to '83. The referendum and the debate about it and so on helped to condition people, I think, so that a year later under totally different circumstances the vote was 60–40 the other way."

Progressive school boards were vocal supporters of the Solidarity strikers. Gwen Chute, president of the Coquitlam board, was known for her own principled stands and admired the teachers' resistance. "Oh yeah. It was desperate. 'We have to stop this.' Teachers and school boards knew that all of these things were going to affect kids in every way. It was going to affect their education at school, it was going to affect their health, it was going to affect their family life." Gwen made the decision to become a teacher when she was in grade five. "I had a really wonderful friend—if there was an injured animal, Sonny would look after it." Sonny was also dyslexic and struggled with reading and math. "In those days, they failed you. He got failed twice and it just destroyed him. A couple of teachers treated him with compassion and respect. So I decided to be a teacher." Graduating from UBC in 1964, Gwen was soon active in the BCTF. Upon moving to suburban Belcarra she was elected school trustee and became board chair in 1978. Some labour "leaders" at the BCFED may not have had much regard for the BCTF leadership in the fall of 1983, but Larry Kuehn and his union had widespread respect among progressive educators. Says Gwen: "I was 100 per cent behind them. Always."

In November 1983, the Vancouver School Board received an injunction barring teachers from picketing their schools. To circumvent the ban, the BCTF and BCGEU arranged a picket exchange wherein each union picketed the other's work site. The Solidarity Coalition also provided pickets, with Women Against the Budget playing a particularly prominent role on the lines. "There was the exchange where the teachers went and picketed liquor stores and other government employee positions and a lot of government employees as well as a lot of people from the Solidarity Coalition picketed the Vancouver schools," says Larry Kuehn. During the strike, pickets didn't obey every whim of the Labour Relations Board (LRB). CUPE, for instance, ignored a board ruling against picketing at the University of Victoria. Students also joined campus picket lines. "I think it's time the

Bennett government realized that people are really upset with it," said Douglas College student president Sean Balderstone. "This legislation hurts so much we're willing to give up a semester."[16]

The teachers' strike almost ended before it began. In North Vancouver, teachers and the school board reached an agreement exempting teachers from the broad firing powers of the bills, which could have been a model for other districts and prevented a province-wide walkout. "There had been an agreement reached that essentially would have exempted us from the Bill 3 provisions, but it was going to require government approval," Larry says. "We had already set the strike date. Unless there was an agreement on this, the strike was going ahead." So the day teachers were scheduled to strike, Larry Kuehn, Art Kube and Jack Munro sat together in a room at the Labour Relations Board offices in Vancouver awaiting news on this agreement. By this time, regardless of any agreement between North Van teachers and the government, many teachers saw they were part of a fight larger than just their own union and were prepared to strike for Solidarity. "We had the television on," Larry says. "There were lots of stories about what was happening." One of the stories on TV featured interviews with New Westminster teachers. "The reporter was asking teachers about going on strike and a teacher said, 'Well, I don't want to go on strike, but these human rights issues are too important. We may have to. We can't accept this destruction of human rights.' He didn't talk about teacher issues at all. Munro was just absolutely so offended by this. It was so wrong to him to use the strike weapon for these soft issues. He was just fuming about this. What happened after that I could see in his reaction there."

After Munro's flare-up, the three continued to sit and watch and wait. In another room at the LRB, the media was also waiting—for Larry to tell them whether teachers would be joining the Solidarity strike. "It was so packed with reporters we could hardly get in it.

BCTV was there, the station in those days that everyone around the province got, and they had a live feed from the LRB." Finally, with no agreement at hand, Larry told Kube and Munro that it was time for him to speak to the press. Larry later learned that the Socred government had advised the North Vancouver School Board not to sign the agreement.

"At six o'clock, I said, 'I have to go out, and there's no agreement, and the strike's going ahead,' and asked Art if he was coming with me. And he said yes. We got up to go out and Munro said, 'Art, you can't leave.' And Art did leave. He came out with me and [kept] that commitment he had made to me all along. I knew he was there with us. That was part of the strength that he had, that led us to go on through that. But the pressure he was under. Here's Munro, the most powerful person in the labour movement, and Art's the president of the B.C. Federation of Labour and he's being told, *No, you can't go.* Explicit orders—Art, you can't go. Yet he walks out with me and faces the media with me. Was I surprised that he collapsed physically after that? The strain he was under was so intense."

The next morning, teachers and support staff went on strike at public schools. They were joined by some post-secondary faculty and staff. "It definitely was uplifting," says Scott Parker, "and the feeling was that we had to join the community. It wasn't so much joining the workers movement because the workers movement wasn't visible, but the parents and the community was visible to us. There was the feeling that we have to stand together with these people who are being attacked by things like doing away with the Rentalsman, doing away with Human Rights Commission, and there were other attacks on social justice which teachers felt very strongly about, and definitely felt that we could join this movement and get something done." So, many teachers who went out in the Solidarity strike were more motivated by the Socred budget's attacks on social programs and human rights than they were about their own union issues. "I would argue that the social issue aspect, the moral outrage, the political consider- ations were more pressing for teachers than what you might call the 'economic' because we didn't have a lot in that regard," says Marcy Toms, who was teaching at Vancouver's Ideal Mini School. Likewise, the community surrounding a school often supported its teachers with some parents joining picket lines. "When they were out, some of the parents and some of the neighbours were standing with them," notes Patsy George. "It's not just the union members."

Local politicians in Vancouver—Aldermen Harry Rankin, Bruce Yorke and Bruce Eriksen—joined pickets at Killarney high school. "I cooked some porridge before coming out," Rankin said.[17] Vancouver City Council passed a resolution calling for the withdrawal of all twenty-six bills. "The bills have very little to do with restraint as such," said the resolution, "but involve severe restrictions on human, social and democratic rights."[18] In Nanaimo, long-time activist Marjorie Stewart filled vacuum flasks with soup ("it was cold") and made her way to a BCTF picket line to hand them out. For Marjorie, a school trustee and former teacher, the appalling new bills were a culmination of a half-decade of Socred assaults on education, stripping away locally developed programs and the financial autonomy of school boards. "We were fairly outspoken within the B.C. School Trustees Association against Bennett's raid on public education."

The teachers' Solidarity pickets held. Marcy Toms drove her 1948 red pickup truck all over Vancouver to speak with picketing teachers. "My job was to go from teacher site to teacher site, build their morale, give them coffee and doughnuts, and find out how people were feeling," says Marcy. "'Are you feeling good, are you feeling nervous, what's going on here?' By the time two days had gone by, that feeling of euphoria was still there. The feeling of solidarity was really keeping people going. But the worry was always there—were, as promised, other unions going to come out and join us? People were starting to worry but they were starting to worry for a reason that we had no control over—are we going to be dangling out here on our own? We had no protections, right. We were not under the Labour Code, and if we had been we would have been violating our contract. It was a moral protest. It was a political protest."

At UBC, a Committee of Concerned Academics staged a demonstration "in support of educational and human rights."[19] The committee urged fellow faculty to respect picket lines of UBC support staff. Those who crossed the lines, the committee wrote, "would be doing so, while members of the support staff of this university, many teaching assistants and many students would be making sacrifices for the preservation of fundamental educational rights. They would be doing so while thousands of teachers, no less professional, no less committed to the interests of their students than any UBC faculty member, put their careers on the line for the same cause. They would do so knowing that many thousands of employees in the public sector were withdrawing their services, not in the pursuit of their particular interest, but in the defense of basic principles and social objectives which we all share."

At SFU, AUCE Locals 2 and 6 (Teaching Support Staff Union [TSSU]) sent delegates to early meetings of the Lower Mainland Budget Coalition. Union coordinator Jeanne Williams wrote a letter to campus workers assailing the elimination of the Employment Standards Board. "This is the removal of all seniority rights and protections of a worker's job from harassment for union activities, personal reasons or any other reasons," she wrote. "A worker can be fired for no reason at all, or worse, for an invalid reason such as a supervisor simply dislikes the employee. There is no recourse. . . . Although the TSSU Executive will throw its full efforts into the fight to protect bargaining rights and human rights in this province, that will not be enough. Every employee affected by this legislation must get involved. We will publicize demonstrations and give notice of meetings. The rest is really up to you. YOUR RIGHTS ARE ON THE LINE."[20]

Tom Wayman was teaching at Surrey's Kwantlen College whose faculty, all members of the College Institute Educators' Association (CIEA), struck along with public school teachers. "Our group met, as far as I can remember, every single day and debated whether to stay out or not. There were always people that stood up and said, 'This is illegal, we shouldn't do this, this is anarchy.'. . . And every day there would be a resounding vote to continue." An "under new management" spirit permeated the province. "Everything," says Tom, "was trembling on the edge of just a major transformation."

―――――

The BCGEU strike touched every corner of the province. In the Cariboo, Barkerville workers living in Wells went out on November 1. "You know it's the right thing to do. You see what's happening in the rest of British Columbia," Ken Mather says. "You wonder how long it's going to last because obviously the bills have to be paid but you're willing to sacrifice that to make a statement." The Barkerville strike for Solidarity differed starkly from most around B.C. "The place wasn't open. In fact, there was a great deal of snow by then. So we basically just set up at the parking lot." Ken picketed at the tourist town's entrance, near a museum and a small shelter with picnic tables. "I think isolated is the term," Ken says. It was an hour's drive and a 2,000-foot elevation to reach Quesnel, the town where Wells went to shop. "We would maybe go in once every two weeks . . . but other than that, we were in Wells and it was snowed in."

The radical politics of Susan Safyan's L.A. youth were in sync with the Solidarity uprising she heard about on the news. "We knew that people were calling for a general strike and it was about workers' rights, and it very much was something I identified with as a person who had come from that kind of background. My partner had very left-wing politics. My friends did as well. And we were very supportive of this but we felt very distant from it. That said, it reached Barkerville on the picket line." Susan's Barkerville contract work had ended but she joined the small BCGEU picket line. "I think we brought a joint to smoke. We stood around and talked." Although hardly anyone outside of Wells–Barkerville even knew there was a picket line there, Solidarity had reached this tiny community and locals were pleased to participate. "I can't remember having arguments or anything like that with someone who took the other side's point of view," Ken says. "We were all aware of what was going on, we were all supportive and happy to do our bit, even though it seemed almost ironic that we were doing it at a time when there was basically nobody at Barkerville."

In the Kootenays, Fred Wah was back in Nelson teaching at David Thompson University Centre when the strike began. By now, Fred was a well-published author, with works such as *Lardeau* and *Pictograms from the Interior of B.C.* He established the creative writing program at the university in 1978. Before the Solidarity strike, there had been a well-attended anti-budget rally in Nelson. When David Thompson faculty (members of CIEA) and staff (members of the Pulp and Paper Workers of Canada) went out on November 8, they set up shop in the Student Union Building across the street from the campus, printing leaflets and posters and holding teach-ins. "That's where we spent that couple of weeks," Fred says. "That was our centre where we held some of our impromptu classes, some of our strike action events. We were printing poems on eight-and-a-half-by-fourteen sheets of card stock—the students were writing poems, political poems, and giving them out to people around the street, walking around town. We were working with the students on this."

In Terrace, Mary Robinson was teaching at ET Kenney Primary School when Solidarity walked out. Northern B.C. towns don't have the pretty antique-store finish of Southern Ontario towns. The rough-hewn B.C. towns are less paved and their bars are louder on a Friday night. To Mary, who grew up in North Vancouver and graduated from UBC, the North at first seemed isolated from the world, but she soon learned that there was less social isolation in her new town than in most urban neighbourhoods. Terrace was welcoming and she quickly formed close ties. Mary's friends in Terrace were fellow teachers and her community was pretty much everyone—school staff and students and parents and assorted townsfolk. So when a couple of popular principals were demoted in 1981 by "a very authoritarian and heavy-handed" school board, the town rallied for them and it seemed only natural that the teachers would strike for them. Mary was always on the line and attended all the rallies. Terrace's six-day strike of 1981 was a benchmark in BCTF history. Although the union did not have the legal right to strike, Terrace showed it could be done. "And we supported that, as a provincial executive," Larry Kuehn says.

Two years later, Mary fell in love on a Solidarity picket line. For her, Solidarity at first was something afar on the evening news. "I remember watching a lot of the Solidarity things happening in Vancouver," she says. "There was always good liaison between the South and us, although we might have been a bit more radical." Solidarity soon had a presence in Terrace. That summer, there were meetings and protests against the budget. "We just thought it was all wrong." As the school year began, teachers were "on board and very, very fired up. So the whole feeling up here was ready to go. And we had information coming from the South from the whole Solidarity movement." Mary met her future husband, Kelly, when the Solidarity line needed bolstering at the school where he was picket captain. "My picket captain asked if anybody would volunteer to be on the other line. So I went down to that other school and picketed with them." The days were cold but the rapport between Mary and the picket-line captain made the two-hour shifts fly by. "The first time I ever walked with him, I liked walking with him the best and I always did. He had a lot of interests like I had and both of us agreed with what we were doing a lot, which is good." So, Solidarity introduced Mary to Kelly. "We joke about it. I'm friendly with a lot of people that teach up here and we say, 'Well, one of the good things that came out of it was our getting together and getting married.'"

———

As the Remembrance Day weekend of 1983 approached, things had become so unusual in B.C. that a union, without being consulted, was told it was striking. With the BCGEU and teachers out, Operation Solidarity announced that the CCU's Independent Canadian Transit Union would be part of the Monday, November 14 walkout, without bothering to tell its president Colin Kelly or secretary-treasurer Gerry Krantz. The CCU's Jef Keighley explains: "Operation Solidarity announced the date that the teachers went out, and the expectation of the right-wing labour movement is the teachers, because of their lack of experience, would collapse, and then they could throw up their hands—'What can we do, you know, the teachers aren't holding the line.'" The teachers, however, stood firm. "That wasn't according to plan. So then they announced the date that the bus system would shut down, without ever once calling Colin Kelly or Gerry Krantz to say, 'By the way, we've got this idea that you guys, as part of this protest, should shut down the bus system.'" The CCU demanded a meeting with Art Kube to discuss this intrusion on its independence. "Art was happy to come along. We sat in the basement of the Burnaby Winter Club and had this meeting with Art and we basically said, 'You know what, you were completely disrespectful with respect to how you involved the bus union. You had no contact whatsoever. But even though we vehemently disagree with how you came to that decision and the lack of consultation, we agree with the decision. So we're going to go ahead and shut down the bus system.'" Ferry workers and municipal employees were also set to walk November 14 with some 250,000 union members expected out by the end of the week, and many others expressing solidarity. Unions at the Vancouver International Airport, for instance, said they would shut down the airport if Operation Solidarity called a general strike.[21] The Canadian Brotherhood of Railway, Transport and General Workers called on the BCFED to organize a general strike of "private sector unions to support the collective bargaining rights of all workers in the province."[22]

—◦∿◦—

The *Solidarity Times* newspaper Stan Persky had proposed at Empire Stadium was up and running. "I found a whole bunch of young journalists, some of whom I'd known from *The Ubyssey*, which I'd written for, from the University of British Columbia. And all of them went on to become successful journalists. There was Tom Hawthorn, who eventually became a writer for the *Globe and Mail*; and his wife Debbie Wilson, who became a reporter; and Keith Baldrey, who went into the television reporting business; and a guy named John Mackie, who is a long-time employee at the *Vancouver Sun*. They were all young and energetic people. And then we found a guy who was working in the tax department in Vancouver. His name was Don Larventz. We said to him, 'Gee, we need a business manager for this newspaper,' and he quit his job on the spot and became business manager for *Solidarity Times*. So this organization was suddenly established from zero, from nothing, to a full-fledged weekly newspaper."

They set up shop in an office at 545 West Tenth and the first issue was out just in time for the October 15 Hotel Vancouver rally. "SOLIDARITY COALITION MARCHES TODAY" read the banner above the newspaper's bright red logo. (So, from the start, Operation Solidarity might have felt a little left out of its own newspaper.) *Solidarity Times'* inaugural editorial said, "If we were cynical, we would say: Thanks, Bill Bennett, for sparking the creation of a new weekly newspaper."[23] Of course, none of the witty young journalists on staff were cynical. They were, however, idealist enough to know where they stood in the fight sweeping B.C., making an editorial proclamation that would never have appeared in the established dailies they would go on to work for after *Solidarity Times* was said and done. "This paper supports the Solidarity Coalition and Operation Solidarity," the editorial said. "We think there is a place for this unprecedented popular movement in B.C. society that will last long after the dust settles on Bill Bennett's legislative monstrosity."

When *Solidarity Times* appeared, the underground press of the 1960s and '70s was a recent memory. Its pages reflected those alternative cultural stylings but with an added dosage of unionism—a cross between the 1970 *Georgia Straight* and the 1970 *Pacific Tribune*. It was a mixture that would, for Persky and Co., ultimately mean trouble with the paper's financial benefactors. Issue No. 1 had Dave Alvin, of the rock band the Blasters, opining on the synergy between

Black Flag and Elvis Presley. "Black Flag played with the same energy that Chuck Berry did in 1956, or Elvis Presley did."[24] Turn the page and you're face-to-face with a large ad headlined, "Building Trades United Against Repressive Legislation." The back cover had locals lauding the notion of a *Solidarity Times*, including activist Jim Green ("our own paper") and writer Terri Wershler ("It's time we had a good weekly magazine").[25]

Stan says the BCFED's Joy Langan was assigned "to keep an eye on us." (She later became an NDP Member of Parliament.) "As a staff we met and we decided what would go in the paper that week," says Stan. "Then my main job was to be the liaison person with the BCFED, and generally what we found was that the BCFED was just as bad as any bourgeois newspaper organization. They wanted to micro-manage. They assumed if you were running a paper for the BCFED, you were doing what the BCFED told you to do in terms of that news-paper. I remember taking Keith Baldrey to a meeting with the BCFED people at the BCFED building and Joy Langan was there and she was complaining about something or other, and I remember very clearly at one point she said, 'Remember who writes your cheques.'"

By 1983, David Lester was a veteran layout artist—from alterna-tive newspapers to punk posters—asked to join the *Solidarity Times* staff. "They said we'd like you to do it because they had seen my work at *Georgia Straight* and *Open Road*," he says. "I was brought in to de-sign, do mock-ups of the pages, and I just went to College Printers and we worked there until it was done." David recalls a BCFED con-cern about the newspaper's cultural content. "One criticism of the paper was, oh, why are you writing about movies, like there's a review of *Christine* there. It's not about the labour movement enough. It's too cultural. There's a cartoon in there or whatever. We had [cartoonist] David Boswell. The criticisms were it wasn't enough of an organ, I guess, of a mouthpiece of the movement or the labour movement." Adds Persky: "There was a huge cultural gap between the trade union movement, especially people like Jack Munro, and the community movement. That was an enormous gap that we were all aware of."

With the BCTF and BCGEU out and talk of a general strike every-where, Stan dispatched one of the paper's young reporters to Victoria to get feedback from NDP MLAs on the matter. "And they came back with a story in which the NDP MLAs more or less pronounced themselves horrified by the idea of a general strike. So that was the story that we had pasted down onto the newspaper. This was in the days when we glued copy to the sheets that we're working on." When BCFED staffer Gerry Scott saw this pasted-down story, the dif-ferences between the labour federation and *Solidarity Times* came to a head. "Gerry Scott arrived from the BCFED and he was shocked to find that the NDP MLAs—the ones we had interviewed—had announced they were against the general strike," Stan says. "He demanded that the story be pulled, and there was a huge, long, into-the-night kind of thing and the story was pulled. BCFED pulled it. And, of course, it was one of those stories where it wouldn't have mattered if it had come out. It would have just been more part of the discussion. But Gerry Scott had decided on behalf of the BCFED that this was somehow politically forbidden to print this. So there was a direct interference. . . . The staff was much more idealistic than I was and they were just horrified that anything like this could hap-pen in the real world, that the labour movement could pull a legiti-mate piece of journalistic news from the newspaper on the grounds that it'd be politically bad for them. The staff was unhappy, to put it mildly."

—❦—

The teachers, much to the surprise of some in the BCFED leadership, held strong as they waited for the rest of the labour movement to join them. Meanwhile, the Solidarity Coalition and left unions like CUPW, Fish and CAIMAW were preparing for the general strike. CAIMAW organizers travelled the province building strike support. "We had a presence all around and we were holding Solidarity meet-ings in our various locals," says CAIMAW's Jess Succamore, "and I would go to the meeting or somebody else was there. Everybody was right on side. There was no reluctance at all wherever we went. It was a really good feeling. There seemed to be a real spirit of . . . solidarity." By late October, resolutions in support of a general strike were passed by Solidarity Coalitions in Prince George, Grand Forks, Prince Rupert and Port Alberni—"resolved that the Alberni coalition endorse a General Strike and that such a strike be carried on until the entire legislative package has been withdrawn, or the present Social Credit government has resigned."[26]

CHAPTER 10

Obsolete Unionism:
The Left-Wing Alternative

WITH THE BCTF AND BCGEU on strike and more unions poised to join them, the BCFED leadership turned squeamish and dispatched Jack Munro to Bill Bennett's Kelowna home. "I guess, at the end of the day, Jack Munro took the hit because they felt he was the only leader who could probably survive it," Diane Wood says. "I mean, he got sent. If Arthur had been well, I guess Arthur would have been there." Adds Jess Succamore: "Kube was very sick. I think he was just run down. I don't fault him. He wasn't weak. But what happened? The rats took over the institution kind of thing. . . . Munro and them, kind of the right-wing group in there, they were terrified about where it was going. Remember, we were on the bloody verge of a real general strike."

To those on Solidarity's left flank, Munro was the personification of the obsolete unionists' contempt for the Solidarity Coalition. "So, there was a real chance for that [general strike] to happen," Stan Persky says. "In the end, it really was what I guess in Marxist vocabulary is known as trade-union consciousness that stopped the whole thing in its tracks. And that was most represented by Jack Munro who—when Kube became ill or had a nervous breakdown or whatever it was—simply stepped in. And Jack Munro hated everything about the Solidarity Coalition. He just saw it all as, oh, crazy women, faggots, druggies, longhairs. He saw all of that as just being an unbelievable kind of portrait of social life that he hated. And so he really represented the opposition to any possibility of a general strike."

So, before the 25,000 bus drivers could strike on Monday, Munro headed to Kelowna on Sunday. Jack met Bill and called Art Kube from the premier's home. Informed that the government would withdraw only one of the twenty-six bills (anti-union Bill 2) and add exemptions to one other (anti-union Bill 3), Kube told Munro to "get the hell out of there." Munro said, "No, I'm not going to do it."[1] Munro and Bennett reached a quick agreement, settling BCGEU's contract but offering little else to most Solidarity members. Then they stepped out on to the premier's patio to announce their Kelowna Accord. "I was completely gobsmacked," says Marcy Toms, who was on the BCTF's Status of Women Provincial Committee. "Confused, angry, trying to figure out what had happened, and also thinking that a great opportunity had been kiboshed. I was inclined to blame what I knew as the labour establishment and a few days later particularly, but not only, Jack Munro." Adds teacher Scott Parker: "Everybody knew right away we had lost. It's not that we didn't make any gains, but what we expected to get out of all this activity disappeared so quickly. You felt like the province had risen for social justice and all of a sudden we were thrown a couple of crumbs and that was enough." *Vancouver Sun* columnist Marjorie Nichols concluded: "Mr. Munro and Mr. Bennett decided that not only do they actually like each other, they have few fundamental differences. The IWA leader will deny it, if you ask him. So will the premier."[2]

Jef Keighley believes there would have been an entirely different outcome had Kube been healthy. "I mean, if Art hadn't been burning the candle at both ends and hadn't had a physical breakdown. He was simply never sleeping, and when he was, his brain was going a mile a minute. 'What are we doing next? How to do this? How do we get around that?' [With a healthy Kube] we would have been the very first jurisdiction in North America to have toppled a democratically elected government through the process of a general strike that would have produced another general election, and it would have returned the NDP to power." How did the NDP feel about this possibility? "They were just scared shitless. They were absolutely scared shitless."

When I spoke with Kube in the late 1980s for a magazine article on Jack Munro, he said he'd brought up the idea of a France 1968-style general strike—when unions occupied workplaces and provided free services—but couldn't find traction for it in the BCFED's inner sanctum. "A syndicalist approach to a strike doesn't hurt the public," he said. "We pulled one off at Tranquille in Kamloops and it went great. We ran Tranquille and basically sent the supervisors and management people home. The buses and ferries could have been run without charging the public and a syndicalist approach to the teachers' strike would have been wonderful."[3] This sounded good in retrospect, but during the course of the Solidarity months Kube gave mixed signals on the growing support for a general strike. ("I just hope I never have to call upon that support," he said.[4]) So, it's unclear whether Kube could have, or would have, changed the conciliatory trajectory of the BCFED leadership.

Kim Zander remains unconvinced that Solidarity's end would have been any better had Kube been available. "I think by that point Kube's leadership would have been largely figurehead when it came to who the actual power was." It is doubtable that the anti–general strike group heading the BCFED would have trusted Kube, had he been healthy, to go to Kelowna to negotiate with Bennett. They wanted someone they could count on to shut Solidarity down. "I think there was a group in the BCFED leadership who, in the end, had their own unity about where things were going to go," Kim says. "I don't think Kube or any one person could have changed that."

Why wasn't there a vote among the varied Solidarity components, or even its trade unions, to accept or reject the Kelowna Accord? Tom Wayman figures the Munro bloc at the BCFED was determined to prevent a rank-and-file vote on the Accord because "they would have lost the vote. . . . But instead of that, the word just came down from the B.C. Federation, you know, shut it down. And people were so unused to democracy in practice that the whole thing shut down, and yeah, it was a real defeat. But I think the lesson is not to let that kind of thing happen again." Operation Solidarity's inaction in the movement's final days went well beyond not arranging a vote to accept or reject the Accord. "During the days we were on strike there weren't meetings of that group," Larry Kuehn says. "There were just meetings of the BCFED and that's where those decisions were made."

Inside the Broadway office of the Solidarity Coalition, Patsy George, Renate Shearer and others were stunned when word of the Accord came down from Kelowna. "We were all in tears," Patsy says. "It was a horrible betrayal." Having worked tirelessly for months to build a mass social movement, these core coalition organizers weren't even told that Munro was being dispatched to Kelowna. "None of us had any idea what is going on," Patsy says. "This decision was made to meet with the premier's people, came about by two or three people in BCFED and Operation Solidarity. Renate didn't know. She wasn't informed. All we knew was that there was this big meeting happening."

Upon finally learning about the Kelowna meeting, some at the Solidarity Coalition office tried to be positive. "Everything was just coming along and we thought the government got frightened, they were going to give in to us," says Patsy, "but they didn't. We gave in to them. . . . The fact that they sent Munro was in itself such a stab in the back because the man didn't believe in the Solidarity Coalition. He thought we were a bunch of communists. I don't think he really, truly believed in human rights. I tell you, I have no problem saying that I hated the man. He had no respect for us. He thought we were just people who didn't have nothing else to do. Sold out. Betrayed. We had no idea that would happen because we were all ready for the general strike."

—⁓—

In 1970, socialist feminist Shulamith Firestone's seminal book *The Dialectic of Sex* challenged Marx and Engels's strict emphasis on economics and class. "The doctrine of historical materialism, much as it was a brilliant advance over previous historical analysis, was not the complete answer, as later events bore out. For though Marx and Engels grounded their theory in reality, it was only a *partial* reality," Firestone wrote. "It would be a mistake to attempt to explain the oppression of women according to this strictly economic interpretation. The class analysis is a beautiful piece of work, but limited: although correct in a linear sense it does not go deep enough. There is a whole sexual substratum of the historical dialectic that Engels at times dimly perceives, but because he can see sexuality only through an economic filter, reducing everything to that, he is unable to evaluate in its own right."[5]

Some in the New Left believed working-class consciousness of the twentieth century had become embedded in values and aspirations of middle-class culture. Many of these activists realized that workers' control of their workplace would ultimately have to be a part of a fundamental social change, but felt their own organizational time was better spent mobilizing sectors of the population—marginalized races, women, alternative cultures—more open to their radical ideas. So, the counter-politics of the late 1960s and early '70s marked the beginning of what would later be called "identity politics." In those days, we called it liberation movement politics. There was women's liberation and black liberation, gay liberation and youth liberation. Organizing around one's identity wasn't entirely new. There had been suffragettes and anti-racist organizations and left-wing groups organized along ethnic lines. What was different in the 1960s and '70s was that some New Left groups felt that their particular community had replaced the working class as the "motive force" for systemic change, and that race and gender were no less key than workers and unions. The early leftists of the nineteenth century were correct in their assertion that you cannot create socialism without collectivizing—*socializing*—workplace production, without understanding class. What they did not know then, but was equally apparent by 1983, is that you also cannot create socialism without smashing racism and sexism.

Besides, racial minorities, women and counterculturists had jobs, too, so perhaps by organizing around their interests you were, in a roundabout way, organizing workers. Radicalization within a union was at times the result of the new social movements. Larry Kuehn notes that when New Leftists became teachers, programs against racism and sexism were established in schools. By 1983, every local in the BCTF had formed a Status of Women Committee. "Those grew out of the '60s activists, particularly in the women's movement. The Status of Women Committee was key to the union's changes in the '70s. There were a bunch of women that were key to that change, and it was the style of organizing that they brought to the organization that really changed so many elements of it. That style of organizing that really grew out of the feminist movement was the core of the change in the organization."

The economistic business unions and some doctrinaire leftists were so wedded to their romantic nineteenth-century idea of "the workers" that it was virtually impossible for them to see the merit of newer social movements whose focus was other than class. Anarchoecologist Murray Bookchin noted the problems in focusing on workers and unions to the exclusion of everything else. "To infect the new revolutionary movement of our time with 'workeritis' is reactionary to the core," he wrote.[6] "There can be no social revolution without winning the workers, hence they must have our active solidarity in every struggle they wage against exploitation. We fight against social crimes wherever they appear—and industrial exploitation is a profound social crime. But so are racism, the denial of the right to self-determination, imperialism and poverty profound social crimes—and for that matter so are pollution, rampant urbanization, the malignant socialization of the young, and sexual repression."[7] While the Marxist focus was on *class*, anarchists such as Bookchin saw an even broader problem: *domination*. This included class conflict, but also the domination of a woman by her husband or a black youth by a cop, and on and on.

The 1879 Socialist Congress of France declared equality of the sexes. "But," noted Simone de Beauvoir, "feminism was a secondary interest since women's emancipation was seen as depending upon the liberation of the workers in general."[8] The tensions around the Old Left's focus on class to the subordination of everything else didn't begin with Solidarity. Kim Zander, for instance, notes her mother's departure from the CP: "Part of the reason was the CP wasn't very damn good on women's issues—surprise on that one. There's not many political parties that are good on women's issues." This state of affairs would be challenged by the emergence of feminism in the 1960s and '70s. "When I was becoming more aware of what was going on in the world in the '70s, the women's movement was really blossoming."

The fixation on "the workers" wasn't confined to left groups founded pre-1960s. Some of Gary Cristall's fellow members of the newly formed Revolutionary Workers League (RWL) weren't pleased when he was named director of the Vancouver Folk Music Festival. Gary had grown up with folk music—Paul Robeson, Woody Guthrie, the Travellers. "The first thing I did culturally, I helped organize the first Be-In in Toronto in '67. We paid Leonard Cohen $500. We thought it was a lot of money." When he was asked to help found a folk festival that would become an iconic event in Vancouver, there was disagreement in the RWL about his new job. "What I did with the folk festival didn't have anything to do with the organization. In fact, they wished I wasn't doing the festival." Gary believed in working-class organizing as much as anyone in the group but, to the consternation of some, he also saw value in other kinds of organizing. "They wanted to do working-class organizing and they thought that what I was doing was petit-bourgeois indulgence, you know, doing this stuff in the arts. I should get a job in a factory and organize the working class. There was no way I was going to do that. I thought I had an opportunity, for a series of reasons, to be able to do something in the field of culture that could actually have some political content."

—◦/◦/◦—

The division between Operation Solidarity's unions and the Solidarity Coalition's social movements wasn't the only split within Solidarity. Within the Solidarity Coalition, there were differences between radicals who wanted transformative change and reformers (including religious and small-business groups) who only wanted to oppose specific legislation. While there were obsolete unionists and unimaginative leftists who couldn't fathom the new social movements, there were also some in those newer movements without an understanding of class. The union movement was also divided. Alongside the business unions that dominated the BCFED, there was an assortment of openly left unions, including the CCU affiliates, Fish, CUPW, Carpenters' Union, SORWUC and AUCE. The core organizers of these unions came primarily from three backgrounds—radical expats (such as CAIMAW's Jess Succamore and the farmworkers' Raj Chouhan), the CP (such as Fish's George Hewison and the carpenters' Bill Zander) and former New Leftists (such as the BCTF's Larry Kuehn and SORWUC and AUCE's Jackie Ainsworth). These militant unions, which could be counted on in a general strike scenario, constituted maybe 20% of the B.C. labour movement. "A lot of the union leadership of that time were guys that had come from Britain and they were quite familiar with that concept that the unions can be at the forefront of building a better community, building a better society," Tom Wayman says. "There were enough people around with that view. Plus, for all its faults, the Communist Party also had a vision, at least on paper, of social change unionism—that the unions can be a way of organizing society since [the job is] the point of which the community is reproduced every day, so if you make changes there, you're making changes throughout the whole fabric of society." Jess Succamore likes to distinguish between a union's brass and its rank-and-file. "It always seemed to me that a lot of people in the union movement were scared of their members. And I was just the opposite, no matter what it was. There was a lot of good guys in the IWA, too, that weren't necessarily in the top leadership, you know." There were unions outside Jess's CCU that he admired. "Fish. I always think of them more as a CCU union than a Fed union. They always took good positions. Same with CUPW." Jess also had a close working relationship with the feminist union SORWUC.

Jess's father, Fred, was a union steward at the Euxton munitions factory in Chorley, England, and would, on occasion, take Jess along when he collected the members' dues. "'Son, the working man has very few rights. One is to gripe. Don't take that away from him.' My dad was a pretty soft-spoken fellow but pretty resolute as far as his politics went." From his mother, Elizabeth, Jess learned something else about life, and death, on the shop floor. During the war, she inspected propellers at a de Havilland aircraft plant. Although his mother never smoked, she came into contact with carcinogens at the plant and died of cancer as the war ended. "She died direct as a result of that. Just turned forty."

After arriving in Canada in 1952, Jess worked a variety of union jobs (machinist, steelworker) before taking up with the Lenkurt Electric Plant in Burnaby. In 1966, 257 members of the plant's International Brotherhood of Electrical Workers (IBEW) walked out when management tried to force them to work overtime. They stayed out and other B.C. unions backed them despite little support from the IBEW's American-based leadership and a court injunction against picketing. The pickets continued and there were jailings. Jess became increasingly involved as the strike continued. "It changed my life completely. . . . There was a whole bunch of single-parent mothers there and to see the way they were mistreated, browbeaten. I instinctively felt it was so wrong. And I wasn't going to let that go."

———

Allied against the new social movements and the left unions were the obsolete unionists hell-bent on preventing a general strike. They operated in a time-warped parallel universe where certain recent phenomena had never happened—feminism, the Gay Liberation Front, Dylan, the Clash, Black Power or ecology. By 1983, most unions of the BCFED were business unions narrowly focused on their next contract, with organizational hierarchies that resembled a big-business boardroom. They fought to keep left-wing ideas out of their unions, their "White Blocs" in sync with the American anti-Communist witch hunts in the 1950s. Now, the idea of a Solidarity Coalition filled with leftists and genders of every variety was anathema to them. "They were completely threatened by it," Sara Diamond says.

Still, their unions were the make-or-break force within the B.C. Federation of Labour. There had been hints in the days leading up to November 13 that BCFED leadership was preparing to capitulate. On November 8, private-sector union leaders met to deliberate how to quell the uprising. Afterward, Art Gruntman, of the Operation Solidarity executive, said:

> We're not going to say you [Socreds] have to do precisely this on human rights or tenants' rights. That would be dumb. . . . We want the government to resolve the labour dispute, which means get the people back to work. Then talk about those other issues, the human rights, the renters, the old people that have been hurt, the young people, the child-abuse centres.[9]

Gruntman wasn't the only Fed leader pushing for Solidarity's social issues to be set aside. "We [unions] have many crucial bargaining issues of our own to resolve," Jack Munro said.[10] He called for a quick end to the escalating Solidarity-Socred clash because it was creating an impression outside B.C. that investing in the province is "like investing in a powder keg." On the tenth and eleventh of November, the upper hierarchy of the B.C. Federation of Labour held discussions with the Socred government, and Munro flew to Kelowna on the thirteenth with Bill Bennett's deputy minister Norman Spector. So, the shape of the Accord was determined before Munro met with Bennett.[11] Following the Fed leaders' dismissive comments about social issues, Solidarity Coalition members called for an emergency meeting of its Steering Committee. The BCGEU's Jack Adams expressed the high regard he had for Solidarity Coalition input: "This is a very serious business. Operation Solidarity, not the Solidarity Coalition, made the decision to start the escalating strikes. Operation Solidarity, not the Solidarity Coalition, will decide to stop it."[12] Adams added: "We're not going to sell out the Coalition. They don't need to be worried about that." Meanwhile, the BCGEU continued to negotiate with the government and Art Kube was looking increasingly fatigued. On November 8, after addressing a Solidarity Coalition meeting in New Westminster, Kube said he hadn't slept for three days.[13]

—⌁⌁⌁—

For Gary Cristall, the right-wing social-democratic blowback within the BCFED and NDP began with the success of the Hotel Vancouver march. "Things began to move in a way inexorably toward a confrontation. That's when the bureaucracy tried to figure out how to stop it. They said, 'Well, the teachers will go first. We're going to take the weakest group of workers who have never gone on a picket line and we're going to have them lead.' And they assumed that the teachers would fold, that people would come out and yell at the teachers— 'Get back to work. What are my kids going to do?'—that their kids were at home, they were missing work, they didn't have money. And it was absolutely *au contraire*." Gary and friends joined a picket line to help stiffen teachers' resolve. "I was at some school on the West

Side in a well-to-do neighbourhood because we figured that the teachers were going to get shit and abuse out there, so we might have had some hard-core commies walking the line with them." Instead, out of the houses came parents bearing cookies and hot chocolate. "They're coming up to us and saying, 'We baked these this morning for you, we support what you're doing, we're with you.' If you're a commie, this is like some kind of fantasy come true. All these well-to-do parents in areas that have voted Socred forever are making hot chocolate and cookies. This happened everywhere. The teachers were out, and the teachers stayed out." He suggests that rank-and-file members of other unions saw the teachers' determination and said: "'When are we going out.' And that's when they ended it. That's when Munro made the deal."

If there was any doubt about Munro's opinion of the Solidarity Coalition, he made his views clear in an interview shortly after the Kelowna finale. "The Bennett government created the climate to put together a whole raft of groups of people who never, ever really had the ability to get together before," Munro said.[14] "These groups of people all of a sudden find this fantastic power where people are talking about strikes in the public sector and general strikes in the private sector and all this. Shit, they thought, this is fuckin' great. The same people who had never ever in their goddamned life . . . ever thought that they would sit down at an executive board and make these kinds of decisions. Like, where the hell would you ever get enough people to attend the Rural Lesbians' Association fuckin' meeting . . . sitting next to the Gay Alliance, sitting next to the Urban fuckin' Lesbians, and all this horseshit that goes on in this fuckin' world these days, making a decision to shut the province down. It was great. Trade unionists . . . we were the turkeys in the goddamned thing. Chicken-shit trade unionists. You could feel that we were the goddamned moderates, for Christ's sake. I should have been for all these causes, a lot of causes that I don't goddamned agree with. I should have been asking our people, who maybe were going into a strike situation of our own, to come off the job. Well, that isn't the way the real world works." This was sent to Kelowna to represent the interests of the Solidarity Coalition.

Munro would often be at loggerheads with environmental activists, too. As for David Suzuki, Munro told me: "B.C. can't be preserved as one fantastic park. I think he's [Suzuki] a frustrated scientist who should go back to the goddamn lab to research the sex life of bees or something. Because Lyell Island is there and a couple of goddamn totem poles are there that fell down, it doesn't mean we should shaft our economy." During the Solidarity months, Jack Munro was fond of telling anti-budget crowds that he wasn't about to call Bennett a fascist, but "if you walk like a duck and you quack like a duck, you're probably a duck." Munro actually did walk like a duck—not Donald or Daffy, but a humongous, lumbering Baby Huey–like duck. "He would stand over you," says Craig Patterson, who spent considerable time around the IWA leader. "He used the trick that some other tall men do of standing as close to you as possible and bearing down on you." (In 1984, when IWA members crossed other forestry unions' picket lines, buttons circulated reading, "If you walk like a scab and you quack like a scab, you're probably a scab.") Having lived and worked in the Kootenays for eons, Tom Wayman is well aware of the union history of Jack Munro, who began his climb in Nelson. "He was the right-wing of the woodworkers, and they had driven out the kind of Communist folks who had started that union and built it up." Joining the union shortly after an internal war between the union's white and red blocs, Munro was allied with the remnants of the White Bloc. "Because it was an international union, they could use all that draconian legislation in the States about you have to get Communists out of the union."

Larry Kuehn didn't have the bombast of Munro, and he certainly didn't have his John Wayne stature, but in his softer, smarter, good-teacher way, he's tougher than the IWA leader. He instinctively knows wrong from right and has an unflinching resolve to serve his membership and fight the good fight. Some labour brass saw Larry's members as sacrificial lambs, but they turned out to be among the heroes of this story. "Once the strike started, Munro was determined to end it," Larry says. "Besides thinking that this was entirely inappropriate to use the strike for all these social issues, his members were in position to go on strike. He was desperately trying to keep them off of striking because they were involved in negotiations at the time and had strike votes. They could have legally been out on strike and joined us without it being any limitation, but he was desperate to stop that for these two reasons: he didn't believe in the social issues and he certainly didn't believe that you use labour power on behalf of social issues." Larry would learn that Munro's behavior in Kelowna wasn't so different from the way he dealt with employers in the forestry industry. "As he did about Solidarity, he would stand up and make militant statements, but really behind the scenes he was doing something very different. And that was not just Solidarity. That's the way he was as a labour leader in terms of his own dealings, as you saw when he finished with the IWA and became a lobbyist for the forestry industry."

—⁓—

"It was simply a political betrayal," Stan Persky says. "Whatever had been airily promised at various public meetings and rallies and things like that had been completely betrayed, and they had lost their nerve. As soon as it was clear that Jack Munro was going up there to negotiate with Bill Bennett, we knew it was over. This is not going to be a political settlement at all. This is going to be capitulation, and it was."

Women Against the Budget activists were blindsided, too, by the anti-climactic Kelowna finale. "At the time that we heard Jack Munro was going to meet with the premier, there was a lot of concern," says Sara Diamond. "And then we found out through the news, I think, that basically an agreement had been reached—the Kelowna Accord—and it was really shocking. People were really angry. But it was done. And it was dismantled fast, like the labour movement pulled all the apparatus away and you couldn't keep the Solidarity movement going. Everybody was very upset, very depressed, very angry."

Says WAB's Nora Randall: "The thing is, once we knew that he had gone up there we knew the whole thing was over. That is not a collective action. People with political awareness in the Women Against the Budget just knew it was curtains. Art Kube was a union guy who we had some good will toward. But Jack Munro!" So, Nora knew the Munro–Bennett meeting would come to no good. "We knew that. We just knew that. I mean, you take a group of women and you tell them that two guys are going to work out their problems, you know that they know it's not happening." Having been active inside the BCFED as well as the women's movement, Gail Meredith knew all about business unions. "I don't see how it could have gone a different way, given the way it was going." Still, she was disgusted. "They sold out. For me, it was not a real surprise. I knew that he [Munro] would do it. But it was a real surprise for [many other] women's movement people because they really felt that they had a promise that nobody was going to sell out anything . . . and that was not the case."

While Bennett met with Munro in Kelowna, the Solidarity Coalition's Steering Committee met and called on Operation Solidarity to "recognize that the existence of the current set of negotiations is an achievement for the Coalition as a whole . . . the negotiating process include representatives from the provincial Coalition whose primary concerns are the issues of social policy."[15] The following day, with the Accord its new reality, the Solidarity Coalition met, then issued this news release:

> A large crowd of about 450 delegates, representing the broad-based Lower Mainland Solidarity Coalition, jammed into the Fisherman's Hall tonight to discuss the weekend agreement reached by the provincial government and Jack Munro of Operation Solidarity. . . . We acknowledge such trade union gains as were won in the agreement between Operation Solidarity and the provincial government; however, that agreement is not a settlement of our issues, namely the withdrawal or repeal of all offensive legislation and full restoration of social services. We express our strong disagreement with the absence of full consultation in the recent negotiating and discussions, with the Provincial Steering Committee.[16]

It was an emotional meeting, with the Solidarity crowd unleashing their pent-up anger at the Socreds and the BCFED leadership and their Kelowna Accord. On stage, Art Kube was in tears. "I don't think I sold out the Coalition," he said.[17] Fed secretary-treasurer Mike Kramer, a Munro ally, showed up about midnight. Minutes of the meeting say: "He [Kramer] reported on the 'deal' and reported that Jack Munro recommended to OpSol after the meeting with the Premier that we should call a truce and that the strike is over. . . . A motion was passed that the steering committee of the Solidarity Coalition meet with Operation Solidarity steering committee as soon as possible."[18]

Jess Succamore had gotten to know Munro because CAIMAW organizer Cathy Walker was friendly with his lawyer wife Connie Munro. After the Accord, Jess was interviewed by the *Vancouver Sun*. "I said words to the effect that Jack should divorce himself from the labour movement or else we should divorce him from us. Connie called me the next morning to say, 'Oh, you got misquoted in the *Sun*. You better go and look at that and get them to print a retraction.'" Jess went out to pick up a copy of the paper, then phoned Connie Munro back. "I said, 'Connie, that's what I said.' It was the worst betrayal I've ever seen." Craig Patterson knew Jack Munro, too, having shared a law office with Connie Munro. "The story I heard was that she didn't know that Jack had gone to Kelowna, and when she found out that he was in Kelowna from his secretary, she shrieked apparently over the phone, 'What the fuck is he doing?'"

Most Jack Munro critics are well aware that he was symptomatic of a strain of conservatism within the BCFED executive, and that in Kelowna he was doing the bidding of more than just himself or the IWA. Later, Munro criticized Operation Solidarity strategy committee members "who didn't have the guts to stand up and say: 'I was part of a unanimous decision.'"[19] Munro told me in a 1989 interview that he was acting on a decision by officers of the BCFED when he made the Kelowna deal. "Where we were leading was a disastrous course," he said.[20] "A general strike meant we were going to try to overthrow the government." Without support from the "business union" elements of the labour movement Munro would not have been able to conclude the Accord with Bennett. Kube added: "Munro was just a messenger in that thing."[21] CUPW's Marion Pollack concurs: "I think that Munro was acting on behalf of a number of people. It wasn't just him." Says Kim Zander: "I think he was a right-wing social democrat who also considered himself a labour demagogue and would do whatever the hell he wanted. Jack Munro could be a force to be reckoned with. He was bold when he wanted to be and he had an ego a mile high. What better person to do your bidding? I don't think he did it on his own. I think he did the bidding of a group of people who said, 'Go in there and do this for us. Do the dirty work.' And Jack was an asshole enough to do it. He was self-righteous and had a big enough ego to say, 'Oh yeah, I'll go do it.' We knew right away that it was a slow-mo train wreck. We knew there was absolutely one and only one reason that Jack Munro was there. And that was to stop the escalation of a general strike at all costs. Nobody thought that he was going to go there shaking his fist and was going to get anywhere with Bennett. Nobody did. We knew then that the labour movement was caving. Nobody was surprised at what happened. I was so disgusted, because I had seen the fear, the desire for control and power of the right-wing social democrats. Spineless all along."

Jean Swanson says the hesitation of "the major unions" had been visible at Solidarity Coalition meetings, although only a handful of labour representatives attended. "I don't know if they would have been able to get their members to go out. I don't know if they tried, you know. . . . There may be four or five union reps [at the meetings], and everybody else, community folks, would be wanting a general strike. And the union folks would all be saying, 'We have to have our members agree to this because they're the ones who aren't going to have the wages, and you guys, you came to this because of being activists—because of wanting women's rights, because of wanting gay rights, because of wanting to end poverty, things like this—but people join the union because they need a job. They don't join a union because they're political.' Not all of them wanted their members to go on strike. Like, I don't think Jack Munro did." Jean was a paid union staffer but identified more with the coalition's community groups. "That's where my heart was. I had only been at HEU for a year or so."

Craig Patterson agrees that Munro wasn't a solo act at the BCFED. "There was Kramer," says Craig, recalling the Fed's Mike Kramer attending an early public meeting against the budget. "Kramer conducted himself like he was a security guard at a rock concert at the meeting. He stood prominently against a wall, apart from everyone else. He didn't sit down. He stood up against the wall and he glowered at everyone at the meeting. That was Kramer." When Kube came down with whatever he came down with in early November, Kramer was named temporary acting chair of Operation Solidarity, a position he held when Munro was dispatched to Kelowna. "I was thoroughly discouraged by the action of the labour movement leadership," says Craig. "I was very upset. Very upset. It confirmed in me that I should not get any closer to them than necessary, and that probably opposition to them was more progressive than quiet support for them. That was the angry side of it. Accord? It was a sellout, fair and simple. Accord is a big word. It sounds like the end of the First World War in Versailles or something. And you know it was nothing near that. Pitiful capitulation is the only two words really that could sum it up. Pitiful capitulation."

———

The reaction to Kelowna was province-wide outrage. When the strikes began in early November, Nettie Wild and Headlines Theatre were touring the B.C. Interior with *Under the Gun: A Disarming Review*, an agitprop exposé production about Canada's role in the arms race. "We're out doing our play. It's being sponsored by various progressive groups throughout British Columbia and, in particular, teachers. As they started to go out, we were on tour. We would come into a town and the venue where we were supposed be doing our play, which would be in a school gymnasium, would have a picket line around it.

So the progressive teachers would then find a place for us to play the piece not in school. We'd be in the church, or we'd be in whatever. It was an extremely exciting and confusing and high-stakes time in a way that I'd never, ever, ever experienced in this province before." Nettie and her Headlines castmates had a close-up view of the divisions occurring throughout the province. "The teachers had struck and we were staying at the teachers' houses and they were talking about teachers who had not struck, that the split between them was really, really bitter and that they didn't know how they'd ever go back to work side by side again. What was happening in my house was happening in these houses, only they were teachers' houses."

The night Munro met Bennett in Kelowna, Headlines Theatre was performing in Terrace, where teachers that had been so bold in 1981 were doing it again in 1983. As was customary, after the performance they went back to a teacher's house where they were staying and watched the news. "Every night, that's what you did. You watched the news because there was a lot of shit going down all over the province and we're with these teachers." That night—November 13, 1983—was different. "We were with teachers who were looking at this, and this was not just a news item. They had been totally sold down the river. I'll never forget that moment. People were in tears and beyond tears. So much had been lost. . . . A sense of right and wrong." Terrace teachers who had signalled a new BCTF militancy two years earlier when they staged an illegal strike were now distraught at the news from Kelowna. "It was stunning. And it was really interesting for me because that's a really, really strong sense memory of Solidarity for me. And how I lived that particular moment. I'm sure lots of people have talked about that moment and how they perceived it, but it was extraordinary."

Some union leaders actually found cause for celebration that night. The BCGEU's Diane Wood was in negotiations with the provincial government at the Labour Relations Board office when she learned of the Accord. "Our president Norm Richards, who was at the negotiations with us, I think came into the room and said, 'Just so you know, there's something that's going to happen pretty soon.'" Diane was so immersed in negotiations that she didn't know Munro was in Kelowna. "We just knew that something was happening and of course there's all kinds of speculation. And then we got the word that there had been this Accord and it was like, woah, what's that about?" While the Solidarity Coalition's social issues and BCTF demands were not addressed by this Accord, the BCGEU did have its contract resolved, which was enough to satisfy some in the union. Later that evening, Cliff Andstein, the BCGEU's chief negotiator throughout the Solidarity months, went to the union's Burnaby headquarters and found a good deal of its leadership and staff merrily drinking "cheap bubbly" in a party atmosphere. Andstein took a quick look at the celebration, turned, and walked out. "I was upset and really angry at what I saw," he would say decades later.[22] "It was a lousy deal." Some long-time union activists simply don't have a bigger dream, so it was impossible for them to see the Solidarity drama as a failure. To them, it was just another contract negotiation. The BCGEU had its share of the business-union kind who were happy with the Accord, but the union's best, Solidarity partisans like John Shields, understood that solidarity means more than one union and that so many put themselves on the line and on November 13 got nothing. "It was a day of mourning," Shields said of the Accord, "for me certainly, and for the other public-sector unions who felt that they'd been betrayed. There's no other way of saying that."[23]

Larry Kuehn stopped by the BCGEU party, too. "I was out at the GEU where they were celebrating." Like Andstein, he didn't feel much like partying. Although the teachers were out on strike, Larry wasn't included in anything to do with the talks between Munro and Bennett to settle the strike. That's how fundamentally undemocratic this Accord was. "For most of it, I wasn't really aware what was going on in Kelowna, but it was I guess about the time of the [Kelowna] press conference that Art Kube actually called me and said, 'I'm sorry, you know, I'm sorry that we haven't gotten anything for you.' I didn't even realize how bad it was until the next day on *The Jack Webster*

Show, where it became clear how much contempt Munro had for us. The thing that supposedly he had gotten for education wasn't even for public schools—it was for our money to go into apprenticeship programs in the forestry industry. I had no idea. I was never told. I was absolutely never told."

The day after the Kelowna Accord, the Solidarity Coalition's environmental rep Cliff Stainsby woke up in Queen Charlotte City, an island community just off the West Coast. He was scheduled to speak at a town hall Solidarity rally. "I got up in the morning, I went in the afternoon to the rally and I got hell. What had happened was the Kelowna Accord, and I didn't know it and they did." There was visceral anger waiting for him at the hall. By this time, Cliff had appeared at a number of Solidarity rallies and was comfortable speaking publicly on its issues. "It's just like talking to your friends, but it wasn't that day. They were furious. Asking me, 'What the hell did you . . . What's going on?' It was teachers and health workers mainly as I recall. Probably some fishers, too. . . . Teachers had got out of their classroom on a non-wage thing. It was about broader social issues. *And they did that.* But anyway, they were pissed. I got the brunt of it for a while, and then they realized I didn't know what was going on, I wasn't part of it, and that I was pissed, too. It's just the emotion. The obvious word is raw, I guess, and then that kind of emotion didn't go away in a hurry."

The fury was unabating in the days and weeks and years that followed. So many Solidarity supporters felt that when the big decisions were made, Solidarity, which had seemed so democratic, was suddenly utterly undemocratic. "The frustration level was so high, you know, you wouldn't believe it," recalls Raj Chouhan. "I personally was visited by many people expressing their frustration—like, 'What the fuck are we going to do now.' Really, really angry. I was upset because I felt left out. We were not part of the final decision-making. No consultation. . . . People thought that was a betrayal, said those words. People thought that was a deliberate action on a part of some of the unions who did not want to see this kind of progressive movement becoming more broad. So that was a setback in people's minds. After that it [Solidarity] kind of fizzled out. Within days, it was gone."

———

Tom Wayman says Munro and company were terrified that people in their unions would say: "Wait a minute. All these social issues affect us, too, even though we're not government workers. All the other legislation—the closing of libraries, the closing of hospitals—that's going to affect us too, so we want to go out." So Munro was sent in to stop Solidarity before it got out of hand. In his epic poem, *The Face of Jack Munro*, Tom writes:

> Those days in November I felt
> the presence of
> another room alongside this one,
> another field and sky
> beside this meadow and air.
> It seemed we had built
> a passageway to that crystal life,
> a door which took shape
> from our careful daily acts of defiance.
> But we left a few to keep
> that opening for us
> and when we tried to cross through
> we learned they had taken it away.[24]

"It's just a cry of outrage," Tom says of the poem, "because it had seemed to me, in so many of these meetings, public meetings and union meetings, that people were rethinking everything about how society functions. The way we've got things set up now is not the best the human race can imagine and people were coming up with other ideas or at least questioning, you know, why do we do it this way, why do we do it that way. And that was all short-circuited by the sellout."

CHAPTER 11

The Solidarity Legacy:
An Imperfect Storm

AFTER A 123-YEAR RUN, *The Columbian* went bankrupt. Its final
issue was published on November 15, 1983. In an article on its last
front page, I asked: "Is Solidarity forever or is it just a temporary anti-
government coalition that died Sunday night?"[1] A year later, Art
Kube reflected on the movement at an event with Women Against
the Budget, which had been the first component of Solidarity to endorse a general strike. During the Solidarity months of 1983 I often
interviewed Kube, and as this event wound down we spoke. "In retrospect," he said. "The women were right." Art Kube was just one of
so many who would evaluate and re-evaluate Solidarity for the rest of
their lives. Patsy George would go on to be a legendary Canadian
activist, but Solidarity's finale still nags at her. "I'm so happy I was
part of it, even though I was disappointed at the end. I get fired, and

then I get hired by the union to fight the government who fired me. I mean, you know, that's quite an experience."

—⁓—

At the height of the Solidarity uprising, in late September 1983, a movie was released about veterans of the student/anti-war movement of the 1960s and early '70s who reunite in a sprawling South Carolina country home for the funeral of someone in their circle who has committed suicide. Despite a great soundtrack (Creedence Clearwater Revival, Carole King, Smokey Robinson, etc., etc.), the characters in *The Big Chill* have lives filled with ennui, wandering about directionless in post-Movement depression over the loss of their youth and their idealism. Instead of stewing in that big old country house, they should have headed north to B.C.

The notion that rebellion was something that occurred in the past—to stew about and be nostalgic over—was a popular, convenient trope for those who never liked rebellion in the first place. It was belied, however, by events taking place in B.C. when *The Big Chill* was released in 1983. For thousands upon thousands of British Columbians—including many veterans of student/anti-war activism—Solidarity was as heady as anything they had experienced. "The old-style labour union approach is a class approach, versus what came out of the '60s which had a lot to do with culture and lifestyle," notes Alan Zisman. "That's why it was such a unique time and you had this coalition of all these other people who weren't part of that [labour] world, and then they all came together. It could have been a perfect storm, I guess. . . . Another moment of what could have been."

Why wasn't it a more perfect storm? Within Solidarity, the Kelowna Accord was waiting to happen. Within Solidarity, there were clashes between left-wing unions and business unions, class-based and identity-based activism, reformers and radicals, economistic and social justice demands. So, Solidarity was a flawed coalition with misunderstandings and animosity, but still the kind of coalition that is ultimately necessary for fundamental social change. Beyond the internal differences, beyond even the Kelowna fiasco, there was exhilaration in those months of solidarity.

Kim Zander has lingering questions from November 1983. Why did the BCFED insist on waiting for BCGEU to be in a legal position to walk out before beginning the strike? "We didn't need anyone's collective agreement negotiations to be the signal for it. It could have just happened." Why the drawn-out strike scenario? "Were they hoping it would fail? Like, seriously, if you're escalating toward a general strike, why are you doing it one union at a time and so slowly?" Kim says a lasting legacy of Solidarity requires "learning how did it actually come to be and have the strength it had. That's why I said there's many perspectives—we all have pieces of where that strength came from and what the lessons were. People felt their power in a way they'd never tried it on before, and that's never a bad thing. Never."

In the immediate aftermath, there was resistance and retribution. In Kamloops, "after the Tranquille occupation, workers weren't putting up with shit anymore," BCGEU's Gary Steeves says. "Workers had opinions. When a social worker said, 'No, the care plan for this person should include this,' the management then said, 'No it won't,' the social worker said, 'Yes it will.' Workers understood what management did and they weren't about to take any guff. They just didn't believe bullshit anymore." In Nelson, Fred Wah and friends at the David Thompson University Centre didn't have much to celebrate about the Munro–Bennett deal. "Sellout," Fred says. "So that was a kind of dismal winter, '83–'84, and then we kept being told by the administration that we were probably on the chopping block. Partly arising out of the whole Solidarity thing because we were all pretty involved with that.... Arts funding across the province had been scuttled. We had an arts school. We were going to be scuttled. We knew that. If Solidarity had continued, it might have changed enough of the direction of the province to keep David Thompson going."

With feelings so raw in the days following Kelowna, Sara Diamond, "a real hoarder of records," did something she doesn't do. She saved nothing. "One of the really sad things that I did . . . I guess I was so upset about what had happened with Solidarity that wildly and weirdly I actually threw out a whole box of records [of the movement], and it's such an unusual thing for me to do. So I don't have a lot of the material from the Solidarity movement, which is pretty funny. But there you go."

For the B.C. Teachers' Federation, the legacy of Solidarity continues every day. The experience left the BCTF so sensitive to the democratic process that it often holds multiple votes on a single matter. "That's a function of what happened in Solidarity," says Larry Kuehn, adding: "What Solidarity showed was the world doesn't fall apart when you go on strike, like some teachers thought beforehand." The Kelowna shenanigans left some teachers so disillusioned that they refused, for decades, to join the B.C. Federation of Labour. After Solidarity, though, the BCTF was "strong and more realistic" and more militant, says Larry. "The teachers crossed picket lines until 1983. That's not the case anymore." Marcy Toms says the BCTF has, since 1983, tried "in every single way to knit together those two sort of solitudes that we talked about earlier—the economist or economic focus of bargaining, and a collective agreement with social justice issues that when pursued would have political, moral, social and cultural benefits. Not only to you, as a member of that union, but to society in general through the work that you did with students, whether it was advocating for LGBTQ rights, working on women's social justice issues, women's rights in curriculum, taking a lead in aboriginal justice in schools—as the BCTF has done."

Not everyone in the labour movement was like the BCTF and drew lessons in democracy from Solidarity. In 1987, Jess Succamore attended a meeting at Burnaby's BCGEU hall filled with labour organizers furious with new legislation—stripping workers of the right to strike and organize—from another Socred premier, Bill Vander Zalm. When Kube's successor as BCFED president, Ken Georgetti, opened the meeting, someone rose from the floor to say: "'I want to tell you something before we go any further. . . . We were really dismayed about Solidarity." Jess knew what this trade unionist was about to say—"lack of accountability and all of that." But, says Jess, Georgetti interjected. "He says, 'Well, I want to tell you right off the bat we learned a lot of things from Solidarity.' And everyone's thinking, 'Oh well, this is a good way to start off.' And Georgetti said, 'There's going to be no open mics.' Because what happened at every Solidarity meeting is you had all the riff-raff getting up and saying things. They were socially active people, getting up and speaking, making sense a lot of them, you see. And they [BCFED leadership] didn't want that sort of input. They wanted to keep it a controlled environment. I thought that was symptomatic of them." Seated next to Jess, pulp workers president Bob Anderson said: "Jess, let's get out of here."

There are those in the labour movement—including some who were upset at the time—who have come to accept the Accord and pay tribute to Jack Munro. "The pretense of the virtues of the late Jack Munro are not deeply impressive for me," Stan Persky says. Marcy Toms shares Stan's opinion on this. "I do not understand the constant sanctifying of this guy," she says. "A red-baiter who had his position because of red-scare hysteria that had been whipped up in-side the trade union movement."

Scott Parker points to another legacy of Solidarity. "How about the next election? We lost."

—⁓—

Working at a weekly newspaper during the next provincial election of 1986—which was again expected to be a New Democratic Party victory—I was at an NDP headquarters in a Burnaby hotel ballroom watching results come in on a television screen. I noticed an elderly, working-class NDP loyalist, who'd likely gone to war with the CCF too, slowly work his way through the crowd until he was standing directly in front of me, looking up at the screen. It took him just a moment or two to see that the results were disappointing. The Socreds had won again. Instantly deflated, he softly said under his breath two words that only I could hear: "Damn people."

You can't always see a phenomenon's long-term impact in its immediate results. In the aftermath of the May–June events in France '68, President Charles de Gaulle's right-wing coalition won the next election. Still, the uprising, with its demands for a sweeping social transformation, set in motion ideas about work and ways of living not just in France but everywhere. Regardless of its initial apparent outcome, the process of resisting created, over time, more resistance. In 1983, B.C. union leaders, for the most part, couldn't see the value in a transformative general strike. But many people in B.C. instinctively knew, and who knows what forms of freedom might have swept the province had the strike proceeded.

"You can't know what actually would have happened," says Stan Persky, "if the unions had really gone on general strike and had made very clear that the demand was the entire restraint program had to be renegotiated with the Solidarity movement, and we will be on strike until you are prepared to negotiate. What would have happened in those circumstances? There were at least various signs that segments of the trade union movement, especially in the social services areas, were much more militant than the old-style unions had anticipated. The people that became frightened were the people who ran the BCFED. It wasn't Larry Kuehn that was frightened as the leader of the teachers' union, for example. He wasn't frightened of the notion of a general strike. But people like Jack Munro were horrified by it and the kind of indiscipline that it would represent. It would be a real challenge to all of the parameters of bourgeois society. It certainly had a degree of popular support and we could get out large demonstrations, which were significant demonstrations."

No one can say for certain what a general strike would have accomplished. It is clear, though, that it would have gotten more than Munro got in Kelowna: virtually nothing for the BCTF, the Solidarity Coalition and so many other targets of the Socreds' twenty-six bills. The striking BCGEU and BCTF weren't the only unions invested in Solidarity. Other union members and community activists awaiting their turn to join in were thoroughly deflated by the Accord. Postal worker Saria Andrew says there was enthusiasm for a general strike in her Commercial Drive neighbourhood. "In my community and my union, almost everyone was preparing for an extended general strike and a community takeover. We were figuring out how to do it little by little. The suspensions at work and the like didn't matter, as we were all in this together. . . . Then with the Kelowna Accord, it all came crashing down."

—◦◦◦—

When Solidarity was on the verge of general striking, I spoke long distance with my Uncle Sam in Philadelphia. He said that the current union leadership in Philly didn't talk about things like general strikes. At the time, I didn't know how militant Philadelphia unions had been in Sam's youth. While researching this book, I came upon an August 4, 1937 issue of *The Columbian* (then called *The British Columbian*). A front-page story, dateline Philadelphia, begins: "Mayor S. Davis Wilson declared a 'state of emergency' existed in Philadelphia today as union leaders met to discuss the proposal of a general strike."[2]

In the early 1970s, having worked on the *Yipster Times* newspaper in New York City, I was driving back to Vancouver and stopped in Philadelphia for a couple of days to visit my Uncle Sam and Auntie Sophie. I was countercultural New Left and Sam Kovnat was working-class Old Left, but he was a hero to me. The toughest man I ever met. Sam organized a boxers' trade union in Philadelphia and was one of the militant Congress of Industrial Organizations's (CIO) national organizers in the late 1930s. So tough and smart was Uncle Sam that he was dispatched to Brooklyn to organize on the waterfront in 1938. A member of the Communist Party as well as the CIO, Sam came face to face with another organization in Brooklyn: the mob. He is quoted in the book *Reds or Rackets?* as saying back then that the Brooklyn rank-and-file was "wild and rarin' to go" but "it will be a slow process. Because in spite of the enthusiasm of the men, we have yet to see how they react when [mobster] Carmada's gunmen start to work."[3]

Sam and the Communist Party had been parted for decades when I visited Philadelphia in the 1970s, but like so many who left the CP he held on to a lot of its politics. Before I went to bed the first night at their home in working-class Philadelphia, I handed Sam the latest issue of *Yipster Times*, the international Yippie newspaper. The following morning, I was surprised to find that Sam had stayed up late reading the paper. He had been thinking about the difference between his movement in the 1930s and mine in the 1970s and told me that back during the Depression they were out of work and *needed* to organize because they were in a fight for survival. "We didn't have a choice," he said. "You can cut your hair, go back to university, and drop out of this movement any time you want." There was truth to Sam's words and I didn't have an immediate answer. I did think about it, though, and decided that there's something to be said for choice. Whether you're talking about a woman's body or joining a social movement, choice can be a powerful thing.

Unlike the 1930s, the 1950s and '60s was a period of relative affluence. Young people, for the first time, had widespread access to postsecondary education and plenty of free time to explore ideas. They questioned everything, saw that the culture was rooted in racism and sexism, and challenged every kind of prejudice and taboo. Having come of age with three square meals a day they still weren't satisfied, and the economistic demands of earlier social movements fighting for basic needs were no longer enough. Instead, they created political movements and subcultures that embraced utopian experimentation, shed cultural repression, demanded social and personal justice—a totalistic human liberation. Among the many slogans of France '68 that captured this spirit: "*It is forbidden to forbid.*" Murray Bookchin, in his essay "Desire and Need," talked about the fulfillment of desire as a motivation for radicals of the 1960s and '70s as opposed to earlier generations' focus on need. "Desire," he wrote, "must become Need! . . . The revolution can no longer be imprisoned in the realm of Need. It can no longer be satisfied merely with the prose of political economy."[4]

—◦◦◦—

Sudden insurrections occur periodically throughout history. While they seem to rise instantly, they simmer for decades or longer, then blow, showing that people are always ready to rise when the right moment arrives. Sometimes they last years, other times four months. They commonly are egalitarian and exhilarating in ways that express the potential for a different, better way of living—were they to become the basis for a new society. In the end, though, they have been extinguished by external forces of suppression or commandeered by better-organized authoritarians with none of the insurrection's initial spirit of freedom. So, how to make permanent the transformative, liberatory spirit of these uprisings?

Socialism in one province? "It was pretty exciting times when what had been an abstraction to us was suddenly taking shape and form right before our eyes," Tom Wayman says. "Was the union movement ready to step in and form a government? Absolutely not. Would the American government allow a kind of social experimentation to take place right on its border? Highly unlikely. So, I don't know, but like you say, it was worth a shot. . . . For me, the big lesson from that Solidarity experience was that when people decide they've had enough, things change really fast. I guess my optimism about the future comes from having gone through that experience. People sometimes get educated through things that don't work. That notion of an inspiration. It certainly kept me going through the bleaker eras because once you see it happen, once you know it's possible, that there's enough pent-up imagination and energy and rage in people that everything could change abruptly, then it keeps you plugging away. . . . The great thing about people is that they take it and take it and take it and then all of a sudden they don't."

In the twenty-first century, there has been a series of sudden risings, including Occupy Wall Street, the Arab Spring and Hong Kong

(2011), climate strikes (2019) and anti-racism protests (2020). In different shapes and sizes, the component groups inside Solidarity would also push on through the twentieth century and into the twenty-first. Not long after Solidarity, for instance, B.C.'s environmental movement engaged in a series of high-profile wilderness fights, at Meares Island, the Stein Valley, the Queen Charlotte Islands and Clayoquot Sound.

———

There are true believers in capitalism who speak as though it has always been here and must always be. But it is, in humanity's millennia, a relatively recent social system. Should anyone you know doubt its harmful consequences, ask them to consider what the streams and sky and forests looked like in the 1820s, as industrial capitalism was getting under way, and give them a hard look in the 2020s after 200 years of unfettered capitalism. Or in 1989. That was the year Tzeporah Berman, a fashion arts design student at Toronto's Ryerson University, went backpacking with her sister and a Eurail Pass. It was also the year people were dying from pollution on the streets of Athens. "I had a dream of always seeing the Acropolis because I was an art history student," Tzeporah says. "I'll never forget going up there. It was just crumbling from acid rain and from pollution, and you look down on Athens and it was just like a yellow smog. I got back to my hostel that night and I was coughing up black goo." Tzeporah left Athens. "We said, 'This is disgusting. Let's go somewhere natural. Let's go hiking.'" Tzeporah and her sister randomly selected Germany's Harz Mountains as the next stop on their Euro vacation. "We're hiking for an entire day through a standing dead forest. Not a bird, not a sound. Black standing dead trees. And we get to the end of this trail, and there's a plaque, and it's in German. We ask this couple to explain it to us and it said, 'This forest has been left standing as a testimony to industrial pollution and what industrial society can do.'"

Returning home, Tzeporah enrolled in the University of Toronto's environmental studies program. In biology class, she saw images of B.C.'s temperate rainforest. "I didn't know Canada had rainforest, and these were thousand-year-old trees 300 feet tall. I just decided to come out here." By 1993, Tzeporah was a determined environmental activist asked to be a blockade coordinator at Vancouver Island's Clayoquot Sound.

Another activist in this book, Alan Zisman, was arrested at May Day 1971, the largest mass civil disobedience arrest in American history. The largest civil disobedience arrest in Canadian history—about 1,000 of the 10,000 who protested—occurred in opposition to logging at Clayoquot Sound in 1993. Tzeporah was arrested and charged with 857 counts of criminal aiding and abetting as one of the core organizers. "So I was on trial for two years. I was twenty-three at the time. We won." Articulate and bold, Tzeporah became the face of the highly publicized protest. Supporters would step forward in the street to hug her. There were also those like the employee of the forestry company MacMillan Bloedel (MacBlo) who pulled the tablecloth out from under her in a Tofino restaurant. "And threw everything back at us, then spit right in my face in the middle of a nice restaurant." Clayoquot blockades, though, had wide support across B.C. "There are tipping-point moments where an issue becomes something that everyone's talking about at their kitchen table. Instead of being behind closed doors, it becomes part of the popular culture. The Clayoquot blockades and our movement at that time caught that wave." Her dining experience at a Vancouver bar was friendlier than it had been in Tofino. Tzeporah ordered a drink called Rainforest Ale because she'd laughed when she saw its name on the menu. "And the bartender hands me the Rainforest Ale and says, 'Right on, fuck MacBlo.' It was everywhere. And it linked into a growing anti-corporate sentiment in the '90s."

When I spoke with Tzeporah about Solidarity 1983, she pointed out twenty-first-century parallels. "I think the strength of this moment is in part because of the ten years of the Harper era. He not only refused to address climate change and many environmental issues, he did it by violating people's right of free speech, by telling scientists who work for the federal government that they're not allowed to speak to the media, by changing major environmental legislation— seventy laws in one omnibus bill with no public debate. So he created a perfect storm, similar to what happened in the early 1980s, where it's not just groups who work on environmental issues anymore. It's groups who work on freedom of speech, groups who work on Indigenous rights, groups who work on poverty issues, because this is a far-right politician who overreached to such an extent that he threatened so many different constituencies at the same time and we found common ground. . . . They cut everything. And so they created that perfect storm." Which brings Tzeporah Berman to a different kind of general strike. The largest mobilization in Canada's history was the 2019 climate strike.

"Greta [Thunberg] called for an international general strike. A million people marched across Canada in one day—300,000 in Vancouver. . . . And globally it was over ten million. It was along this idea of a general strike. So the kids have started this, 'I'm not going to school. I'm striking from going to school because you're not protecting my future.' That's the basis for Friday's strikes, for climate strikes, and they called for the adults to strike with them. And Canadians responded in droves. I've never seen anything like it. We left our house thinking we'll take the bus [to the protest]. I get onto Broadway and there's masses and masses of people at every bus stop. What is this? And then the buses start going by us, start going by us, and we waited for an hour. The buses were full. I've never experienced anything like that in my life. And I said to my son, 'Okay, let's start walking.' The streets are flooded with people. . . . We ended up at the corner of Broadway and Cambie, and we could kind of hear the rally starting. And then this wave of people walked down toward us and we marched with it. At one point it was over. We had to wait an hour and a half to take our first step because there's so many people around you. You have to wait till they move before you can move. It's unbelievable. That was Vancouver."

That climate strike rally was the largest protest in Vancouver's history. Says Tzeporah: "Literally, right now, our life systems are collapsing. You know the weather is not right. Everybody sees the fires in Australia and B.C. and California. And the rise in extreme weather. So now it's become an issue—climate change has—everyone's talking about over their kitchen tables and they're engaging in numbers that we've never seen before. We're fighting for survival. Literally, for survival." So, we've come full circle, from my Uncle Sam's fight for survival during the Depression, to our fight for desire in the 1960s and '70s, and finally to a fight for survival *and* desire in the twenty-first century. The resources and resourcefulness exist now to create an egalitarian society without want, but the prevailing system threatens our very survival, so the tension between what could be and what is has never been greater. The Solidarity uprising of 1983 gave us a glimpse of what could be.

Solidarity was far greater than its anticlimactic ending. It showed, for one thing, how to create a popular movement to resist a Reagan-Thatcher-Bennett agenda. For the four Solidarity months of 1983 all these people organizing alone were suddenly organizing together, and they were as passionate about one common thing—stopping Socred devastation—as they had been pursuing separate issues in their own silos. What made Solidarity so powerful was that thousands upon thousands of B.C. residents unaffiliated with a particular politics were also at those Solidarity protests. Within Solidarity, many activists learned of each other's issues and that creating fundamental change will take a grand coalition—if not a formal coalition of organizations, at least a coalition of ideas that address gender and class, race and ecology . . . everything.

Some things never change, including the desire for justice and a taste of freedom. For a moment in 1983, dreams felt real and goals within reach. "You could have the goal of a general strike being just to have a general strike," says Marcy Toms, "and that might sound kind of anarchic, but I think it can play a political and social-consciousness raising role—We pulled it off!"

Like revolts throughout history, Solidarity 1983 appeared suddenly and disappeared too suddenly, but in those heady few months in-between, the dream of sweeping change felt so real and was bigger, even, than any twenty-six bills.

Notes

INTRODUCTION: Just a Step Beyond the Rain (pp. 1–7)

1 "Edward Baravalle," The Internet Movie Database, accessed October 13, 2021, https://www.imdb.com/name/nm0053126/?ref_=fn_nm_nm_7.

2 Harriet Hyman Alonso, *Yip Harburg: Legendary Lyricist and Human Rights Activist* (Middletown, CT: Wesleyan University Press, 2013), 247.

CHAPTER 1: Bill's Bills (pp. 9–24)

1 Gillian Shaw, "Angry 6,000 hear Fed's call to arms," *Vancouver Sun*, July 20, 1983.

2 Women Against the Budget minutes, July 20, 1983.

3 Budget minutes.

4 "Program of Action," B.C. Federation of Labour, July 15, 1983.

5 "Operation Solidarity—Ten-point Program," B.C. Federation of Labour, July 15, 1983.

6 Trade Union Solidarity Committee minutes, July 28, 1983.

7 "Thousands cheer as rally brands Bennett 'fascist,'" *The Columbian*, July 25, 1983.

8 "Enjoy Your Trip . . . ," Operation Solidarity leaflet, July 1983.

9 Dirk Meissner, "Dave Barrett Memorial: 'His vision indeed far exceeded that of so many Canadians,'" *Vancouver Sun*, March 3, 2018.

CHAPTER 2: In Solidarity (pp. 25–38)

1 David Spaner, "'Next thing I knew, I was biting the cop's arm,'" *Vancouver Province*, August 19, 2007.

2 Jesse Donaldson, "Hard Day's Night at Empire Stadium," *The Tyee*, August 20, 2014.

3 Mike Evans, *The Beatles Literary Anthology* (London: Plexus Publishing, 2004), 152.

4 "JOIN US AND SPEAK OUT Against Discriminatory and Repressive Legislation," Operation Solidarity leaflet, August 1983.

5 "Hospital Workers: your jobs, your seniority, your wages, your human rights, ARE ON THE LINE!," *Hospital Employees' Union Newsletter*, August 1983.

6 Operation Solidarity minutes, August 8, 1983.

7 "Solidarity Rally" memo from city manager Fritz Bowers to City of Vancouver department heads, August 10, 1983.

8 "Join the People of Vancouver!," Vancouver Municipal and Regional Employees' Union leaflet, August 1983.

9 Barbara Efrat, Janet Cauthers and W.J. Langlois, *Sound Heritage: Voices from British Columbia* (Vancouver: Douglas & McIntyre, 1984), Volume VII, 48.

10 "Giant Parade and Mass Demonstration Staged by Labor in Vancouver," *Vancouver Sun*, May 2, 1938.

11 "Giant Parade."

12 Eli Sopow and Olivia Scott, "Solidarity riled by NDP move," *Vancouver Province*, September 18, 1983.

13 Tom Hawthorn, "Yippie for mayor," *The Globe and Mail*, June 22, 2011.

14 Operation Solidarity recommendations, August 17, 1983.

CHAPTER 3: The Solidarity Coalition (pp. 39–62)

1 "Interim Operational Statement," August 3, 1983.

2 Jeff Lustig, "The FSM and the Vision of a New Left.," in Robert Cohen and Reginald Zelnik's *The Free Speech Movement: Reflections on Berkeley in the 1960s* (Berkeley: University of California Press, 2002), 216.

3 "Solidarity (1983)," Confederation of Canadian Unions Policy Resolutions, October 2017.

4 "The Budget and You," *DERA Newsletter*, July 1983.

5 Solidarity Coalition minutes, October 31, 1983.

6 Barrie M. Morrison report on "Solidarity Coalition Meeting 30 August, 1983."

7 Art Kube letter to Textile Workers Union director George Watson, February 24, 1974.

8 "Government Budget/Legislative Package Threatens the Environment," Solidarity Coalition leaflet, October 7, 1983.

9 Sue McIlroy, "Tenants brave Socred cold spell," *The Ubyssey*, October 4, 1983.

10 Jim Quail, "Bill 5—Residential Tenancy Act," Solidarity Coalition document, 1983.

11 "Solidarity stages candlelight vigils," *Vancouver Sun*, September 10, 1983.

12 Solidarity Coalition minutes, September 13, 1983.

CHAPTER 4: The Socialist Coalition (pp. 63–86)

1 David Latham, *Writing on the Image: Reading William Morris* (Toronto: University of Toronto Press, 2007), 167.

2 "You have to go beyond capitalism," *International Socialist Review*, July 2009.

3 Robert Low, *La Pasionaria: The Spanish Firebrand* (London: Arrow, 1992), 109.

4 John Dos Passos, *The 42nd Parallel* (Charlottesville: University of Virginia, 1939), 28.

5 Jim Murray, "My evening with Tommy Douglas," *The Murray Chronicles*, October 20, 2016. www.murraychronicles.com/2016/10/my-evening-with-tommy-douglas.html.

6 "36 INJURED AFTER BATTLE ON WATERFRONT," *Vancouver News-Herald*, June 19, 1935.

7 "The Uncompromising Anti-Capitalism of Martin Luther King Jr.," *IBW21.ORG*, January 15, 2018. https://ibw21.org/commentary/uncompromising-anti-capitalism-martin-luther-king-jr.

8 "Building Trades United Against Repressive Legislation," *Solidarity Times*, October 15, 1983.

CHAPTER 5: From Grace to Grace (pp. 87–102)

1 Women Against the Budget press release, July 21, 1983.

2 "SOCRED BUDGET UNITES WOMEN'S OPPOSITION," Women Against the Budget press release, July, 15, 1983.

3 Shulamith Firestone, *The Dialectic of Sex* (New York: Bantam Books, 1970), 2.

4 "JOIN WOMEN'S CAUCUS," *The Pedestal*, Fall 1969.

5 Women Against the Budget minutes, July 20, 1983.

6 Deb Bradley, Esther Sara Diamond, Esther Shannon and Frances Was-serlein, "Women condemn Socred budget," *Kinesis*, September 1983.

7 "The Socreds are attacking Women," Women Against the Budget leaf-let, 1983.

8 Samuel Beckett, *Waiting for Godot* (New York: Grove Press, 1954), 22.

9 Kate Millett, *Sexual Politics* (New York: Columbia University Press, 2016), 127.

10 "PROTEST at Grace McCarthy's," Women Against the Budget leaflet, August 1983.

11 "500 OBJECT AT PICNIC," *Vancouver Sun*, September 26, 1983.

12 Chris Rose, "Women main targets, rally told," *Vancouver Sun*, Septem-ber 8, 1983.

CHAPTER 6: Cultural Combustion (pp. 103–126)

1 D.O.A., "General Strike," 1983, https://genius.com/Doa-general-strike-lyrics.

CHAPTER 7: Racism (pp. 127–140)

1 David Spaner, "Racism: Documenting Prejudice," *POV Magazine*, Fall/Winter 2018.

2 Spaner, "Racism: Documenting Prejudice."

3 "Stop the attack on Human Rights," Solidarity Coalition leaflet, 1983.

4 B.C. Civil Liberties Association, "BILL 27—HUMAN RIGHTS ACT—SUMMARY FACT SHEET," 1983.

5 "Thousands cheer as rally brands Bennett 'fascist,'" *The Columbian*, July 25, 1983.

6 "Sikhs join battle of restraint bills," *Vancouver Sun*, September 7, 1983.

7 Lynne Fernandez and Jim Silver, "Indigenous People, Wage Labour and Trade Unions: The Historical Experience in Canada," Canadian Centre for Policy Alternatives, March 2017.

8 Jeremy Hull, "Aboriginal People and the Labour Movement," in Errol Black and Jim Silver's *Hard Bargains* (Winnipeg: Manitoba Labour Education Centre, 1991), 89.

9 Gerald Thomson, "SO MANY CLEVER, INDUSTRIOUS AND FRUGAL ALIENS . . . ," *B.C. Studies*, Spring 2018, 69.

10 Bryan D. Palmer, "The ghost of Jack Munro," *BC Booklook*, August 22, 2018. https://bcbooklook.com/bc-labour-movement-history.

11 James Dyer, "'Chief Foster's a White Man' Says Steve Brodie in Hospital Interview," *Vancouver Sun*, June 20, 1938.

12 Audrey Kobayashi and Peter Jackson, "JAPANESE CANADIANS AND THE RADICALIZATION OF LABOUR IN THE BRITISH COLUMBIA SAWMILL INDUSTRY," *BC Studies*, 1994, 57.

13 Eric Dirnbach, "This Little-Known Black Wobbly Dockworker Led the Most Powerful, Democratic Union of His Day," *Labor Notes*, December 17, 2020.

14 Jeff Shantz, "Bows and Arrows: Indigenous Workers, IWW Local 526, and Syndicalism on the Vancouver Docks," *Anarcho-Syndicalist Review*, Summer 2016.

15 Jack Scott, *Plunderbund and Proletariat* (Vancouver: New Star Books, 1975), 153.

16 Justine Hunter, "A forgotten history: tracing the ties between B.C.'s First Nations and Chinese Workers," *The Globe and Mail*, May 9, 2015.

17 Hunter, "A forgotten history."

18 Dale Johnson, *Social Inequality, Economic Decline, and Plutocracy* (London: Palgrave Macmillan, 2017), 258.

19 Raj Chouhan speaking on CJOR radio's "Solidarity View," October 18, 1983.

20 "FARMWORKERS FIGHTBACK," Canadian Farmworkers Union Document, August 1983.

CHAPTER 8: The Hotel Vancouver Rally (pp. 141–157)

1 "Local Artists Unite Talents On Murals for New Vancouver," *Vancouver Province*, February 11, 1939.

2 Solidarity Coalition minutes, September 13, 1983.

3 Solidarity Coalition minutes.

4 Stephen Naft, *The Social General Strike* (Chicago: Debating Club No. 1, 1905), 7.

5 Ralph Chaplin pamphlet, "The General Strike For Industrial Freedom" (Chicago: IWW, 1972), 12.

6 John Mackie, "This Week in History: Homeless veterans occupy the old Hotel Vancouver in 1949," *Vancouver Sun*, January 22, 2016.

7 "Fence-builders go to work at 4 Seasons instant park," *Vancouver Sun*, May 31, 1971.

8 Lisa Fitterman, "Office occupiers declare success," *Vancouver Sun*, September 17, 1983.

9 "More protests predicted," *Vancouver Sun*, September 19, 1983.

10 "More protests predicted."

11 Mike Tytherleigh, "Will council back DERA and its role in anarchy?," *Vancouver Province*, September 21, 1983.

12 Art Kube letter, "OCTOBER 15TH RALLY," September 29, 1983.

13 "March for Your Rights," Operation Solidarity/Solidarity Coalition joint leaflet, October 1983.

14 "Report on Solidarity Coalition Steering Committee meeting," Confederation of University Faculty Associations of B.C., October 11, 1983.

15 "March for Your Rights," Operation Solidarity/Solidarity Coalition joint leaflet, October 1983.

16 Nick Auf der Maur and Robert Chodos, *Quebec: A Chronicle: 1968–1972* (Toronto: James Larimer & Company, 1972), 142.

17 David Spaner and Paul Marck, "50,000 protest Socred policies," *The Columbian*, October 17, 1983.

18 "UNITE for the GENERAL STRIKE," Committee for a General Strike leaflet, 1983.

19 "NOW IT'S WAR," Socialist Challenge leaflet, October 5, 1983.

20 Ralph Chaplin, "The General Strike For Industrial Freedom," pamphlet (Chicago: IWW, 1972), 40.

21 Jeremy Brecher, *Strike!* (Boston: South End Press, 1977), 111.

22 "SONGS FOR THE MARCH," Cultural Workers Against the Budget, October 15, 1983.

CHAPTER 9: Solidarity on the Line (pp. 158–176)

1 "General strike backed," *The Columbian*, October 18, 1983.

2 "General strike backed."

3 "General strike backed."

4 David Spaner, "BCGEU's 35,000-member strike spills rapidly into private sector," *The Columbian*, November 1, 1983.

5 Solidarity Coalition minutes, October 31, 1983.

6 Jane O'Hara, "Radicalizing the workers," *MacLean's Magazine*, November 21, 1983.

7   My interview with BCGEU member Ken Holmes for *The Columbian*, November 6, 1983.

8   "Strike called national test," *Vancouver Sun*, November 5, 1983.

9   "Strike called national test."

10 "Emily Carr Socred Fighter 1983," *CLASS WAR*, ECCAD Student Strike Bulletin No. 2, 1983.

11 "Socred Fighter 1983."

12 William Anderson letter to Norman Harcus, October 25, 1983.

13 "Strike called national test," *Vancouver Sun*, November 5, 1983.

14 Larry Kuehn letter to Bill Bennett, February 17, 1983.

15 Larry Kuehn statement at press conference, February 17, 1983.

16 Paul Marck, "Walkout leaves students puzzling out class chaos," *The Columbian*, November 8, 1983.

17 "3 aldermen picket," *Vancouver Sun*, November 9, 1983.

18 "City council asks bills be scrapped," *Vancouver Sun*, July 27, 1983.

19 "A MATTER OF CONSCIENCE," Committee of Concerned Academics letter, November 7, 1983.

20 "OUR RIGHTS ON THE LINE," Jeanne Williams letter, 1983.

21 "Strike called national test," *Vancouver Sun*, November 5, 1983.

22 "Vancouver labor council supports general strike," *The Columbian*, October 19, 1983.

23 "What we stand for," *Solidarity Times*, October 15, 1983.

24 John Mackie, "Blasting off," *Solidarity Times*, October 15, 1983.

25 "How the other half thinks," *Solidarity Times*, October 15, 1983.

26 "RESOLUTIONS FROM LOCAL COALITIONS AND CONSTITUENT GROUPS," Solidarity Coalition conference minutes.

CHAPTER 10: Obsolete Unionism (pp. 177–198)

1   Art Kube, interview by author, May 1989.

2   Marjorie Nichols, "Within a year Solidarity will become a historical asterisk," *Vancouver Sun*, December 30, 1983.

3   Art Kube, interview by author, May 1989.

4   David Spaner, "New Westminster labor council backs general strike," *The Columbian*, October 20, 1983.

5   Shulamith Firestone, *The Dialectic of Sex* (New York: Bantam Books, 1970), 3.

6 Murray Bookchin, *Post-Scarcity Anarchism* (Palo Alto, CA: Ramparts Press, 1971), 186.

7 Bookchin, *Post-Scarcity Anarchism*, 219.

8 Simone de Beauvoir, *The Second Sex* (New York: Vintage Books, 1974), 138.

9 Ian Mulgrew, "Striking B.C. labor modifies demands," *Globe and Mail*, November 11, 1983.

10 Mulgrew, "B.C. labor modifies demands."

11 Terry Glavin, "Memo lists secret labor offer," *Vancouver Sun*, November 12, 1983.

12 Glavin, "Memo lists secret labor."

13 Rod Mickleburgh, "Private-sector unions gear up," *Vancouver Province*, November 9, 1983.

14 Allen Garr, *Tough Guy: Bill Bennett and the Taking of British Columbia* (Toronto: Key Porter Books, 1985), 141.

15 Solidarity Coalition minutes, November 13, 1983.

16 Solidarity Coalition statement, November 14, 1983.

17 Keith Baldrey, "Coalition upset," *Solidarity Times*, November 16, 1983.

18 Solidarity Coalition minutes, November 23, 1983.

19 Doug Ward, "MUNRO DENIES SOCRED TIE," *Vancouver Sun*, September 25, 1984.

20 My interview with Jack Munro for *Vancouver Magazine*, May 1989.

21 My interview with Art Kube for *Vancouver Magazine*, May 1989.

22 Cliff Andstein speaking at "A Time to Act," a panel discussion on the 35th anniversary of Solidarity, November 8, 2018, at New Westminster's Anvil Centre.

23 John Shields interview for the B.C. Labour Heritage Centre Oral History Collection. https://digital.lib.sfu.ca/bclhc-7/interview-john-shields.

24 Tom Wayman, *The Face of Jack Munro* (Madeira Park, B.C.: Harbour Publishing, 1986), 121.

CHAPTER 11: The Solidarity Legacy (pp. 199–212)

1 David Spaner, "Solidarity forever, or is it just for the history books?," *The Columbian*, November 15, 1983.

2 "STRIKE BLOCKS PHILADELPHIA'S FOOD SUPPLY," *The British Columbian*, August 4, 1937.

3 Howard Kimeldorf, *Reds or Rackets?: The Making of Radical and Conservative Unions on the Waterfront* (Oakland: University of California Press), 124.

4 Murray Bookchin, *Post-Scarcity Anarchism* (Palo Alto, CA: Ramparts Press, 1971), 274.

About the Author

David Spaner has worked as a feature writer, movie critic, reporter and editor for numerous newspapers and magazines. He has also been a cultural/political organizer, helping to stage protests and concerts and produce underground publications. Born in Toronto, he grew up in B.C. and is a graduate of Simon Fraser University. He is the author of *Dreaming in the Rain* and *Shoot It!: Hollywood Inc. and the Rising of Independent Film.*

Index

Wayne, John, 189
Weather Underground, 78
Weavers, the, 111
Webster College, 95
Weller, Jackie, 98
Wellington strike, 131
Wells, Fred, 117
Weppler, Doreen "Dodie", 89
Wershler, Terri, 174
Western University, 84
White Bloc, 3–4, 186, 189.
White Spot, 47, 67–68, 76
Wild, Nettie, 26, 29, 124–26, 194–95
Williams Lake Solidarity rally, 27
Williams, Jeanne, 168
Wilson, Debbie, 173
Wilson, Harold, 51
Wilson, S. Davis, 205
Wilson, Sandy, 112
Winn, Paul, 132
Winnipeg general strike, 144, 154
Wizard of Oz, The, 4
Women & Children Week, 59
Women Against the Budget (WAB), 19, 32, 44, 60, 66, 88–89, 92, 94–95, 97–98, 101–2, 128, 153, 158, 164, 190–91, 199
Women's Caucus, 63, 75–76, 89, 90–91, 94

Women's Health Collective, 10, 37, 95, 100
Wood, Diane, 2, 10–13, 15, 40, 159, 177, 195–96
Woomb, 95
Workers Week, 59
Workers' Compensation Board, 20, 139

X, 123

Yipster Times, 205–6
Yorke, Bruce, 167
Yorkville Yawn, 78
Young Communist League (YCL), 81
Youngblood, 78
Youth International Party (YIP/Yippies), 35, 64, 72, 74–75, 115, 121, 206
Youth Liberation (magazine), 73
Yu, Henry, 134

Zander, Bill, 80, 184
Zander, Kim, 17, 20, 22, 80–82, 146, 148, 179–180,183, 193, 201
Zero, 74
Zinn, Howard, 65
Zisman, Alan, 120–21, 151–52, 200, 209